An Introduction to Post-Keynesian and Marxian Theories of Value and Price

An Introduction to Post-Keynesian and Marxian Theories of Value and Price

Peter M. Lichtenstein

M. E. Sharpe, Inc.
ARMONK, NEW YORK

Second Printing

Copyright © 1983 by M. E. Sharpe, Inc.
80 Business Park Drive, Armonk, N.Y. 10504

All rights reserved. No part of this book may be reproduced in any form without written permission from the publisher.

Design: Angela Foote

Library of Congress Cataloging in Publication Data

Lichtenstein, Peter M., 1944-
    An introduction to post-Keynesian and Marxian theories of value and price.

    Bibliography: p.
    1. Value. 2. Prices. 3. Keynesian economics.
4. Marxian economics. 5. Sraffa, Piero. 6. Economics—History. I. Title.
HB203.L47   1983   338.5'21   82-19707
ISBN 0-87332-214-2 (cloth)
ISBN 0-87332-257-6 (pbk.)

Printed in the United States of America

For Karin

Contents

Preface	xi
Part I: Competing traditions	**1**
1 / A methodological introduction	3
2 / The post-Keynesian/Marxian alternatives	11
Part II: Two value traditions	**25**
3 / The objective theory of value	27
4 / The subjective theory of value	43
Part III: An organizing principle: the economic surplus	**57**
5 / The economic surplus historically considered	59
6 / Contemporary surplus concepts	77
Part IV: Post-Keynesian theories of value and price	**87**
7 / The post-Keynesian (neo-Ricardian) theory of value and price	89
8 / Wages, profits, and prices	103
9 / The Ricardian value problem: the invariable measure	117
10 / Extensions of the basic model	139
Part V: Marxian theories of value and price	**149**
11 / Marx's theory of value and price: an overview	151
12 / From values to prices	167

Contents

Part VI: An overview and comparison   **181**

13 / Marxian vs. post-Keynesian (neo-Ricardian) price
      theory: an overview   183

Recommended Readings   194

Notes   199

About the Author   206

Figures and Tables

Figure	2.1	Neoclassical Circular Flow	13
	2.2	Post-Keynesian/Marxian Circular Flow	19
	2.3	The Post-Keynesian/Marxian Paradigm	23
	3.1	Ricardo's Labor Theory of Value: An Illustration	36
	4.1	Gossen's First Law	46
	5.1	Physiocratic Surplus	67
	5.2	Smith's Surplus	69
	5.3	Ricardian Surplus	71
	5.4	Marxian Surplus Value	73
	6.1	Neo-Marxian Surplus	79
	6.2	Potential Economic Surplus	81
	6.3	Sraffa's Surplus	82
	6.4	Clark-Wicksteed Product Exhaustion Theorem	83
	6.5	Psychological Surplus	85
	8.1	A Linear Wage-Profit Relation	108
	8.2	A Nonlinear Wage-Profit Relation	109
	9.1	Production Over Time with Differing Capital and Labor Applications	121
	9.2	The Simplified Wage-Profit Relation	135
	10.1	Generations of Production: Dated Labor	140
	10.2	The Value of Dated Labor: An Illustration	143
	13.1	Sraffa's Ricardian Model	187
	13.2	The Marxian Model	190
Table	2.1	Comparison of Neoclassical, Post-Keynesian, and Marxian Traditions	24
	3.1	Labor-Commanded vs. Labor-Embodied Value	33
	3.2	Labor-Commanded vs. Labor-Embodied Value: An Extension	37
	7.1	Summary of Models	101

Figures and Tables

8.1	Wage, Profit Rate, and Price Data	107
9.1	Pricing and Capital-Labor Applications Over Time: An Illustration	122
9.2	Features of the Unbalanced Actual System	128
9.3	Features of the Balanced Standard System	132
9.4	The Balanced Industry	133
12.1	The Transformation Process: The Iterative Approach	173
12.2	The Formal Solution to the Transformation Problem	177

Preface

The purpose of this book is to demonstrate to students of economics that there does exist a logically consistent and relevant body of contemporary thought which is rooted in the classical tradition and which forms the basis for both Marxian and post-Keynesian theory.

Once the basic principles of this tradition are understood, the deficiencies of the neoclassical tradition can be better appreciated. But more than that, the student will have access to the tools of an alternative theory of the capitalist system, a theory which raises, and answers, crucially important questions about the nature and source of profits and the distribution of income. Without such alternative theories we would be forever condemned to rely upon the seductive and mystical dogma of the dominant neoclassical point of view.

One premise of this book is that the neoclassical tradition, whose intellectual hegemony extends to virtually every college and university in the United States, is *not* the lineal descendant of what is normally called classical economics (Smith, Ricardo, Mill, et al.). Neoclassical economists did not simply pick up where classical economists left off.

This latter interpretation of the history of economic thought I choose to call the *linear theory* of history. According to this theory, there has been, since Adam Smith, a more or less continuous progression of scientific advance. In this progression, the basic questions of economics have always remained the same (allocation of scarce resources to alternative uses), as have the basic assumptions about human nature (self-interest, rationality, unlimited wants). The only thing that has changed, according to this view, is that the methods of analysis have developed from cruder to more sophisticated forms.

It is usually thought that classical economists gave too much attention to the supply side of the marketplace. It is generally believed that they were mistaken in thinking that the prices of commodities could be explained by costs of production alone—especially labor costs—without any reference being made to demand. As Paul Samuelson observes,

> Classical writers had emphasized cost, to the neglect of utility and demand. It was as if they had been working with *horizontal ss* curves and *neglecting* all *dd* curves.[1]

To the rescue of this damsel in distress (classical value theory) came the utility theorists of the late nineteenth century, with Alfred Marshall taking the lead in linking up the one-sided cost-of-production theory of supply with the utility theory of demand. This marriage provided, it is claimed, a balanced and more sophisticated theory of value and price in which both supply and demand play an equal role. As a result of this achievement, the classical tradition expired and became of interest only to historians of economic thought.

But this interpretation is inadequate. For one thing, the neoclassical theory of supply and demand did not really join the classical cost-of-production theory of supply with the utility theory of demand. The twin blades of Marshall's scissors—supply and demand—never really existed. What really happened was that utility theory came to be used to explain *both* the supply side as well as the demand side. The classical cost-of-production theory was dropped entirely and in its place was substituted a utility theory and opportunity cost theory of factor supply. As Marshall himself stated,

> While demand is based on the desire to obtain commodities, supply depends mainly on the unwillingness to undergo "discommodities." These fall generally under two labels: labor, and the sacrifice involved in putting off consumption . . .[2]

The costs of production, therefore, are themselves based on disutility, opportunity cost, alternative costs, etc., all of which are subjective, psychological explanations of costs. The true classical idea of cost—the amount of society's labor diverted to the production of goods—plays no role whatever in neoclassical supply and demand theory.

All neoclassical value theory is reducible, therefore, to a common denominator: the MIND. It is a form of idealism which penetrates neoclassical theory at every juncture. The classical tradition, on the other hand, is an alternative which rejects idealistic and metaphysical interpretations of value. It is an explanation of value which begins with Smith, continues with Ricardo and then Marx, and, most significantly, exists today in the works of many Marxists and post Keynesians. Classical value theory never really died, therefore. Overshadowed, yes. Misunderstood, yes. But dead, certainly not! This latter interpretation I choose to call the *dual theory* of the history of economic thought.

The main point behind the dual theory of history is this. The orthodox linear interpretation of classical economics is in fact that of neoclassical economists. Neoclassical economists are totally preoccupied with marketplace relations. In fact, they tend to see all social relationships as marketplace relationships. Because of this they fail to realize that the classical theories of price are not based on supply and demand theory at all! Price, as a distinct category of analysis, is *not* simply a marketplace phenomenon. It is this point which neoclassical economists fail to understand and which I hope to make clear in this book.

However, to clarify this point we must distinguish between two kinds of prices. Classical theory generally deals with (1) *prices of production* or *natural prices* and (2) *market prices.* Prices of production serve as the foundation for market prices. The former prices are determined by some variant of the labor theory of value. The latter prices are indeed determined by supply *and* demand. But it is prices of production which are most important to classical theory. The same is therefore true of contemporary Marxian and post-Keynesian theory. Market prices play an important but supporting role.

Classical theory thus does not neglect supply and demand theory as is usually believed. It is simply explaining an economic phenomenon—prices of production—which neoclassical economists do not see. All that neoclassical economists see is market price. They make no distinction between the two categories of price. If all you see is market price, then of course supply and demand theory alone is relevant, and any labor theory explanation will appear to be one-sided and incomplete.

According to the dual theory, the classical tradition runs parallel to the neoclassical tradition and continues to evolve into the modern period. Today, there are two branches of thought within this tradition, the post-Keynesian and the Marxian. Both of these branches, although differing on many important points, share a unique idea of the definition of economics. They see the "economic problem" to be something other than the allocation of scarce resources to alternative uses. Instead, they see the economic problem to be both physical and social.

The physical problem of economics is to make sure that the productive system, particularly that portion which serves human *needs*, can be maintained and can produce a surplus. The social problem is that of designing appropriate institutions which can cultivate the *higher* needs of human society while at the same time providing for society's subsistence needs. By higher needs I mean the need to self-actualize, the need to *grow* in a variey of ways, aesthetic needs, the needs for love, justice, etc.

My purpose, however, is not to develop a general theory consistent with such a definition of economics. This has already been done by others. I suggest that the reader study the recent book by Lutz and Lux as a modern example of such work.[3]

Instead, my purpose is narrower. It rests on the idea that any social-economic theory of capitalism must begin with a coherent and consistent theory of value and price. The neoclassical school, however misleading and inappropriate, is based on a coherent and consistent theory of value and price. Its value theory is a psychological, or subjective theory; its price theory is a market theory.

Post-Keynesian and Marxian economics are, as we shall see, also based on a coherent and consistent theory of value and price. This theory of value appeals not to psychological feelings but to concrete, objective circumstances; its theory of price is not a market theory of price but a technical price-of-production theory. The two types of prices—prices of production and market prices—are *not* the same. All prices are market prices in neoclassical economics.

The "core" of the post-Keynesian and Marxian tradition is, therefore, a theory of value and price. This theory sets out to simultaneously determine prices, profits, and wages by a system of production equations. The development of this theory is the subject matter of this book. It is important because, in my opinion, the approach comes much closer to capturing the essence of a capitalistic economy. It also can serve as the theoretical basis for a more humane approach to the study of economics and the design of humane social institutions.

In Chapter 1 I introduce some basic philosophical concepts having to do with ideology. With these concepts I hope to shed some light on why neoclassical economists see things very differently. More fundamentally, I hope to convince the reader that people can indeed see things differently.

In Chapters 2, 3, and 4, I isolate the basic differences between the neoclassical orthodoxy and the post-Keynesian and Marxian alternatives. These chapters focus primarily on the way in which different overall visions of the workings of capitalism are translated into different perspectives on the nature of value. The neoclassical view of the workings of capitalism is translated into a subjective, psychological theory of the valuation of commodities. The alternative viewpoint is translated into an objective, physical theory of value. It is based on the notion that value reflects real human activity and is therefore founded on concrete, objective notions of productivity, labor time, technology, etc. These two competing value traditions are therefore rooted in two different perspectives on the nature of capitalism.

Part III (Chapters 5 and 6) gets deeper into the theoretical heart of the alternative value tradition. These chapters deal with the idea of economic surplus, a concept which neoclassical economists categorically dismiss. In classical theory the economic surplus, together with the labor theory of value, serves as the foundation for the theory of price. The way in which this foundation is laid for the theory of price is described in the next two parts of the book.

In Part IV (Chapters 7 through 10) I examine the post-Keynesian branch of contemporary classical economics. The term "post" in "post-Keynesian" is potentially misleading because it does *not* refer to all followers of Keynes. It does not refer to that brand of macroeconomics which results from synthesizing Keynesian theory and neoclassical theory and which is contained in almost all contemporary macroeconomic textbooks. That synthesis regards the neoclassical analysis as essentially correct, something which post-Keynesians categorically deny. Also, post-Keynesians are generally far more radical in their policy recommendations than are mainstream economists and take a much more critical view toward capitalist society.

The post-Keynesian approach to value and price is largely based on Ricardian value theory. However, Ricardo's treatment of value theory was not without its difficulties. Because of these problems his approach was never given the serious attention it deserved. The recent work of Piero Sraffa has resolved these difficulties, however, making the Ricardian basis of post-Keynesian theory respectable once again. The chapters in Part IV are based on Sraffa's model of value and price.

Also growing out of the Ricardian tradition, and in many ways going far beyond it, is the Marxian tradition. This second branch is the subject of Part V (Chapters 11 and 12). The philosophy and logic of Marx's theory of value and price are described in Chapter 11. The so-called transformation problem is discussed in Chapter 12.

The final part of this book compares and contrasts the post-Keynesian branch with the Marxian branch. Although I have placed both of these branches in the same general tradition—the classical tradition—the differences between them are nonetheless important and controversial. The book concludes with some suggested readings for those who wish to study the topic more deeply.

Several points need to be made about this book. First, I make no attempt whatever to provide general critiques of neoclassical economics. This has already been done. I only wish to introduce the student of price theory to an alternative to the neoclassical orthodoxy. However, I select certain points of neoclassical economics for criticism whenever this is necessary to understand the alternative approach.

Secondly, I do not try to defend my interpretation of the history of economic thought. To do so would require that I write a history of economic thought text. This has also been done. I instead assume throughout that there does exist a distinct classical tradition with clearly defined contemporary descendants.

Thirdly, I use the expressions "neo-Ricardian" and "post-Keynesian" interchangeably even though the former is more appropriately viewed as a subset of the latter. Post-Keynesianism is a curious blend of Ricardian, Keynesian, Marxian, and Institutionalist economics. It is a school of thought which is emerging into a clearly defined contemporary alternative to conventional neoclassical economics. One component of post-Keynesian economics is price theory. Post-Keynesian price theory is tied to the work of Piero Sraffa, a Cambridge (England) economist whose theory of price is written in the Ricardian tradition—hence the term "neo-Ricardian." I advise the reader not to be too concerned about these potentially confusing divisions until he or she has finished this book.[4] I intend to unravel and elucidate some of the finer differences between the various categories in Chapter 2.

Fourthly, I do not deal with certain issues which naturally arise when discussing Sraffa. Specifically, I do not deal with the so-called Cambridge capital controversies, except for a brief introduction to the topic in Chapter 8. Neither do I deal with the implicit critique of marginalism contained in Sraffa's book, nor the reswitching paradox, nor growth theory.

Fifthly, an important motivation for writing this book was to make the works of Sraffa, as well as the surrounding literature, more readily accessible to students. Sraffa's book, although tremendously important, is tortuous to read, especially for those raised in the neoclassical tradition. The related literature is just as difficult. In order to accomplish my goal of making this economic tradition more accessible I tried to present the material in an ascending level of difficulty. Thus, the beginning chapters are very simple while the latter chapters are more difficult, allowing the student to gradually build to the point where he or she can understand the more advanced literature. This strategy seems to me to be the only sensible one if this book is to be regarded as a true "introduction."

Finally, the audience for whom I am writing consists of intermediate and advanced undergraduate economics majors, especially those studying microeconomics or the history of economic thought; graduate students looking for a brief introduction to a body of literature rarely discussed explicitly in graduate courses but very frequently referred to in scholarly articles and books; and professional economists who likewise would appreciate a brief overview of the issues surrounding Sraffa and

Marx. I also assume that the only mathematical skills required to understand this book are simple algebra and a basic understanding of linear equations and how to solve them.

At this point I would like to acknowledge the invaluable assistance given to me by Professor Alfred S. Eichner. His criticisms of earlier versions of this manuscript helped me immeasurably in improving the quality of this book. Thanks also go to two anonymous reviewers for their helpful criticisms and suggestions. I am also indebted to my teacher, Professor George W. Zinke, for having induced me to read and study Marx and Sraffa in the first place, and to my colleagues Professors Jeffrey T. Young and Pamela Nickless for their guidance and inspiration. I am also grateful to Professor Charles Kerr for his assistance on some of the mathematical aspects of this book. Finally, I wish to acknowledge the support of Professor Richard Payne, and of Ms. Barbara Pickens, whose skill and diligence are the real reasons why this book ever got written.

Competing traditions

Part I

A methodological introduction

1

The trouble isn't what people don't know; it's what they do know that isn't so.

Will Rogers

1.1 The objectivity of economic theory

It is essential that we begin this chapter with a rather simple point. This point is that the theories which together constitute the main body of traditional economics are *interpretations* of social reality as seen through the eyes of economists. Now, on the surface this point may seen rather innocuous. It is not. How we interpret the world around us determines what we perceive to be the important social problems of the day and dictates the methods to be used (and to be avoided) in solving these problems. In other words, our perceptions of reality guide our social actions. If our perceptions are wrong, so too will be our actions.

Economic theories, as we shall see, are formal expressions of these perceptions of the world. Because there are many different ways of perceiving reality, it follows not only that there will be many competing economic theories, but that these competing theories will rarely be capable of being disproved in a detached and scientific manner. The best theory will therefore rarely succeed in completely supplanting its competitors, largely because the criteria for a "good" or "best" economic theory are rather vague.

This suggests that many people often subscribe to theories not because they are "scientifically" valid, but because theories somehow appeal to their personal feelings and their sense of what is just. These feelings and senses are, of course, themselves rooted in popular ideologies. For this reason, a theory may continue to be accepted even if it can be proved false, for proving a theory incorrect may threaten people's loyalties. This is true not only of the social sciences, but of the physical sciences as well. For example, Galileo was persecuted by church authorities in the early seventeenth century for claiming that the earth revolved around the sun. This fact was subject to proof, but proving it *did not* make it so. People did not *want* to believe that the sun was the center of the universe, and so they didn't. No amount of proof could sway their conviction.

Economists are, of course, just like everyone else. We are all raised in a particular social environment and we internalize its values, beliefs, and customs. As a group, economists are therefore unlikely to construct theoretical models which cast doubt upon these values, beliefs, and customs. This is understandable and quite natural; no matter how objective an economist tries to be, he or she is still governed to some extent by a set of beliefs which may in fact have little to do with current conditions.

Although the modern economist perhaps comes better equipped with analytical tools and may be capable of summoning a variety of sophisticated intellectual resources unavailable to others, this does not mean that he or she produces the only accurate interpretations of reality. If the student approaches the study of economics with this false expectation in mind, as indeed many do, he or she is bound to be bitterly disappointed. But perhaps more dangerous than being merely disappointed, the student may fail to perceive the tentative nature of all economic theories and therefore proceed as though TRUTH had been revealed. In this book, there will be no pretense of revealing TRUTH. We simply hope to provide an introduction to an alternative body of economic theory which views capitalism quite differently.

It is essential, therefore, to point out at the very outset that economic theory has a very subjective, ideological aspect to it. Only if this were not true could economics be described as "value-free." To say that a particular study is value-free implies that these ideological elements have been purged. This is rarely, if ever, the case with economics. The observer is inextricably involved with, and has an immediate interest in, the subject matter under observation. Although we can attempt to be objective, we can never fully succeed in being so.

1.2 Ideologies and economics

In spite of the fact that economic theory cannot portray reality with perfect accuracy, its study can nevertheless provide substantial insight into the world around us and how we relate to that world. However, in order to gain this insight, we must fully understand and appreciate the social perspectives that economic theory represents. It is, after all, the process of critically examining these perspectives that will ultimately reveal these insights to us.

The formal theory of Post-Keynesian and Marxian economics presented in this book is useful, therefore, because it translates the ideological components of a given social perspective into a logically manageable form and permits us to obtain a tentative picture of society that can be subjected to our personal scrutiny. In the sections that follow we delve more deeply into the ideological character of economic theory, in an effort to grasp the full meaning of the economic tradition to be presented in this book. Our first task is to examine the structure of ideologies, the role they play in society, and the extent to which they dominate our perceptions of social economic reality.

1.2A Ideology defined

The word "ideology" once meant the study of ideas. Modern usage of the term is somewhat different, however. Although ideology still refers to ideas, today we think of it as a set of doctrines which a certain group or class of people holds in common. It consists of values, attitudes, social and religious beliefs.[1]

Although more than one ideology may coexist in a given society, it is typical to find a single dominant ideology that serves as a point of reference. Because the ideas that make up that ideology specify "correct" or socially acceptable values, beliefs, and attitudes, the dominating ideology gives direction and purpose to the activities undertaken by members of society. These ideas may be embodied in social customs and taboos, religious doctrines, civil laws, and political views. In fact, they shape all social institutions. Moreover, the values, preferences, and attitudes of individuals within a society are rooted in the ideology to which society as a whole collectively subscribes. By "rooted" is meant learned and enforced. The same social institutions which share an ideology tend, in their normal functioning, to perpetuate that ideology. And this perpetuating process is in fact a learning proces.[2] Any individual who learns but still fails to subscribe to the dominant ideology, or some subset of it, may be referred to as a *heretic*.

It is very difficult, if not impossible, to catalog with precision all the ideas which constitute an ideology. This is due to the fact that ideologies are never officially documented or codified. They are only partially incorporated into the laws, regulations, and customs of a society. Moreover, ideological elements are often implicit in the things we do and the things we say. Such elements cannot be easily observed or articulated because we are not always fully conscious of our attatchment to them.

1.2B Ideological propositions and economics

As we have just seen, an ideology is said to contain sets of ideas which define what a group of people believe to be the correct or proper modes of individual and collective behavior. A given ideology may be said to be "layered," with very abstract, general ideas on the top layers and more specific and concrete ideas on the bottom layers.

On the highest or most abstract level are those ideas which relate to broad philosophical issues such as destiny, existence, human nature, and good and evil. On a lower and more concrete level we find more specific ideas about democracy, individualism, free enterprise, private property, competition, and economic freedom. Moreover, ideas on this level usually flow from higher level ideas. For example, the general higher level belief that the nature of human beings is to be greedy and acquisitive will most likely result in a lower level economic belief in competition and in the necessity of material rewards as an incentive for productive activity.

Any statement which conveys an idea that is a component of an ideology, no matter at what level, is called an *ideological proposition*. Such propositions are usually incapable of verification and are often tautological (i.e., true by definition). For example, the proposition "capitalism is the best of all possible systems" is ideological, primarily because there exists no empirical evidence to substantiate it. It is impossible to show how present society would be different if another system existed. Hence there is no way to test the validity of this proposition.

Similarly, the proposition "all men are created equal" is ideological because it is based on a tautology. This statement does not specify what it is that is equal among men. Is every man of equal intelligence? Of equal height? All the statement asserts is that every man is equally equal, by definition. As Robinson observed, " 'All men are created equal' is a slogan which expresses a protest against privilege by birth. In an egalitarian society no one would ever have thought of saying any such thing."[3]

Ideological propositions, then, appeal directly to what is considered correct or true according to a society's particular stage in history and to the form which that society takes at the time. They enter into economic theory at almost every juncture and are very difficult to identify and isolate. This is largely due to the fact that ideological propositions are subtle, emotional in nature, and frequently fused to propositions of a more scientific character.

Before we leave the impression that ideology is "bad," or something to be avoided, we must consider the role played by an ideology in society. Every society requires a set of rules to guide activity and to provide order. Such rules evolve over time and are therefore historically determined. An ideology plays a decisive role in maintaining a status quo (and hence order) by providing certain rules of conduct which prohibit some modes of behavior and encourage others.

What insures universal compliance with the dominant ideology? Typically, existing social institutions will be mobilized to enforce and perpetuate the dominant ideology, or new ones will be created that will do so. Such institutions as the army, police, judicial system, and educational systems provide the necessary sets of rewards and penalties to screen out heretical perspectives and values.

Ideologies are also dynamic and change shape frequently over time. What is deemed socially acceptable in one era may become unacceptable in another. Oftentimes, the demands of political and economic change force society to alter the content and form of its ideology. Such ideological transformations have generally followed social, political, and economic transformations and will almost certainly continue to change in the future. As Marx once asserted, the only thing that really never changes is the fact of change itself.

1.3 Paradigms, visions, and theories

We have thus far made the point that economic theory is inherently ideological. In fact, the very definition of the scope of neoclassical economics, found in all modern textbooks, has an ideological aspect to it. Economics is usually said to deal with the allocation of scarce resources to the provision of goods and services for the satisfaction of our unlimited wants. The notion of scarcity thus derives from the psychological premise of unlimited wants. Economics is, according to this viewpoint, the "science" of choice. We must choose how to allocate resources.

1.3A Economic visions

We might have begun with another orientation and with another definition of the scope of economics. If we had done so, we could rest assured that a different kind of economic theory would have followed. But the scarcity—choice perspective is the jumping-off point for neoclassical economics. It is, as Joseph Schumpeter might have called it, the neoclassical *vision*.[4] So we will focus on it for a little while longer before moving to the alternative tradition.

A vision may be defined to be a general perspective of reality which gives direction and purpose to further intellectual activity within a discipline. It guides the search for understanding. A vision is an expression of how we think society works and of what the major problems confronting society are. As far as economics is concerned, a vision is the conceptual "raw material" for economic analysis. It is the preanalytic, precognitive act, to use Schumpeter's terminology.[5]

A vision tells the economist where to look for answers to economic problems. It even defines what is and what is not an economic problem. A vision also points to those phenomena which are deemed important to research, and just as importantly prevents us from seeing others which are deemed unimportant.[6]

Since a vision is a world view of the economic process, it is on the one hand based on an ideological foundation and on the other hand the basis for economic theories of the economy. The relationships between an ideology, a vision, and a body of economic theories may be illustrated as follows,

Ideology → vision → economic theories

where the arrows show the main directions of causality. A dominant ideology will result in a standard economic vision, which in turn will yield a certain set of economic theories. However, general acceptance of a general body of economic theories may in turn feed back onto the ideology, reinforcing its general acceptance.

1.3B Paradigms

Just as an ideology influences a person's vision of the economy, a vision will in turn influence a set of theories that will come to dominate economic thought. As long as the ideology persists, so too will the vision, and so too will the theories. This dominating set of theories may be called a *paradigm*.[7]

A paradigm is a standard approach or explanation which members of the discipline accept and use in advancing or applying their knowledge. The activities of those involved in a discipline are generally patterned on the models and techniques that constitute the standard, at least until such time as a new standard proves more acceptable. Moreover, a ruling paradigm does not provide all the answers to the questions which it poses. It is open-ended enough so that a sufficient number of problems remain to be solved. This provides incentive for the continued application of the ruling paradigm.

1.3C Theories

Economic theory is what we shall be dealing with throughout this book. It is therefore of paramount importance that we discuss the meaning of the word "theory" and come to an understanding of what economic theories can be expected to accomplish.

An economic theory may be broadly defined as a set of abstract theorems used to explain social action and behavior. It is a logical edifice which in its entirety represents, or interprets, certain aspects of the real world. Additionally, a theory is bound to appear "unreal" insofar as it will never fully account for everything that one observes. This is because a theory approximates reality; it does not replicate reality. Given an ideological foundation and a certain vision, a theory is then the economist's portrayal of how the economic system functions.

A theory will also vary in generality. Some theories attempt to explain a large part of reality; others attempt to explain only a small segment of reality. The Marxian theory of capitalist economy, for instance, attempts to explain the entire dynamic of a capitalist society. Adam Smith's theory of political economy also tried to explain the general overall principles of a capitalist economy. These are all examples of "general theories." They are all made up of other subtheories of lesser generality and more modest scope. Examples are demand theory, production theory, and distribution theory.

An economic theory will usually consist of three elements. First, it will contain a *taxonomy*. A taxonomy is a system of classification. It defines certain categories which are then employed in constructing a theory. An example of such an economic category is "profit." Profit, as a category, defines a form of income that accrues to certain individuals in society. An example of a system of such categories is the national income accounts. The student should recognize that the system of classification can severely restrict economic analysis as well as enhance it. The Eskimo system for classifying snow is far more complex than that of people who live in temperate zones. In areas where knowing snow conditions intimately may mean survival, having over one hundred different words for snow hardly seems extravagant.[8] Given their system of classification, Eskimos could easily develop an elegant and formal analysis of snow conditions whereas most others would have to settle for a vague and not very descriptive alternative.

A second element of a theory is the set of *assumptions* made by the economist. The purpose of these assumptions is to set aside what the theorist believes to be unimportant, or outside the realm of his or her consideration, permitting him or her to focus only on what is felt to be important to the construction of a theory. Just as the physicist assumes away friction in formulating the theory of gravity, the economist also assumes away certain real-world phenomena in order to formulate economic theories.

The first two elements of a theory create a view of social reality within which the economist can form *hypotheses* about economic behavior, the third element of a theory. The hypothesis is a proposition that can be logically derived from a set of assumptions the economist is using. Once a hypothesis is generally accepted as true, it becomes a *theorem*. A theorem is the basic building block of all theories. By logically assembling a group of theorems, we create an economic theory.

In the next chapter we explore the general nature of the post-Keynesian/Marxian tradition and see how it differs from the neoclassical tradition. This analysis will help us to understand the context in which value theory and price theory are situated.

The post-Keynesian/Marxian alternatives 2

> *It is easy enough to make models on stated assumptions. The difficulty is to find the assumptions that are relevant to reality.*
> Joan Robinson

2.1 Neoclassical ideology, vision, paradigm

The neoclassical approach to economics can be adequately summarized using the concepts defined in Chapter 1. Beginning with ideology, mainstream neoclassical economists make certain assumptions about human nature which are generally consistent with and supportive of a capitalist society. These include the assumption that people behave rationally and act in their own self-interest. It also includes the assumption that people's material wants are unlimited and hence can never be satisfied. Ours is an acquisitive, growth-oriented society in which more material wealth is always preferred to less. The neoclassical ideology also holds that competition (as opposed to cooperation) is a necessary fact of life and may even be desirable. Inequality in material well-being is also typically assumed to be a fact of life, as are the beliefs that material incentives are essential for human motivation and that property ownership is a natural right.

These components of our social ideology give direction to scientific inquiry in the economics discipline by way of the neoclassical *vision*. This vision can best be described as scarcity–choice–harmony. Given the views of human nature to which economists subscribe, the disciplinary question then becomes one of efficiently allocating resources. Because wants are unlimited, these resources are scarce. This in turn requires certain allocative choices to be made (what to produce, how to produce, for whom to produce). Hence the words, "scarcity" and "choice."

The word "harmony" enters into the neoclassical vision because all that is seen is the process by which individuals voluntarily exchange the goods and services which they own. It is believed that a competitive market system is inherently harmonious in the sense that everyone's interests are (or could be) best served. Market exchange is always mutually advantageous to all participants, so that any society organized by a market system is harmonious and benefits all concerned.

The neoclassical vision therefore rests on the perceived freedom and harmony of the marketplace. Consumers are free to choose how to dispose of their incomes; businesses are free to decide what to produce and how to produce; workers are free to choose for whom to work and what occupation to pursue. The free market therefore allows economic freedom to be exercised and, because free exchange is always mutually advantageous, everyone benefits. Economic freedom and social harmony are the kingpins of the neoclassical vision of ideally functioning capitalism.

The *paradigm* which results from this vision is what we call neoclassical economic theory. It consists of a body of economic theories which includes supply theory, demand theory, general equilibrium theory, welfare theory, etc. But the heart of the neoclassical paradigm is its theory of value and price. This theory claims that the value of commodities, represented by their market prices, is ultimately determined in the minds of individuals. Specifically, pleasure (utility) and pain (disutility) are the two factors which together serve as the foundation for market prices and therefore the allocation of resources. As we shall see later, this subjective theory of value gives full expression to the harmony vision of neoclassical economics.

2.1A The neoclassical paradigm

The theoretical description of a capitalist economy as seen through the eyes of a neoclassical economist is illustrated in Figure 2.1. The economy is divided into two groups, households and firms. Each group relates to the other by way of market exchange. All economic agents are both buyers and sellers in this scheme and meet each other on an equal footing in the product and factor markets.

In the factor market households exchange factors of production (land, labor, and capital) for income. Thus, the firms' input costs are equal to the households' income. The terms at which these factors of production are sold to business firms are established by the interaction of supply and demand in the market for these inputs.

On the output side, households spend the income which they receive on the goods and services produced by firms. Once again, the market forces of supply and demand determine the terms (prices) at which goods are sold to households. Households are therefore buyers in one market and sellers in another.

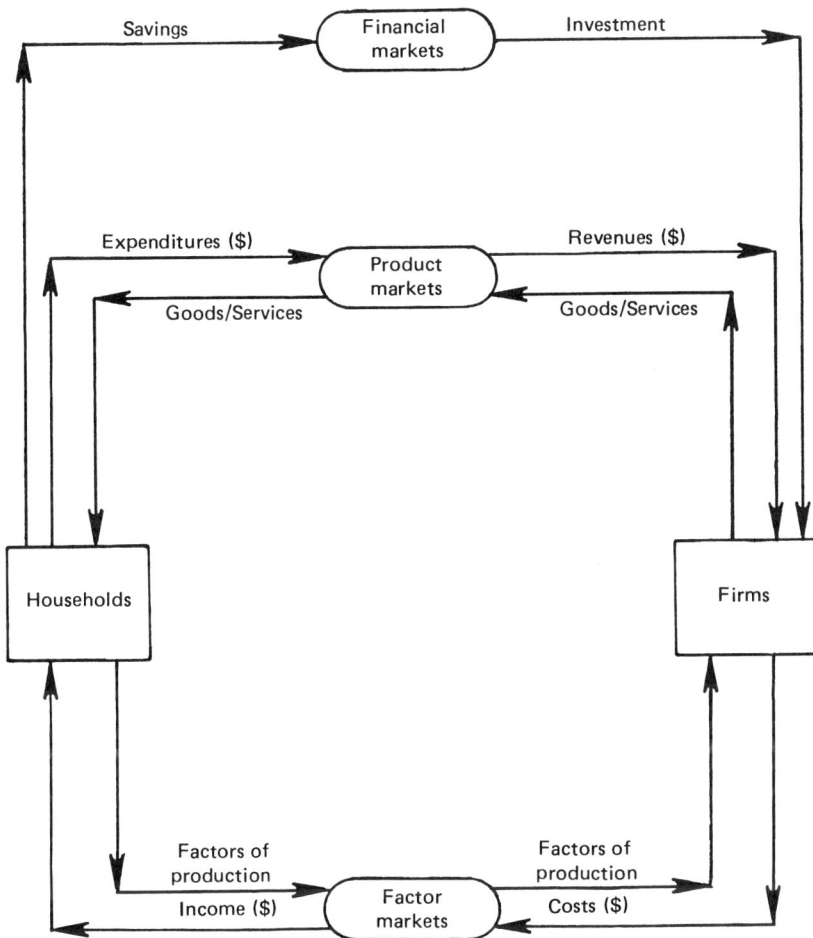

Figure 2.1

Neoclassical Circular Flow

Finally, a portion of the income received by households remains unspent (savings), and a portion of the total output produced and sold consists of investment goods rather than consumer goods. Additionally, the production of investment goods is assumed to be financed by firms' borrowing from household savings. This is represented in Figure 2.1 as a sale of financial assets from firms to households in the financial markets. All income, then, flows either into savings (which is then used for investment) or consumer demand for output. All output goes to supply consumer demand and investment demand.

The neoclassical perception of capitalism, expressed by the circular flow model in Figure 2.1, is clearly based on the market relationships between the two main sectors of the economy, households and businesses. The reason for this emphasis stems from the very definition of neoclassical economics, described earlier: the allocation of scarce resources among unlimited competing uses. *Allocation* and *market exchange* are the key ingredients in a capitalist economy, according to neoclassical economics, and the main partners of this system of exchange and allocation are individual households and firms.

2.1B Equilibrium analysis

Central to neoclassical economic theory is the identification of equilibrating forces in a market economy. Thus, for each of the factors and product markets in existence there will be a certain price and quantity combination that will guarantee that supply equals demand. This combination is termed an *equilibrium price* and *equilibrium quantity*.

Two approaches have been taken in analyzing equilibrium. Together, these two approaches constitute neoclassical microeconomic theory. The first approach is named after its founder, Alfred Marshall (1842-1924). It consists of isolating a single market and examining the forces that work to bring demand equal to supply in that market. Such an analysis is called *partial equilibrium analysis*. It assumes that all other things remain the same (ceteris paribus) and that whatever occurs in the market under observation does not affect conditions existing in other markets.

The second approach to equilibrium analysis originates with the French economist Leon Walras (1834-1910). This approach examines the mutual interconnections between all factor and product markets and is therefore called *general equilibrium analysis*.

A Walrasian general equilibrium model is intended to describe, in a formal way, how everything relates to everything else. It tries to explain, for example, how the price of coffee is tied to the price of substitute and complementary commodities, and how these prices are in turn tied to the prices of the factors of production. In other words, whatever happens in any one market affects all other markets, and general equilibrium models try to demonstrate the nature of these interdependent linkages.

The Walrasian model is constructed with the following four pieces of information given: (1) the available quantity of factors of production; (2) the technologies used to transform inputs into outputs (i.e., production functions); (3) consumer preferences for final goods and services; and (4) the manner in which factors of production are distributed among consumers (that is, the initial distribution of ownership of factor resources).

Given this information there are n factor markets in which resources are bought and sold, and m output markets in which final goods and services are bought and sold. There will therefore be $n + m$ markets, each with a supply and demand relationship of its own. These relationships can be expressed in equation form. The variables of the equations will be the equilibrium prices of all outputs, the equilibrium prices of all factor inputs, the quantities of output purchased, and the quantities of each factor input allocated to each of the productive activities.

Solution of these equations gives us a set of equilibrium market prices which will equilibrate supply and demand in all markets. In other words, if all exchanges take place at these equilibrium prices then supply will equal demand, and all markets will clear. Each of these equilibrium market prices is therefore a measure of relative scarcity and hence a marginal valuation of goods and services. Different patterns of factor ownership, changes in consumer preferences, changes in the technology of production, and/or alterations in the available quantity of factors of production will change the way these factors will be allocated to different lines of productive activity. Such changes will also alter the allocation of final outputs to households. As these allocations change, so too will equilibrium market prices.

Economic activity is portrayed in these models as a *linear, one-way* flow of given factor inputs to the consumption of final output. Thus, the word "circular" in the term "circular flow model" is somewhat misleading. All that the circular flow model of Figure 2.1 portrays is the dual role of households (as buyers and as sellers) and firms (also as buyers and sellers). The causal relationship between all markets is indeed circular in that a change in one variable will affect the values of all other variables. It is also circular in the sense that every flow of commodities is accompanied by an equal and opposite flow of money. However, once the actual physical output finds its way to consumption, nothing else happens. And how the initial endowment of factors of production comes into existence in the first place is obscured. The full meaning of these observations will become clear as we proceed to later chapters.

2.2 Selected criticisms of the neoclassical paradigm

Our purpose is not to provide a general critique of neoclassical economics. However, it is essential to stress certain selected weaknesses of the neoclassical tradition in order to better understand the strengths of the post-Keynesian/Marxian challenge to that tradition. To this end let us briefly enumerate some of the problems we have thus far encountered.

First, the neoclassical paradigm reduces all economic activities to exchange activities. Thus, there is no real concept of production in this paradigm because it only looks at producers in their roles as buyers and sellers in factors markets and product markets. Production, therefore, becomes reduced to an exchange activity.

Without a concrete theory of production, *independent* of exchange, it is impossible to tell if an economic system is *viable*. By viable is meant the ability of an economic system to maintain itself over time. As Walsh and Gram point up,

> There is no presumption [in neoclassical economic theory] that the use of factor services is accompanied by any activity that reconstitutes their productive powers so that it cannot be known that the allocations which now yield an output of commodities will, in the future, be repeatable.[1]

Second, because the neoclassical general equilibrium analysis begins with a given endowment of resources, nothing systematic can be said about where these resources came from and how they are produced. Once again Walsh and Gram observe that

> [i]n a model of neoclassical allocation theory it is of no importance to distinguish inputs on the basis of the process by which they came into being. . . .Indeed, the *only* historical fact that has any bearing on the analysis is that a given quantity of resources has come into existence and is now available at a point in time to be used in ways that may or may not have been anticipated when these resources were produced.[2]

This criticism stems directly from the one-way direction in which *given* factors of production are assumed to result in outputs which *end* in consumption.

Third, neoclassical theory does not have a long-run perspective of the capitalist capital accumulation process. That is, capital accumulation, or investment, is not the center of the neoclassical model; it is instead incidental to it and is submerged in a welter of individual allocative decisions. As Harris states,

> When it comes to the problem of accumulation, this is treated in neoclassical theory essentially as a matter of the exchange of commodities through time, or the exchange of "time-dated" commodities. As such, the problem of accumulation has no special significance in this theory apart from the problem of exchange per se....The basic object of the

economy is consumption; accumulation is an incidental feature of individuals' consumption decision.³

Fourth, the neoclassical paradigm has a very limited explanation of distribution theory. Income distribution in this paradigm is determined by (1) the intensity of demand for factors of production; (2) the willingness of factor owners to make the services of these factors available to firms; (3) technology, which determines factor productivity; and (4) the initial distribution of factor ownership. With the latter two factors given, income distribution becomes entirely a market affair in which individual owners of resources meet buyers in resource markets. How different ownership patterns can influence the outcome of the market is not relevant to the analysis. This points to the general lack of importance given to the idea of *social class* by neoclassical theory.

A social class is a grouping of individuals who share one or more common attributes. In the economic theory to be explained in this book the attribute which unites individuals into a class is ownership of means of production (i.e., produced resources such as factories, machines and equipment, etc.). Those who own means of production and whose income is subsequently derived from this ownership make up the *capitalist class*. Those who do not own means of production, and who must earn a living by working for those who do, make up the *working class*. Other criteria can also be used to partition the population into classsses, and those which have just been described (capitalist and working classes) can be further subdivided to provide increased realism. The main point is that no such class divisions are made in neoclassical distribution theory.

The subservience of production to exchange, the failure to focus on the production of resources and on long-run capital accumulation, and the denial of the relevance of social class all threaten to obscure from our view some of the most essential features of a capitalist system. In particular, they threaten to divert our attention away from the pathology of capitalism. In so doing, social problems such as poverty, unemployment, inflation, and imperialism are not seen as endemic to our economy but as aberrant and curable.

2.3 The post-Keynesian/Marxian alternative

2.3A General overview

It has already been suggested that the post-Keynesian and Marxian paradigms have their roots in the classical school of political economy. We are posing both of these paradigms as a single alternative to the neoclassical orthodoxy. The reason for this association between post-Keyesian and Marxian theories is that they each share a common concern for the kinds of problems and issues which the classical economists were also concerned with, and which the neoclassical school generally pays little attention to. Specifically, they share a vision of capitalism that is based on (1) the identification of production as a distinct social activity; (2) the importance of the *reproduction* of the so-called factors of production; (3) the identification of capital accumulation and its volatility as a focal point for economic theory; and (4) the existence of social classes which interact in a social setting that is not limited to market institutions and which are defined by their relationships to the means of production (i.e., ownership and control of the means of production). These are the same four points which we have just noted were omitted from the neoclassical point of view.

Although the similarities between post-Keynesian and Marxian economics are significant enough to permit us to consider them as a singular alternative in this book, we will not let this association obscure the very real differences between them. These differences are numerous and will be discussed in considerable depth as we proceed toward our consideration of value and price theory.

2.3B Post-Keynesian/Marxian circular flow

The post-Keynesian/Marxian approach is premised on the assumption that capitalism is a class-divided society. The division of society into classes depends, as we have seen, on ownership of the means of production. Those who own the means of production (capitalists) receive an income that is proportional to the extent of their ownership. Those who do not own the means of production are the workers and are obliged to work for the capitalist class.

This approach is also premised on the assumption that a capitalist economy produces a *surplus* of output above and beyond the customary needs of the population. This surplus is the source of profit income. It is a residual which accrues to the capitalist class who owns the means of production.

The existence of this surplus is an important source of conflict between social classes. The view that capitalism is best understood as a system of conflicting social relationships is in contrast to the neoclassical view that harmony among economic agents is the primary attribute of the capitalist system.

The post-Keynesian/Marxian vision is illustrated in Figure 2.2.[4] The right-hand box represents all firms. The left-hand triangle represents the social pyramid. This pyramid includes unemployed workers at the very bottom, the working class in the center, and the capitalist owning class at the top. Some upward and downward mobility is shown by the vertical arrows within the triangle. Wage income accrues to the working class; profit income accrues to the capitalist class.

The financial markets gather the accumulated savings from the capitalist class and distribute these savings to industry for expansion. Note well that according to this view workers are assumed to spend all their income, saving nothing. Capitalists are the only savers in this model. The workers' income is spent on necessities (broadly defined) and the portion of the capitalists' income that is not saved is spent on necessities and luxuries. The relevant transactions occur in output markets for these commodities. Revenues from these sales return to business and industry for continued production and accumulation.

The scope of the post-Keynesian/Marxian paradigm as shown in Figure 2.2 clearly differs from, and goes beyond, the exchange orientation of neoclassical economics. The difference lies mainly in the fact

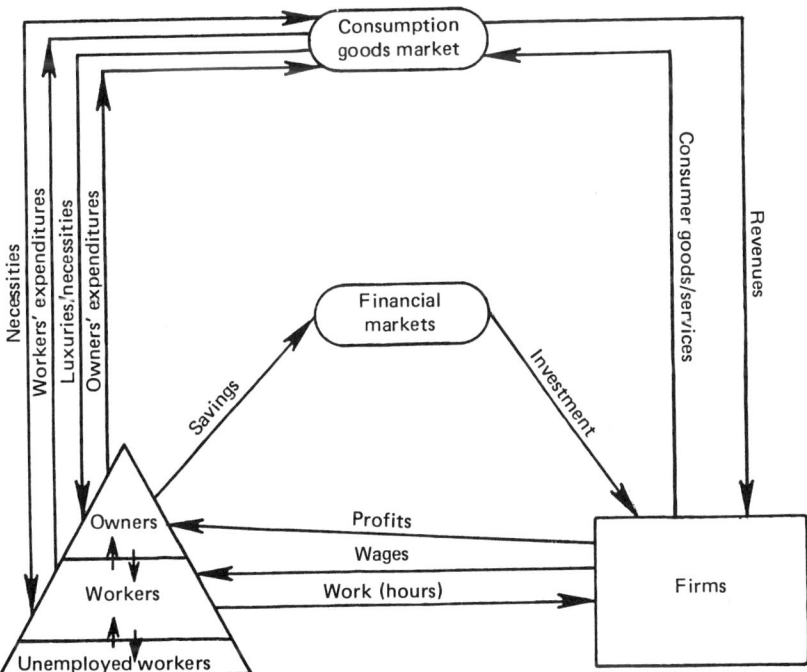

Figure 2.2

Post-Keynesian/Marxian Circular Flow

that resource allocation is only one of several concerns regarded as important. Other concerns include class structure, class conflicts over the production and distribution of society's surplus output, etc. This paradigm also has a multidisciplinary approach since it includes concepts traditionally belonging to sociology and political science.

2.3C Key theoretical elements of post-Keynesian/Marxian economics

The post-Keynesian/Marxian paradigm rests firmly on a theoretical foundation which consists of (1) a theory of value and price; (2) a theory of distribution; and (3) a theory of capital accumulation, or investment.

2.3C(1) Value and price. In neoclassical economics the value of commodities is determined in the minds of individual market participants. Specifically, pleasure (utility) and pain (disutility) are the two factors which together serve as the foundation for value. Market prices, therefore, measure the subjective value of commodities to individuals and result from the harmonious interaction of buyers and sellers.

Value in the post-Keynesian/Marxian tradition is "objective" rather than "subjective." Objective means (according to Webster) "expressing the nature of reality as it is apart from personal reflections or feelings." Value is therefore an attribute of commodities and stems from the fact that these commodities are physically produced by the application of social labor under certain technical conditions.

If the application of human labor, working under certain technical conditions, is what produces value, then any income paid out to people who do not physically participate in production is regarded as a *residual income*. Thus, wage income is not a residual because it is payment for a value-producing activity. Profit income is a residual because it represents a deduction from the value produced by others.

Another feature of post-Keynesian/Marxian value and price theory is that there are three kinds of price instead of the one (market price) which is assumed in neoclassical theory. The two additional prices are *prices of production* and *markup prices*. The former prices are long-run measures of the necessary costs of producing a commodity and reflect the technical conditions of production as well as the distribution of income between wages and profits. The remainder of this book is devoted to an explanation of the relationship between prices of production, costs of production, and income distribution.

A markup price is the price which actually obtains on a day-to-day basis. Unlike the market price, however, the markup price is established by a large corporation which can exercise a great deal of market power. It is argued that such corporations, or "megacorporations," have discretionary control over the prices which they charge their customers. They add a certain percentage markup to their unit costs of production. The net revenues collected from this markup are used in part to finance their investment plans. The determination of markup prices is therefore not made by the market forces of supply and demand as neoclassical microeconomics suggests.[5]

In summary, the post-Keynesian/Marxian tradition is based on a distinction that is made between long-run pricing and short-run pricing. Long-run prices are based on the technical conditions of production and are supply oriented. They are the centers of gravity around which short-run prices will fluctuate. These short-run prices are set either by the forces of the market (market price) or by administrative decision (markup price).

2.3C(2) Distribution theory. Income distribution in capitalism is determined by the interaction of social classes instead of by the private, individual decisions made by factor owners and firms. Because the class structure of capitalism is rooted in the social division between workers and capitalists, it is appropriate to speak of the distribution of income between these two classes. Thus, the two main categories of income are wages and profits, as we have already seen in Figure 2.2.

Apart from the nature and history of class relations, the distribution of income between wages and profits is determined by savings and investment decisions. To see this, let us consider a very simple model developed by Nicholas Kaldor.[6] It is based on three simple equations:

(1) $$Y = W + P$$

(2) $$S_w = s_w W$$

(3) $$S_p = s_p P$$

The first equation states that national income *(Y)* is divided into wage income *(W)* and profit income *(P)*. The second and third equations state that savings out of workers' wages (S_w) is proportional to wage income and that savings out of capitalists' profits (S_p) is proportional to profit income. The factors of proportionality, s_w and s_p, are the average (and marginal) propensities to save out of wage and profit income, respectively.

Adding together the second and third equations we obtain an expression for total savings:

(4) $$S = s_w W + s_p P$$

Because $W = Y - P$ (from the first equation) we can rewrite equation (4) as follows:

(5) $$S = s_w(Y - P) + s_p P$$

or, multiplying out,

(6) $$S = s_w Y + (s_p - s_w)P$$

It should be recalled that macroeconomic equilibrium is defined by the equality of savings and investment. Thus, $S = I$ in equilibrium. Substituting equation (6) for S we obtain this expression for equilibrium:

(7) $$s_w Y + (s_p - s_w)P = I$$

Dividing through by Y and rearranging we obtain

(8) $$\left\{\frac{1}{s_p - s_w}\right\} \left\{\frac{I}{Y}\right\} - \frac{s_w}{s_p - s_w} = \frac{P}{Y}$$

Equation (8) is the new expression for macroeconomic equilibrium and derives from the simple proposition that $S = I$. It suggests that the share of profits in national income (P/Y) is related to the propensities to save (s_w and s_p) and the rate of investment (I). Now, if we invoke the simplifying assumption made in Figure 2.2, namely, that workers consume all of their income ($s_w = 0$), then equation (8) reduces to

(9) $$\left\{\frac{1}{s_p}\right\} \left\{\frac{I}{Y}\right\} = \frac{P}{Y}$$

In other words, the capitalists' decisions to save and invest determine the share of their income in national income! As M. Kalecki observed,

> Thus, capitalists, as a whole, determine their own profits by the extent of their investment and personal consumption. In a way they are "masters of their fate"....[7]

If capitalists in this simple model choose to increase the amount of investment they will also increase the share of income going to profits.

2.3C(3) Investment theory. In the post-Keynesian/Marxian tradition investment is controlled by profit recipients. Thus, as Figure 2.2 clearly shows, savers and investors are one and the same individuals (or institutions). By making their investment decisions these groups of people influence not only the prices of commodities and the distribution of income, but also the rate of growth of the economy.

An additional feature of investment is that it is an autonomous

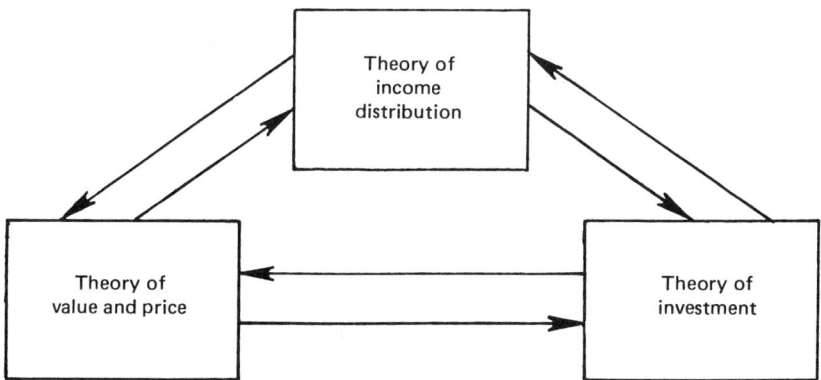

Figure 2.3

The Post-Keynesian/Marxian Paradigm

process which takes place for its own sake. This is the reason that many people say ours is a growth-oriented society, a society which must continue to expand because success itself is measured by the rate of that expansion.

Finally, investment is extremely volatile in a capitalist economy. This is partially due to the uncertainties which corporations must face when making their investment decisions. These uncertainties result from lack of foreknowledge about future economic conditions.

2.4 What lies ahead

We are now in a position to situate the subject matter of this book in its appropriate context. The post-Keynesian/Marxian alternative to neoclassical economics is a general theory of capitalism which consists of a theory of value and price, a theory of distribution, and theory of investment. Each theory is uniquely related to the other two, as Figure 2.3 illustrates.

This book focuses on the post-Keynesian/Marxian theory of value and price. We do not concern ourselves with investment theory and distribution theory. This post-Keynesian/Marxian theory differs from the neoclassical orthodoxy in that it is an objective theory which is rooted in the class relations of capitalist society. Table 2.1 summarizes the main features of neoclassical, post-Keynesian, and Marxian economics. The next two chapters explore each of the two value traditions (objective and subjective) in much greater depth.

Table 2.1

Comparison of Neoclassical, Post-Keynesian, and Marxian Traditions

Main Issue	Neoclassical	Post-Keynesian	Marxian
Dynamic properties of capitalism	stable system with episodes of cyclical variations; equilibrating forces are the main focus	systematic cyclical variations around a constantly expanding growth path; disequilibrium, volatility of investment, corporate control over growth path.	same as post-Keynesian except that capitalist system has a tendency to break down: constant growth not sustainable in long run.
Economic spheres most important	exchange	production and exchange	production and exchange
Main institutional assumption	competitive markets	megacorporations: dominance of large-scale enterprise	monopoly capitalism: dominance of large-scale enterprise
Theoretical focus	allocation: scarcity and individual choice	reproduction and capital accumulation	reproduction and capital accumulation
Primary actors	individuals	social classes	social classes
Relations among actors	harmony	conflict	conflict and oppression
Concept of value	subjective: rooted in mind	objective: rooted in technical structure of production	objective: rooted in labor theory of value
Source of profits	productive contribution of capital; abstinence from present consumption	a residual claimed by capitalist class, used to finance investment and capitalists' consumption	a residual claimed by capitalist class; result of working-class exploitation
Purpose of theory	rationalizes an ideal natural order	explains real, crisis-ridden workings of capitalism	explains capitalism and seeks to change it
Main policy stance	promote market efficiency and stability	radical reform; national planning	social revolution

Two value traditions

Part II

The objective theory of value

3

Whosoever buys a thing, not that he may sell it whole and unchanged, but that it may be a material for fashioning something, he is no merchant. But the man who buys it in order that he may gain by selling it again unchanged and as he bought it, that man is of the buyers and sellers who are cast forth from God's temple.

Gratian

3.1 What is value?

The ultimate purpose of our study of economics is to assess the performance of a society's productive activity. To this end it is necessary to be able to explain how the volume and composition of output is determined and how its distribution among social classes is decided.

Before we can begin to answer these questions, however, we must first identify the social forces which regulate the working activity of people in an economic system that is based on private ownership and market exchange. It is after all, this working activity which, in association with natural and man-made resources, produces the output necessary for the survival and growth of society.

The basic regulating mechanism in a market economy is, of course, *price*. The level of prices reflects the worth which society places on commodities and through the market mechanism directs the use of resources to various lines of productive activity. This price is sometimes referred to as *exchange value*, since it measures the power of commodities to command other commodities in the sphere of exchange (i.e., in the marketplace).

For example, if one shirt sells for $10 in the marketplace, and five pens also sell for $10, then we can write

$$1 \text{ shirt} = \$10 = 5 \text{ pens}$$

Thus the exchange value of 1 shirt is 5 pens; 1 shirt, in other words, can "command" 5 pens, as well as a variety of other commodities.

The determination of exchange value is the subject matter of value theory. However, identifying the social forces which ultimately determine the exchange value of goods, and hence the allocation of society's working activity, is no simple task. The single most important feature of a competitive market economy is the fact that no single individual or group is directly responsible for deciding exchange values. It appears as if an "invisible hand" makes these decisions and guides production in a certain direction. If these social forces, then, are hidden from view, how are we to identify them? The answer to this question, as we shall see, depends entirely on one's approach to the value question.

3.2 Post-Keynesian/Marxian and neoclassical value theory

The post-Keynesian/Marxian and neoclassical schools of thought differ markedly in their approach to value theory. So different are these approaches that they lead to entirely different opinions about the proper scope of economics.

The currently dominant neoclassical theory of value asserts that the exchange value of commodities is subjectively determined and revealed in the marketplace, or the sphere of exchange. In other words, exchange value is a function of individuals' *psychological* assessments of the final utility to be derived from using the commodities in question. The neoclassical paradigm claims, therefore, that utility is the final determinant of exchange value and that this use value is determined in the minds of consumers.

The post-Keynesian/Marxian paradigm, on the other hand, grants only a limited role to use value and individual psychology. These factors are instead regarded as prerequisites of value, but not determinants of value. The source of value must instead be sought in the *sphere of production* rather than the sphere of exchange. This approach falls into the general category of *objective* theories of value, where "objective" here refers to the concrete and material, rather than the psychological attributes of economic activity. It is the actual expenditure of human effort which confers value on commodities.

The direction in which these two approaches lead us is a matter to be discussed later. Let us first take a closer look at both theories of value. Since the objective approach to value theory has a much longer history, dating all the way back to Thomas Aquinas (1225-1274) and beyond, we shall begin with a brief discussion of its evolution and refinement over time. We shall then take up the competing subjective theory of value in the next chapter. It is a newer economic theory because it did not begin to occupy the attention of economists until the latter part of the nineteenth century. At that time it supplanted the objective theory of value and became what is today the mainstream approach.

3.3 Before the labor theory of value

3.3A The just price theory of value

One of the earliest treatments of the subject of value was that of Aristotle. As was typical among ancient and medieval scholars, discussions of economic topics were framed in the setting of ethics and philosophy, and Aristotle's notion of value was no exception.

According to Aristotle, exchange is necessary to the survival of the community. However, when one person sells a commodity to another, the terms of exchange (price) should be such that both parties will be enabled to maintain their respective stations in life—no more, no less. Implicit in this argument is the idea that the cost of producing a commodity, defined to include a small increment for the producer's "necessary" income, determines the proper selling price. The idea of buying or producing a commodity for the sole purpose of reselling it at a profit was frowned upon and considered acquisitive and hence unethical. Reimbursement for costs incurred, together with an increment for the maintenance of the seller at his or her given standard of living, was the "just" reward.

This line of reasoning continued through the Middle Ages in Europe and well into the Renaissance era (roughly until the early seventeenth century). During this period economic morality was being "preached from the pulpit," and the just price theory of value had become well entrenched in Catholic religious teaching. However, the kinds of commercial activities that were becoming essential to the development of society in the latter Middle Ages encouraged a "commercial morality" that was denounced by the church as sinful. The rise of a sizable merchant class who transported their wares over long distances—and sold them for a profit—was a phenomenon which could not be easily reconciled with the just price theory. There was no problem so long as people purchased or produced commodities for the purpose of using them. But what should be done about those who purchased commodities for the purpose of reselling them for a net gain?

This is an excellent example of the dilemma created by an ideological system that is at odds with the material demands of a dynamically changing society. Not unexpectedly, the ideology eventually changed with the growth of Protestantism, and the moral foundations upon which the just price theory of value was based eventually crumbled. But the seed for a more fully developed objective theory of value had been planted. The notion that value was related to the cost of production survived until the economists of the eighteenth and nineteenth centuries transformed it into a labor theory of value.

3.3B From the just price to Adam Smith

During the sixteenth, seventeenth, and eighteenth centuries in Europe a number of important changes occurred in the organization of society. The source of the merchants' profits had at first been the price differentials which they were able to exploit. They bought commodities cheaply from independent producers and sold them at higher prices to consumers. Profits in this kind of system originated, therefore, in the sphere of exchange.

As commerce became an increasingly dominant source of income, competition among merchants made it increasingly difficult to take advantage of price differentials. The need to control the production process itself became paramount and ultimately resulted in the rise of manufacturing and industry. It also resulted in an enormous growth in technology. This development, together with the evolution of a large working class who had no access to capital resources, culminated in the Industrial Revolution. This was truly a revolution, for within a relatively short period of time European society transformed itself into a modern capitalist society.

Along with this social transformation came a change in the way social theorists explained the phenomenon of exchange value. The problem of value was understandably much more complex, largely because society itself had become much more complex. Although brief flirtations with a subjective theory of value were indeed made during this time, economists still looked to the costs of production as the major determinant of value.

There was one substantial difference, however. This difference originated in the fact that *labor* now became crucial in industrialized society. Without a large supply of workers available to work in the newly opening factories, the growing capitalist class would be unable to continue producing. By this time (eighteenth century), moreover, the moral difficulties associated with profit making had been almost entirely overcome.

Labor became such an important element in society—it was, in fact, considered the universal element of cost—that many economists now came to look upon labor costs as the final source of exchange value, rather than costs in general. Additionally, rather than looking to the sphere of exchange for the source of profits, looking to the sphere of production now became more reasonable, not only because the employment of labor in production was responsible for creating an abundance of material goods, but also because the employment of labor yielded attractive profits to the employer. What once began as a cost-of-production theory of value would now gradually evolve, at the hands of Smith, Ricardo, and Marx, into a legitimate labor theory of value.

3.4 The labor theory of value

3.4A Adam Smith's theory of value

Among Adam Smith's major objectives was to discover the laws which governed a self-regulating market economy and to be able to identify those social institutions which prevented these "natural" laws from operating. To this end Smith employed the concept of *natural price*. This price was, in modern terminology, the long-run equilibrium price, or that price which would exist in the absence of any outside disturbances and after all market adjustments had taken place. It was the center of gravity around which market prices fluctuated.

This natural price was, therefore, different from the *market price*. The market price of a commodity was determined by given supply and demand conditions at a certain moment in time, and in the short run could be expected to differ from the natural level. In the long run, however, the marketplace would tend toward its natural level in a freely competitive market.

One way of showing how such a mechanism works is to assume that at a given point in time the market price and natural price for a commodity are equal. The market is in a stable equilibrium. Now, all of a sudden, consumer preferences change causing an increase in demand for the commodity. The market price will rise above the natural price. Higher profits will be made, inducing new firms to enter the market. Market supply increases, and the market price will then return to its original natural level. The opposite will occur if market demand were to initially fall. In this way the market supply and demand always tend to drive market prices toward their natural levels.

The distinction between these two kinds of price was indicative of Smith's concern with the harmful effects of monopoly power and of government intervention in society's productive activity. These are regarded as unnatural, or artificial, obstacles to the smooth functioning of the economy, and they result in prices that remain well above or below their natural levels.

Smith's explanation of the natural price, or value, of commodities is best examined in the light of the following two questions. First, what is the *source*, or cause, of value? Second, what determines the *level* of value? One would think that the answer to the first question would also be the answer to the second, that whatever "caused" value would also determine how much value a commodity would possess. Smith did not see things in this way, however.

Smith's analysis began with a search for a suitable measure of value. He observes that the measure which best captures the essence of exchange is the ability of a commodity to command other commodities. Now, it is true that in a society characterized by the division of labor the exchange of commodities is in fact an exchange of other people's laboring activities. These laboring activities are embodied in the commodities themselves. It therefore follows that the best measure of value is the ability of a commodity to command the laboring activities of other people. This approach is referred to as the *labor command* theory of value.

Before we proceed any further, it is important to note the compatibility of this measure with what Smith was actually observing at the time. Essential to the growth of the newly developing capitalist system was the ability of the capitalist class to accumulate and reinvest the material wealth produced. Smith noted that the funds that were thus accumulated came from profits. And, unlike other costs of production, profits represented a payment for something that was not actually used up in the act of production. Where did profits come from then? In order to explain the origin of profits, Smith employed the concept of *surplus*, although he didn't attribute as much importance to it as Marx later did. This surplus was the amount of output left over after deducting the expenses of maintaining society's fixed and circulating capital. It was out of this surplus product that the capitalists received their profits and workers received their wages. It was also out of this surplus that the landlords received their rent.

The natural price of a commodity, therefore, was determined by the three main components of price, each representing the social average rate of income accruing to the three main classes in capitalist society: (1) *wages* earned by the working class; (2) *profits* received by the capitalist class; and (3) *rent* received by the landlord class.

Since the value of the output, represented by the natural price, is greater than the labor value of the inputs, represented by wages, accumulation (reinvestment) could take place. This difference arose from the fact that rent and profits were deductions from the output produced by labor and not payments for inputs. The capitalists and landlords did not actually contribute directly to production. The amount so accumulated could then put more workers to work. The labor command theory of value, then, was an indirect measure of this accumulation process, since the capitalists' fund would over time be able to command increasing amounts of labor.

Now that Smith had located what he believed to be the best measure of value, he proceeded to ask what it is that regulates its level at any point in time. That is, what determines the amount of labor which a commodity's natural price can command?

Smith at first claimed—but later rejected—the notion that it is the amount of labor actually incorporated into the production of a commodity which determines the amount of labor which it can command. This view is referrred to as a *labor-embodied* theory of value. Hence, the labor-commanded value (i.e., the amount of labor which the natural price of a commodity can purchase) was first thought by Smith to be determined by the labor embodied in the production of a commodity.

To see why Smith rejected this idea, let us employ the following illustration.[1] Assume that in a given year 100 bushels of corn can be produced by 300 hours of labor. The real wage rate per hour is determined in a competitive labor market and is paid out in corn rather than money. Finally, assume that the wage rate is 0.25 bushels per hour and that only the workers and the capitalists share the output.

Table 3.1

Labor-Commanded vs. Labor-Embodied Value

Corn Output (bushels)	Labor Input (hours)	Wage Rate (bushels/ hours)	Total Wages (bushels)	Surplus (profits) (bushels)	Labor Embodied (hours)	Labor Commanded (hours)
100	300	0.25	75	25	300	400
100	300	0.33	100	0	300	300

The data are shown in Table 3.1. If the wage rate is 0.25, then the total wage bill is 75 bushels. This leaves 25 bushels available to the capitalists for profit. The labor-embodied value of the 100 bushels of corn is 300 hours; the labor-commanded value is 400 hours (at a wage of 0.25 per unit, the 100 bushels of output can exchange for 400 hours of labor).

Since the two quantities are widely divergent, Smith rejected the embodied labor explanation of labor command value. Only in a precapitalist society in which the workers owned their own tools and received the entire output *without* having to share it would the two quantities be equal. In such a society, depicted in the second row of Table 3.1, the implicit wage rate would be 0.33 bushels per hour, total wages 100 bushels, and profits zero. But to Smith this was entirely unrealistic in a capitalist system.

How then, did Smith leave the question? What actually regulated the natural price of a commodity? Smith's answer was that it was the natural price of labor, land, and capital which in turn regulated the natural price of a commodity as measured by commandable labor. This claims in effect that prices determine prices, a circular argument which, as we shall see, was not very satisfactory.

3.4B David Ricardo's theory of value

David Ricardo continued the effort to develop an objective theory of value. Like Adam Smith, he attempted to explain and measure value by focusing on the actual conditions of production. It was therefore the expenditure of human labor in the process of production which, to Ricardo, conferred value on commodities.

Unlike Smith, however, Ricardo developed a labor-embodied theory of value and rejected the labor-commanded version. The amount of society's labor time allocated to the production of a commodity was the true source of value and also the best (although imperfect) measure of value. Thus, the only circumstance which could change the natural price of a commodity was a change in the way it was produced and hence a change in the amount of labor time necessary for its production. This view is best expressed by Ricardo as follows:

> To me it appears a contradiction to say a thing has increased in natural value while it continues to be produced under precisely the same conditions as before.[2]

Ricardo's labor-embodied theory of value was based on four assumptions. First, he assumed that "[u]tility . . . is not the measure of exchangeable value, although it is absolutely essential to it."[3] Second, Ricardo argued that the exchange value of a commodity is due to (1) scarcity and (2) the labor embodied in production. However, he assumed that those commodities which derive their value from scarcity alone "form a very small part of the mass of commodities daily exchanged in the market."[4] Hence, Ricardo focuses only on those commodities the supply of which can only be increased by the application of human effort.

The third assumption made by Ricardo was that the labor incorporated into the raw materials as well as the capital goods which are used in the production of a commodity must also be included in the value accounting. Thus, the past labor time embodied in capital goods and "transferred" to the output during production must be added to both the current labor expended and the labor embodied in the raw materials in order to obtain the total value of output.

It should be noted, however, that it is not all the labor used to build the capital goods that must be counted, but only that portion which is consumed in the production of a unit of output. For example, suppose an expensive machine that lasts 10 years is produced with 360,000 labor hours. In one year, 36,000 of the 360,000 hours are used up. In one day, 1/360, or 100 hours, is used up. If 20 units of output are produced per day, then each unit has 5 labor hours of value embodied in it. This value must then be added to the number of current labor hours necessary to produce one unit of output and the labor value of raw materials to obtain the total value per unit. This total is then sold at the natural price, and the value thereby realized in exchange is divided among the workers (wages) and the capitalists (profits) and the landlords (rent). For simplicity, however, we assume away the landlord class and work only with the working class and the capitalist class.

The final assumption in the development of Ricardo's theory was that qualitative skill differences among workers are fully reflected in wage differentials, *and* that these differences remain constant over time. Hence, one hour of labor provided by a worker with skill A may be worth two hours of labor provided by a worker with skill B. If these skill differences remain constant throughout the economy, then we may reasonably neglect them in our labor value accounting.[5]

With these assumptions in mind, it was believed that the natural prices of commodities would be proportional to the labor embodied in their production. Thus, if a certain commodity A required 10 hours of labor to produce, and another commodity B required 20, then the natural price of B would be twice that of A.

Ricardo's labor theory of value is shown graphically in Figure 3.1. We assume a factory produces a certain kind of output, commodity A, with three inputs: machine X, raw materials, and labor. As before, the machine contains 360,000 hours of labor and lasts for 10 years; the labor content of the raw materials is 50 hours; and 50 hours of current labor are used to produce 20 units of output per day. The daily output then contains 100 hours of machine time, 50 hours of raw materials, and 50 hours of current labor. A single unit of output then contains 10 hours of labor. This is what determines commodity A's natural price.

Ricardo preserved this labor-embodied approach and rejected

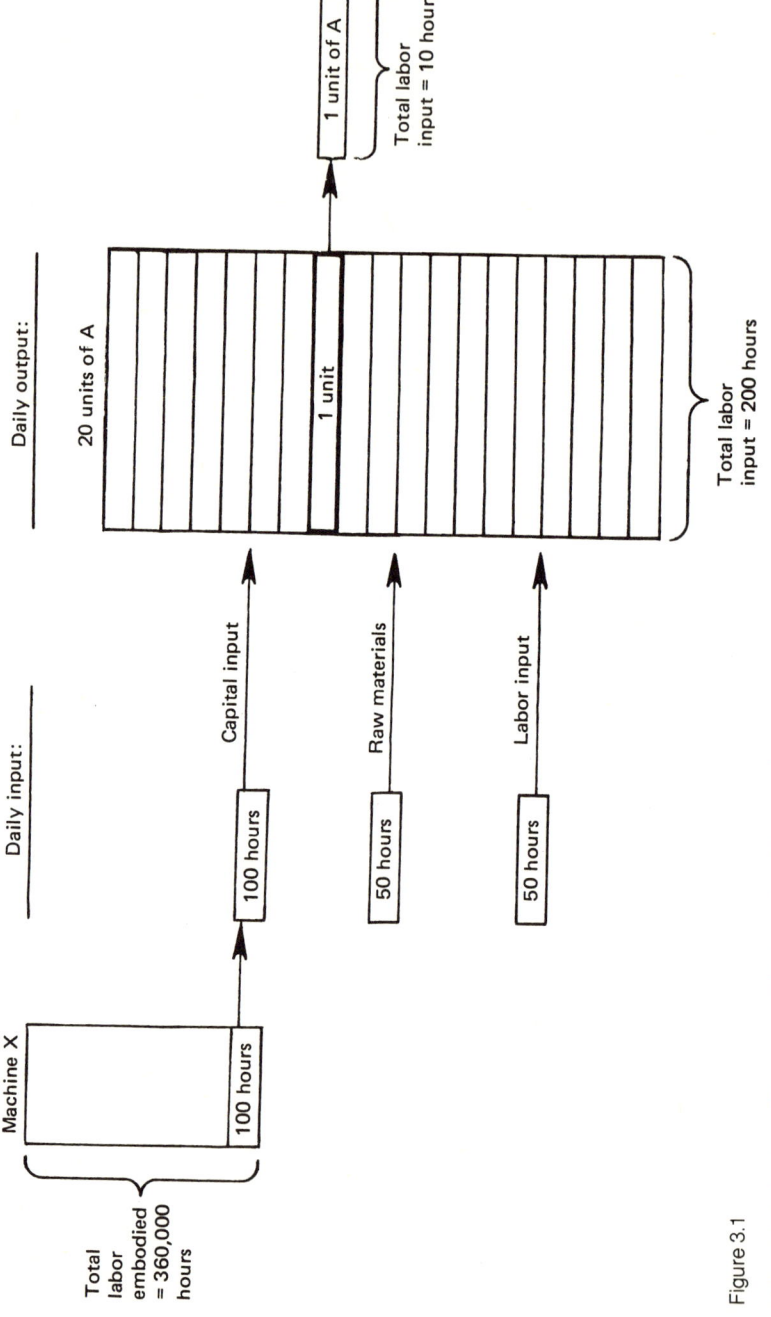

Figure 3.1
Ricardo's Labor Theory of Value: An Illustration

Smith's labor-commanded approach, because the latter was a highly variable measure and rarely equal to the labor embodied. This is seen in Table 3.2, which is simply an extension of Table 3.1. When the wage rate falls to 0.15 bushels per hour, the labor embodied remains at 300 and the labor command rises to 667. Since labor embodied is invariable, it would also appear to be a more suitable measure of value.

Table 3.2

Labor-Commanded vs. Labor-Embodied Value: An Extension

Corn Output (bushels)	Labor Input (hours)	Wage Rate (bushels/ hours)	Total Wages (bushels)	Surplus profits (bushels)	Labor Embodied (hours)	Labor Commanded (hours)
100	300	0.25	75	25	300	400
100	300	0.33	100	0	300	300
100	300	0.15	45	55	300	667

Before we move on to Marx and the modern views of value, it is important to point out that Ricardo introduced another consideration into his labor theory of value. This consideration entailed the effect on value of a change in wages. Specifically, different industries employ different proportions of current labor and fixed capital (i.e., plant and equipment). Moreover, the durability of the fixed capital used in different industries may also be expected to vary significantly. If the price of one hour of labor changes, then prices of outputs may change disproportionately, even if total labor time stays the same. A change in wages only affects current labor, not the labor already used in the past to produce the fixed capital. Hence, variations in the durability of capital goods among industries, and variations in capital–labor ratios among industries, result in prices that do not correspond to labor–time values. Thus if commodity A contains 10 hours of labor, and another commodity B contains 20, then the value ratios are 1:2. Because of the above considerations, it would not necessarily follow that the prices of A and B would also be in a 1:2 ratio. This deviation of prices from values led George Stigler to argue that Ricardo had only a 93% labor theory of value.[6]

Ricardo never resolved the problem of invariability and never succeeded in finding a standard of value that would not vary as the distribution of income between wages and profits varied. The search for an absolute, objective standard of value ended for Ricardo in a dead end.[7]

3.4C Karl Marx's theory of value

Any discussion of Karl Marx's labor theory of value, in isolation from his broader theory of society, would not do him justice. In fact, the same holds true for our discussion of Smith and Ricardo. Nevertheless, our goals are modestly restricted to the topic of value, and we ask the reader to grant the distortions inherent in such an approach.

Marx's theory of value stems from two different sources. The first source is, of course, the Ricardian labor theory of value. From a *quantitative* point of view, Marx's theory is an improved extension of Ricardo's analysis of exchange value and natural price. There is also a second, *qualitative*, dimension to Marx's labor theory of value. This dimension originates with the German philosophers Georg Hegel (1770-1831) and Ludwig Feuerbach (1804-1872), both of whom had an enormous influence on Marx's approach to the study of society. In many important respects, therefore, Marx's labor theory of value is an expression of a social philosophy and *not* merely a tool with which to determine prices. Many people have been led astray in their treatments of Marx because they have failed to recognize this broader, philosophical aspect of his theory of value.[8]

Essentially, the social philosophy of Marx rests on the following points. First, the essence of human society is its creative ability to transform its environment through production. This attribute of people is well recognized and highly esteemed by society. Our readiness to express appreciation for workmanship and artistic accomplishment gives evidence to this view.

Secondly, a capitalist economy is characterized by the existence of a large working class who owns none of the means of production and who must therefore work for someone else in order to earn a wage. In fact, the existence of such a class of people who *must* sell their labor as a commodity is the primary attribute of capitalism. This, it is argued, makes labor in capitalism a dehumanizing and alienating experience. Thirdly, production in capitalism is for exchange, not for the immediate use of the producers. That is, the object of all production is profit, and commodities are sold in markets *only* for this reason. These three points are combined to form Marx's analytic model of capitalism, which has the advantage over the earlier work of Smith and Ricardo that it attempts to explain, within a labor theory of value context, what determines the value of labor itself.

If we assume perfect competition, then because labor is a commodity like any other commodity, the natural or long-run equilibrium price of labor (the wage rate) will be proportional to the labor embodied in the production of labor. In this way, Marx simply applies the labor-embodied theory of value to labor itself, an approach that Ricardo also followed, but for different reasons. Thus, the labor power sold by workers to firms is "produced" in the sense that clothing, food, housing, and whatever else is customarily included in subsistence must be purchased. The labor time necessary to produce these subsistence "inputs" will therefore determine the value of labor, and the wage rate of labor.

For simplicity's sake, let us assume that one hour of labor is valued at $1 in the marketplace and that it takes five hours of labor to produce the market value of the worker's subsistence. The price of labor will then be $5 per day. If, however, the workers labor for more than five hours in a day, then clearly they will be able to produce more than just the commodities necessary for subsistence.

Now, by virtue of the fact that the capitalist class owns the means of production, it also has the power to set the duration of the workday at whatever length it desires, or at whatever length is practical. Hence, if the capitalist buys the workers' labor power for (say) a 10-hour day at a price of $5 per day, the first 5 hours of work (called *necessary labor time*) will produce the equivalent of the wages advanced to buy the labor. The remaining 5 hours (called *surplus labor time*) will result in surplus output. This surplus is the private property of the capitalist and is the source of the capitalist's profits. To be precise:

(1)   10-hour day = 5 hours necessary labor time
        + 5 hours surplus labor time

Thus, for every 10 hours of labor employed, the capitalist only needs to pay for 5 hours. This, after all, is the market value of labor. Marx called this ratio of surplus labor to necessary labor the rate of exploitation, and in this case it equals 100% (5 hours/5 hours).

Referring once again to Figure 3.1, let us calculate the value of the output produced. The capitalist employs 50 hours of current labor input. Let us say that 5 workers are hired for a 10-hour day. The wage rate is $5 per day, based on a rate of exploitation of 100%. Thus, total wages are $25 per day. If one hour of labor is still valued at $1, then the 20 units of output is worth $200 in the marketplace. The total costs of production are $175, however, and can be calculated as follows:

(2)   Total Costs of Production = $100 (100 hours machine time) +
        $50 (50 hours raw materials) + $25 (wages)

The difference between the $200 value of output and the $175 costs of production is the $25 of output produced by the 25 hours of surplus labor time. This $25 surplus is the source of the capitalists's profit.

The social philosophical implication of this labor theory of value is twofold. First, as noted earlier, the workers' labor power is objectified in the production of commodities. A portion of these commodities—and thus the workers' labor power—is claimed by the capitalist due to the fact that the latter owns the means of production and is therefore enabled to set the workday. This appropriation of the worker's product, the objectification of his or her soul and being, is the basis for alienation in capitalist society. As a consequence, the workers' ability to freely express themselves and to enjoy their own creativity is eliminated, and work becomes dehumanizing.

Secondly, the exchange of commodities in the marketplace will result in long-run prices which (given certain strict assumptions) will be proportional to the value of labor embodied in these same commodities. That is, labor embodied in production will determine the center of gravity around which market prices will fluctuate in a capitalist economy. If we drop the assumption of perfect competition, however, market prices could be permanently kept above their prices of production. Similarly, if the ratio of capital to labor varies among industries then prices of production will *not* be strictly proportional to the amount of labor embodied. This further complication will be dealt with later.

In the meantime, it is important to point out that, according to this theory, the worker's wage is not determined by the value of the output he or she produces but rather by the necessary labor required to reproduce the worker's customary subsistence. The workers' interests are served when their "customary subsistence" expands, so that the share taken by the capitalist contracts; the capitalists' interests are served when their share of output expands, leaving less for the workers. Therefore, the workers and the capitalists are constantly at odds over the allocation of output, and the outcome of this struggle—a given wage rate and profit rate—is reflected in commodity prices. This is the second implication of the labor theory of value.

Marx studied price determination, then, not for the purpose of explaining how a market system allocates scarce resources to alternative uses, but rather for the broader purpose of illuminating the essential features of the social relationships that exist in a capitalist system. It was his primary tool in developing his theory of history, politics, economics, and sociology. On this level the Marxian labor theory of value provides some rather extraordinary insights into the nature of capitalist society and is considerably more far-reaching in purpose than Smith's or Ricardo's theory of value.

3.4D Modern objective theories of value

The labor theory of value lives on in the works of many contemporary Marxian economists. Many of the flaws in the labor theory approach have been corrected so that price theory can once again be rooted in the concrete circumstances of human economic activity.

The post-Keynesian branch breaks company with the Marxists when it comes to the labor theory of value. Although they share the notion that pricing is linked to income distribution and capital accumulation, they do not share the Marxist theoretical explanation of how these linkages operate. Thus, in a broad sense, post-Keynesians and Marxists have a great deal in common. In a more specific sense they do not. These issues are explained in depth in later chapters.

3.5 General characteristics of objective theories of value

There is a common thread which unites the various economists of post-Keynesian/Marxian persuasion. We briefly enumerate those points of agreement which together form this thread and which allow us to speak of an objective theory of value.

The first common viewpoint is that the value of a commodity can be explained by looking only at the sphere of production rather than at the sphere of exchange. It is in production that the laws of capitalism are to be found.

The second common viewpoint is derived from the first. It suggests that demand is not directly linked to the determination of relative prices as it is in neoclassical theory. This arises because we are speaking of long-run, "natural," prices of production and not of the short-run market prices which exist on any given day. In fact, the two types of prices are not likely to be equal to one another. The explanation of these long-period prices is thought to have greater importance than explanations of short-period market prices because it is the longer period price which reflects the technical needs of capitalist production on a continuing basis and which is causally linked to capital accumulation and growth and income distribution.

It is in this sense that we can say that the post-Keynesian/Marxian theory of value and price is uniquely tied to the social, institutional, and technological characteristics of capitalism whereas the subjective, neoclassical theory is related only to atomistic economic agents who are defined in isolation from these same characteristics.

The subjective theory of value

4

> *The . . . conception of man is that of a lightning calculator of pleasures and pains, who oscillates like a homogeneous globule of desire of happiness under the impulse of stimuli that shift him about the area but leave him intact . . . . Self imposed in elemental space, he spins symmetrically about his own spiritual axis until the parallelogram of forces bears down upon him, whereupon he follows the line of the resultant. When the force of the impact is spent, he comes to rest, a self-contained globule of desire as before.*
>
> Thorstein Veblen

4.1 Introduction

This chapter briefly explains the development of the subjective approach to value theory. We do not seek to provide a complete history of this theory, but rather to provide a contrast to the objective theory of value about which this book is primarily concerned. The subjective theory of value differs significantly from the objective theory just discussed and its widespread acceptance by 1900 altered the face of economics. We will begin with a brief account of how the subjective theory of value came to dominate the economic way of thinking. The chapter ends with an attempt to isolate the chief characteristics of this theory.

4.2 Historical development of subjective value theory

The elements of a subjective theory of value exist in the background of economic theory throughout the nineteenth century. The basis of this approach is, in fact, *use value*, a concept which post-Keynesian/Marxian economics regards as the prerequisite for market exchange. However, it should be recalled that post-Keynesian/Marxian economics denies that use value plays an important role in determining the *level* of prices. It is a prerequisite, but not a determinant, of price.

In contrast, those who pioneered the subjective approach to value theory asserted that there does exist an important relationship between the price of a commodity and the degree to which it is useful. In other words, use value does determine price. It is not merely a prerequisite; it is a determinant as well.

Among the early pioneers of this approach were Daniel Bernoulli (1700–1782), Jeremy Bentham (1748–1832), William F. Lloyd (1795–1852), Augustin Cournot (1801–1877), A. Juvenal Dupuit (1804–1866), and Herman Gossen (1810–1858). Because Bentham and Gossen occupy a highly visible role in the history of economic thought, we begin with a brief overview of their contributions.

4.2A Jeremy Bentham and the pleasure–pain calculus

Bentham is remembered primarily for his theory of human motivation and his use of that theory to argue for social reform. His theory of human motivation is referred to as *utilitarianism*.

According to utilitarianism, an individual's actions are judged right or wrong by the goodness or badness of the consequences. If action A results in a set of consequences which are "good," and an alternative action B results in a set of consequences which are "bad," then A is the right act and B is the wrong act. Philosophers sometimes call this analysis *consequentialism*.

A nonutilitarian, or nonconsequentialist, may arrive at a different choice between A and B. Such a person might claim that, whereas A's consequences are good and B's are bad, action B should nevertheless be chosen. The justification may be based on an appeal to criteria other than goodness of the consequences. Action A may, for example, involve breaking a legal or moral rule or other social custom. The nonutilitarian might argue that conformity with rules, traditions, and customs is more important than the goodness which results from action A.

If one agrees with utilitarian ethics, how are goodness and badness to be defined? What constitutes a good consequence? The answer given by Bentham was based on the psychological principle of *hedonism*. Hedonism is a doctrine which asserts that people act only to enhance their personal pleasure or to diminish their pain. It is a form of egoism whereby all action is geared toward eliminating unfulfilled personal desire.

Combining the hedonistic psychology with the ethics of consequentialism gives rise to a particular brand of utilitarianism. This brand is described by John Stuart Mill as follows:

> The creed which accepts as the foundation of moral "utility" the "great-

est happiness principle" holds that actions are right in proportion as they tend to promote happiness, wrong as they tend to produce the reverse of happiness. By happiness is intended pleasure and the absence of pain; by unhappiness, pain and the privation of pleasure.[1]

This philosophy is referred to as *hedonistic utilitarianism* and defines the correctness of an action as being that which promotes the happiness of all those affected by the act.

As we have already said, Bentham was a social reformer. His attempts to reform society were based on his hedonistic utilitarian philosophy. Using this philosophy he claimed that income should be more equally distributed because this would provide the greatest good for the greatest number. Any social action which redistributes income equally would be justified since the results would be "useful."

In order to provide a scientific basis for such a policy, and to be able to establish the usefulness of programs, Bentham endeavored to devise a method of measuring the pleasures and the pains that would be involved. Bentham's measure was *marginal utility*, which we can loosely define here to mean the increment of satisfaction gained from a small change in consumption. If the poor would gain more utility than the rich lost, then legislation favoring redistribution would be warranted. This was the basis of Bentham's reform program. If only utility could be measured, the usefulness of a given social program could be readily determined.

The difficulty with this analysis, however, is that there is no way to compare the utility lost by the wealthy people who give up income to the utility gained by those whose incomes are increased: utility is assessed on an individual basis. If a wealthy person must give up a Rolls Royce so that a poor person can have more food, the utility lost by the wealthy person may be greater than the utility gained by the poor person. The Rolls Royce may be worth more to the former than the food is to the latter. Then again, the opposite may be true. We have no way of knowing.

Utilitarian analysis, therefore, can be very conservative because it can prohibit the analyst from making any judgments about social issues. In this regard, utility theory lends support to the status quo because it can never really be proven that change is worthwhile.

4.2B Gossen's two laws of utility

Another leading figure in the development of utility theory was the German economist Herman Gossen, who independently "discovered" the concept of marginal utility.

46 TWO VALUE TRADITIONS

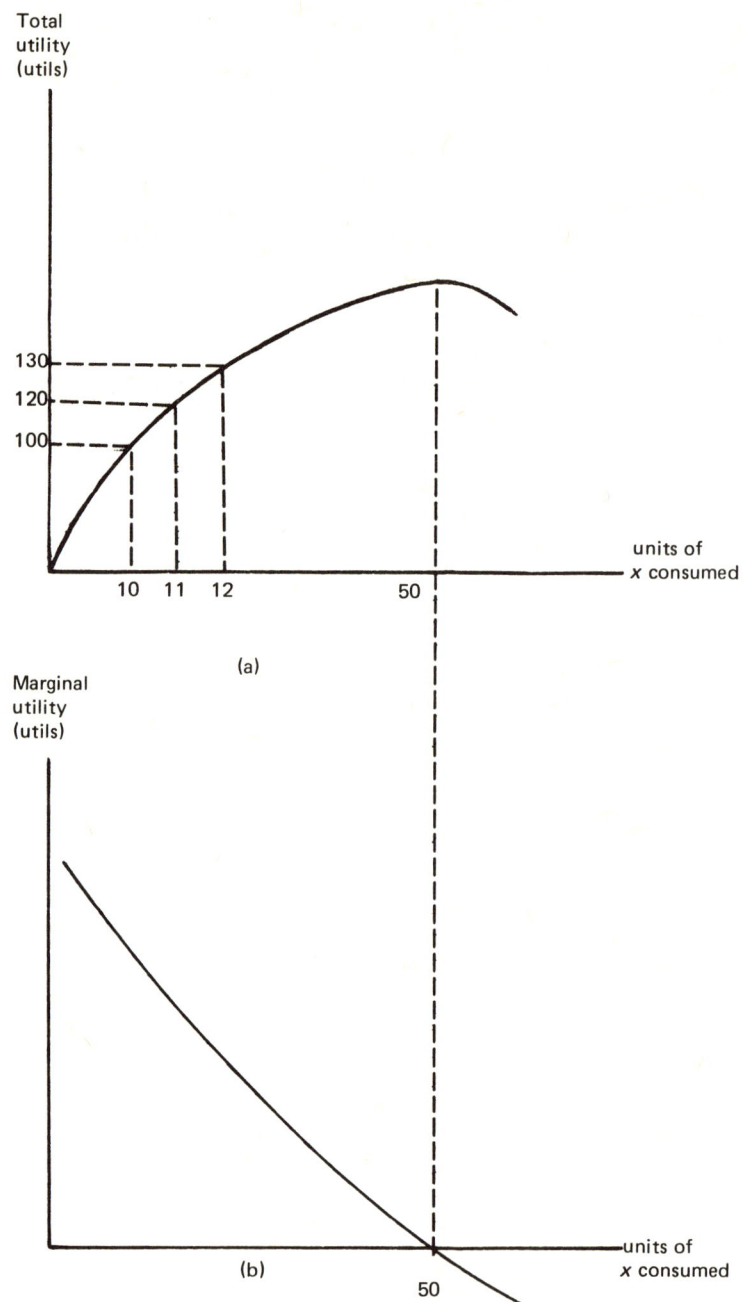

Figure 4.1

Gossen's First Law

Gossen's analysis begins with the observation that the consumption of successive units of a commodity yields diminishing pleasure or utility until a point of satiety is reached. This "law of satiable wants," also stated by Bentham and Bernoulli, has come to be known as *Gossen's first law*. This familiar law is illustrated in Figure 4.1(a).

If we can measure utility in cardinal units, say "utils," then the number of utils of pleasure derived from the consumption of some commodity x expands as the amount of x consumed expands. Total utility will reach a maximum in Figure 4.1 (a) when 50 units of x are consumed. This is the point of satiety.

It should be clearly noted that the amount by which utility increases with successive equal increments of x consumed declines. Thus, increasing consumption from 10 to 11 units will increase total utility from 100 utils to 120 utils. The increase in total utility in this case is 20 utils and is referred to as *marginal utility*. Increasing consumption further by an equal amount, from 11 to 12 units, will once again increase total utility, this time from 120 utils to 130 utils, or by 10 utils. But, as can be observed from the graph, the added utility is in this case smaller than the previous increment. According to Gossen, these increments of utility continue to decline as consumption increases, approaching zero in the diagram, with the fiftieth unit consumed. Figure 4.1(b) shows this inverse relationship between marginal utility and quantity consumed.

Gossen's second law aserted that a consumer can maximize utility by purchasing a variety of utility-yielding commodities until the marginal utility per dollar expended is equal for all commodities. This familiar equimarginal principle can be mathematically described in modern terms as follows.

If a person were consuming only two goods, X and Y, then utility would be maximized when

$$\frac{\text{Marginal Utility of Good X}}{\text{Price of Good X}} = \frac{\text{Marginal Utility of Good Y}}{\text{Price of Good Y}}$$

or, more compactly, when

$$\frac{MU_x}{P_x} = \frac{MU_y}{P_y}$$

If this equality does not hold, a consumer can increase satisfaction by changing the pattern of consumption. Suppose that the consumer had chosen to consume quantities of X and Y such that the marginal utility of good X per dollar was greater than the marginal utility of good Y per dollar. That is,

$$\frac{MU_x}{P_x} > \frac{MU_y}{P_y}$$

In this situation, total utility could be increased by purchasing more of X and less of Y. The utility per dollar gained by consuming more of X would be greater than the utility per dollar lost by consuming less of Y. Thus, total utility is increased. Because of the law of diminishing marginal utility, however, as the amount of X consumed increases, the MU_x will fall. Likewise, as the amount of Y consumed decreases, the MU_y will rise. The consumer's efforts to maximize utility will eventually result in the following situation:

$$\frac{MU_x}{P_x} = \frac{MU_y}{P_y}$$

The consumer will be unable to further increase total utility by changing the amounts of X and Y consumed. We shall see that this is the same type of reasoning that Jevons used to explain the determination of prices.

This type of analysis can be applied to many different types of economic problems. Marginal analysis, in its simplest form, consists of balancing the gains against the losses, or the returns against the costs. When the cost of an action just offsets the return from such an action, a point of maximization is reached. Thus, a firm maximizes profits when the revenue gained from the last item sold (the marginal revenue) is just equal to the cost of producing the last item sold (the marginal cost). The economic theory introduced in most principles of microeconomics courses is based on this marginalist principle.

4.2C Jevons, Menger, and Walras

In the late 1800s an intellectual revolution had occurred in economics. The objective theories of value, so popular among the early classical economists, had been replaced by the subjective approach. This subjective approach is the foundation of modern neoclassical economics. This was no simple change, for the entire scope of the economics discipline shifted its emphasis as well. The scope changed from one which stressed the importance of capital accumulation, economic growth, and the role played by *social classes*, to one which stresses the allocation of scarce resources and the role played by *individuals*. These are two very different visions of economics. A significant number of economists rejected this newer approach, however, and have continued the earlier classical tradition until the present day. The ideas they hold constitute post-Keynesian/Marxian economics.

The revolution in value theory was largely initiated by the almost simultaneous publication of three books written separately by William Stanley Jevons (1835–1882), Carl Menger (1840–1921), and Leon Walras (1834–1910). All three books were published between 1871 and 1874 and were amazingly similar.[2] In effect, they explained prices in terms of utility theory, clearly linking price to "marginal utility."

Jevons was a disciple of Bentham's. He stated quite clearly that "pleasure and pain are the ultimate objects of the Calculus of Economy." Utility is "the abstract quality whereby an object serves our purposes, and becomes entitled to rank as commodity."[3] The utility of an object, he explained, is not an inherent quality. It arises instead out of the particular circumstances which account for the object's ability to meet a person's requirements. For example, fur coats probably offer little utility in tropical climates, whereas lightweight short-sleeved shirts offer little utility to someone living in the North Pole. Following Bentham and Gossen, Jevons developed the law of diminishing marginal utility. He did so by distinguishing between total utility and the utility that is associated with an additional unit of consumption. According to this law, marginal utility decreases as an individual consumes more and more of one good. Now this seems almost obvious. It only stands to reason, the argument goes, that the more we possess of a particular good the less satisfaction we will derive from an additional unit of that good. The second glass of wine gives us less pleasure than the first, the third is less satisfying than the second, the fourth less satisfying than the third, and so on until our appetite for additional glasses of wine is completely gone. At that point the marginal utility of one more glass would be zero.

It should also be noted that, at this point, total utility will also have been maximized. Even though marginal utility declines as consumption of wine increases, each added glass still makes a positive contribution to the person's total satisfaction. Further consumption beyond this point would simply subtract from this total amount.

It is the marginal utility of a good that determines a commodity's exchange value. Jevons demonstrated this by examining the case of two individuals who are engaged in exchange. The two individuals will participate in trade only when the marginal utility of the commodity which they receive exceeds the marginal utility of the commodity which they give up. In other words, a person would only participate in exchange if the person gains more pleasure (utility) than he or she loses. This principle is identical to the equimarginal rule described above.

Following this reasoning, an individual would be expected to continue to exchange one commodity for another until the marginal utility gained (which falls as more and more is acquired) is no longer greater than the marginal utility that is given up. When trade ceases, all parties will have given up certain amounts of their initial holdings in order to obtain other commodities which they desire more. If we were to calculate the ratios at which all commodities exchanged, we should discover that these ratios are uniquely related to the marginal utility of the commodities that are bought and sold. Jevons showed, like Gossen before him, that ultimately goods will only exchange in ratios inversely proportional to their degrees of marginal utility. For example, suppose that two individuals engage in exchange. Person A possesses only corn and person B possesses only beef. Exchange in this example will consist of A's giving up some corn in return for some of B's beef. Similarly, B will give up some beef for some of A's corn. If both parties continue to exchange voluntarily until no further satisfaction can be derived, then the total amount of corn given up for beef will fully reflect both A's and B's psychological evaluation of the worth of each commodity. That is, exchange value is determined by marginal utility.[4]

Jevons believed that this case of isolated exchange illustrated the logic of price determination and could be applied generally to all exchanges in the economy. Notice that the costs of production have not been mentioned at all. This came about because the costs of production were not a major factor in the determination of price. Jevons reasoned that once a commodity was produced, the costs of production no longer mattered to anyone but the producer.

In determining exchange values, therefore, costs of production are unimportant. All that matters is how much consumers think a product is worth. In Jevons's view, the value of a product could change even if the costs and methods of production were unchanged. The value of all goods, including inputs into the production process, was determined by subjective value.[5]

Menger explained more clearly than Jevons what determines the cost of production, and hence the value of inputs. The value of consumer goods is determined by their ability to satisfy consumer wants. Like Jevons, Menger had an entirely subjective approach to value—value is determined entirely by human desire. Menger classified consumer goods as "goods of the first order" and producer's goods or inputs as "goods of the higher orders." The value of "goods of the higher orders" is determined by their contribution to production of "goods of the first order."[6] Simply stated, the value of labor is determined by its contribution to the production of a final product. If that final product is of small utility to consumers, then the value of labor is small.

Menger, Jevons, and Walras all agreed that the value of labor (or any other input) is therefore determined by the value of the product it enables one to produce. The value of the product is in turn determined by human desire for the good (the marginal utility of the product) and *not* by the objective conditions of production. And while they all expressed doubts about the measurability of utility, the neoclassical economists who followed them found that it was not necessary to measure utility in order to explain prices.

4.3 Cardinal and ordinal utility theory

The theory of utility developed by Jevons, Menger, and Walras during the 1870s was based on the idea that utility rather than the labor expended in production was the source of value. The subjective nature of value was regarded as a psychological fact. Additionally, it was generally believed at that time that the utility derived from consumption was measurable. For this reason, some economists even believed that utility theory was a branch of psychology, a notion that was encouraged by some psychologists.[7]

Two additional attributes of utility were emphasized by economists of this era. First, the utility which a consumer obtained from consuming a commodity was thought to be *independent* of the rate of consumption of other commodities. Hence, a person's utility function for some commodity x_1, $u(x_1)$, could be defined independently of how many other commodities were consumed.

Secondly, utility functions were thought to be additive. This assumption logically follows from the previous assumption of independence. Additivity means that the total utility derived by an individual from consumption in general is simply the sum of the utility derived from each commodity consumed. Thus, if $u_i(x_i)$ is the utility obtained from consumption of some commodity x_i, then the total utility of consuming all commodities may be written as

(1) $$u = u_1(x_1) + u_2(x_2) + \ldots + u_n(x_n)$$

Because each individual utility function is independent of all others, they may be simply added to arrive at total utility.

4.4 The transition to ordinal theory

By the turn of the century many economists began to question some of the restrictive assumptions that supported utility theory. Following the works of F. Edgeworth (1845–1926), I. Fisher (1867–1947), and others, the assumption that utility obtained from consuming a commodity is a function only of the amount of that commodity consumed was replaced with a broader assumption. It was now assumed that the utility derived from consuming a commodity is a function of the person's rate of consumption of *all* commodities. This assumption admits the possibility that a person's consumption of one commodity may influence the satisfaction obtained from consumption of another.

Instead of simply adding the utility derived from consuming individual commodities to obtain total utility, as in equation (1) above, we may simply state that

(2) $$u = u(x_1, x_2, \ldots, x_n)$$

without specifying how consumption of one good affects the utility obtained from another. Total utility, u, is simply a function of that consumption.

After the independence and additivity assumptions were eliminated, the assumption of measurability came under attack. This development is largely attributed to V. Pareto (1848-1923). According to Pareto, it is possible to rank a person's preferences for commodities and combinations of commodities without having to assign a numerical value to the utility obtained from each. This approach is called *ordinal utility* theory. In the old cardinal approach to utility theory it was claimed that if commodity x is preferred to commodity y then we can measure the amount by which the utils obtained from x exceeds the utils obtained from y. The ordinal system of measurement on the other hand simply states that x is ranked first and y is ranked second. We need not know by how much. This is just like saying that it can be determined whether or not one is at the top of a hill without having to know the altitude of where one stands. The newer ordinal theory, however, has no more lent itself to empirical observation than the older cardinal theory.

The ordinal approach to utility theory is the cornerstone of modern economics. Today it is sometimes called preference theory or choice theory, but the terms are basically the same. The modern version is still utilitarian insofar as consumers are seen to make choices on the basis of the consequences that are expected to occur. But the assumption of hedonism is no longer thought to be essential, since the motives which lie behind a person's preferences need not be specified. All that is required is a given set of preferences, and whether or not a person is hedonistic or altruistic is of little consequence.

Thus, neoclassical economists today assert that utility theory merely describes people getting what they want. The motives behind a consumer's expenditures, although still utilitarian, may or may not be hedonistic. What consumers want may be states of mind other than pleasure. As the eminent historian of economics Joseph A. Schumpeter observed,

It is not difficult to show that the utility theory of value is entirely independent of any hedonistic postulates or philosophies. For it does not state or imply anything about the nature of the wants or desires from which it starts.[8]

But even though modern utility theory may have been liberated from its hedonistic assumptions, it is still based on another assumption which is equally restrictive. This is the assumption of individualism.

4.5 Utility theory and individualism

Individualism is a view that describes people as independent and self-contained organisms. That is, all values, attitudes, aspirations, desires, and preferences originate with individuals. Society as a whole is therefore viewed as simply an aggregation of independent, individual units. No person, group, or institution can influence the preference characteristics of an individual unless that individual willingly goes along.

There are two aspects to this assumption about human nature. First, when studying society as a whole, the observer is inclined to conclude that all social processes, institutions, and characteristics can be explained by examining individual behavior. In other words, the "laws" which regulate society can be deduced from the laws which govern an *individual's behavior*. The former is simply the sum of the latter. Thus, the idea that an individual's demand for a commodity can be influenced by the market demand (e.g., fads) is incompatible with individualism. This approach to the study of society is called *methodological individualism*.[9]

The second aspect of an individualistic view of human nature is *laissez-faire individualism*. This is an ethical proposition which holds that the interests and responsibilities of individuals are morally paramount. Each person, according to this view, should be held responsible for his or her actions and for his or her successes and failures. Any attempt by an external governing force to diminish these responsibilities, or to alter the consequences of individual actions, is unethical.

The justification for this view is based on the notion that, when those who succeed continue unregulated and those who fail continue unsupported, the "fittest" individuals will survive. Through this process of natural selection, society will grow strong and the welfare of all people will be maximized.

To what extent is modern utility theory an expression of individualism? To begin with, utility theory assumes that individual preferences are taken as given and independent of other people's preferences. Thus, the only thing which affects a person's utility is the quantity of commodities which *that* person consumes. The source of these personal preferences and the social influences exerted on individuals are regarded to be either beyond the scope of economic analysis or nonexistent. In either case, the behavior described is ultimately individualistic.

The implication of the individualistic foundation of utility theory is that, as a theory of consumer behavior, it is incomplete. It is of course valid and important to be able to explain how individuals make decisions in the marketplace *given* their tastes and preferences. But it is equally important to explain how these tastes and preferences are formed to begin with.

Consumer tastes and preferences are not, however, determined in isolation from society. Instead they are formed and influenced in a variety of ways. Religious beliefs, social customs, and traditions all influence people's tastes and preferences, to say nothing of advertising. Unless this interaction between individuals and society is included in the analysis, the neoclassical theory of consumer behavior will remain incomplete.

Finally, the individualistic focus of neoclassical demand theory contains a distinct bias toward laissez-faire. This bias is incapable of being justified when interpersonal influences on consumption are introduced.

To see this bias, consider the following conclusion reached by a popular textbook:

> ... restrictions of any kind placed on a person's freedom of choice in the market can never increase his or her utility. In other words, an individual with freedom of choice is always at least as well off, and generally better off, than an individual whose choice is restricted.[10]

This commonly held view *does not* follow unless one is willing to maintain an individualistic philosophy. The above conclusion about individual freedom is actually built into the assumptions to begin with and cannot otherwise be upheld. Utility theory, therefore, reflects the views of individualism; it cannot prove the validity of laissez-faire.

4.6 Subjective and objective theories compared

We may now look back upon the objective and subjective theories of value and summarize the differences between them. As we shall see, these differences are of paramount importance. Because a theory of value serves as the foundation for virtually all economic theories, divergent value theories will result in different economic theories.

Using the terminology developed in Chapter 1, we say that the economist's vision of capitalism is expressed in his or her theory of value. Which of the two visions is selected will determine which of the two economic paradigms will be adopted. An objective theory of value will place the economist in the post-Keynesian/Marxian school; the subjective theory of value will place the economist in the neoclassical school.

The following four areas of disagreement between these two schools can be identified:

(1) *Source of value.* The objective theory claims that the value of a commodity is directly linked to the way it is produced. The subjective theory suggests that value is linked to utility. Utility, in turn, is subjectively determined in the minds of individual economic agents. Philosophically speaking, the objective approach says that value is produced in the material universe, whereas the subjective approach says it is produced in the minds of individuals.

(2) *Aspects of economic activity regarded as most important.* The post-Keynesian/Marxian vision emphasizes production and diminishes the importance of exchange. According to this view, it is the way in which production is organized that distinguishes capitalism from other kinds of social systems. Although markets are important in capitalism, they are also important in noncapitalist societies. Thus, market exchange is not the focal point of post-Keynesian/Marxian economic analysis.

The neoclassical school reverses this order of importance, stressing instead the significance of free exchange among individuals. In fact, production theory in neoclassical economics is just an application of exchange theory.

(3) *The beginning point for economic analysis.* Classical value theory naturally leads the economist to study the social relationships that characterize production. Neoclassical value theory, because it believes the individual to be the basic unit of analysis, naturally leads the economists to study the relationships among individuals in society. This distinction may be clearly observed in the circular flow models depicted in Chapter 2.

(4) *Social relations.* Output is produced by one class of society according to the classical scheme. Because the nonworking classes must share in the output produced by the working classes, class relationships are not viewed as harmonious. Rather, class conflict is characteristic of a capitalistic economy. This conflict is basically over the shares of the output produced. This is another way of saying that class differences arise in the area of income distribution.

The neoclassical vision perceives instead a society in which the pursuit of individual self-interest leads naturally to a state of harmony. A free market system spontaneously leads to a situation which benefits everyone concerned. It is a society in which people freely and voluntarily interact to make economic choices. Moreover, knowledge of the laws which govern capitalist society can be obtained by understanding the laws which govern individual behavior. This is in direct contrast to the class orientation of post-Keynesian/Marxian economics.

An organizing principle: the economic surplus

Part III

The economic surplus historically considered 5

> *If men conduct their economic affairs only with an eye to money it will glare at them as harsh and mercilessly as do the stars in the black void of outer space. That is why setting national priorities, and implementing them, isn't a matter of just allocating money but requires instead thinking about what physical quantities of surplus exist that can be utilized humanely.*
>
> George W. Zinke

5.1 Introduction: the production point of view

Any economic theory which focuses on production as a unique human activity will also attach a great deal of importance to the concept of economic surplus. This concept is one of several intellectual devices used by post-Keynesian/Marxian economists in analyzing a capitalist economy. In contrast, neoclassical economists deny the importance, if not the validity, of economic surplus.

Interest in production as a unique activity, and hence in economic surplus, dates back to the Industrial Revolution. As we shall see in this chapter, it was during this time that it became apparent to economists that a nation's wealth can be expanded by applying to production the new scientific technologies then being developed. Prior to this time it was thought that a nation's wealth could only expand at the expense of another nation's wealth. It was believed that there existed a given endowment of resources (particularly precious metals) which could not by themselves expand in quantity. But the enormous technological advances made during the Industrial Revolution quickly destroyed this belief. Wealth was not a fixed stock but rather a variable stock that could be increased in quantity by production. Surplus was simply a measure of the amount by which a nation's wealth could be increased.

This change in emphasis from wealth as an exogenously given endowment to wealth as a produced output revolutionized economics by making production the starting point of analysis. Today, a revival of interest in theories of production characterizes modern post-Keynesian/ Marxian economics. Three production models in particular have attained popularity in recent years: the Leontief model, the Sraffa model, and the von Neumann model. These are in addition to the Marxian models of capitalist production.

The Leontief model is the well-known input-output analysis developed by Nobel laureate Wassily Leontief in the 1930s. It is a method of analyzing the technical structure of an economic system. Input-output analysis is concerned solely with the physical interdependencies among intermediate and final goods sectors of an industrial economy and introduces prices only as exogenously determined parameters. Thus, the Leontief model leaves open the issue of pricing and its relationship to income distribution and growth.

The Sraffa model, named after the Italian economist Piero Sraffa, also examines the structure of production in an industrial economy. The main difference between the Leontief model and this model is that the latter analyzes production in price terms. Thus, the Sraffa model *does* explore the relationship between pricing and income distribution. It does *not*, however, examine the relationship between these two facets and economic growth.

The third model is named after the Hungarian mathematician-economist John von Neumann (1903-1957) and actually predates the works of Leontief and Sraffa. The von Neumann model focuses on the problem of economic growth and examines the effect on growth rates of different rates of profit and different techniques of production. The pricing and distribution issues play a secondary role, however.

In this chapter and the next we continue to develop the production theory point of view by exploring the surplus concept. Once this is accomplished we will be prepared to consider the Sraffa production model. We select the Sraffa model instead of Leontief and von Neumann models because of our interest in the problem of pricing and distribution.[1] Once having developed the Sraffaian point of view we will compare it to the Marxian production model in Part V.

5.2 The social significance of economic surplus

To grasp the full importance of economic surplus, begin by imagining what life would be like in a simple society that produced no surplus at all. That is, the entire output produced by the members of that society is just sufficient to provide for their survival needs. Any less output would mean starvation for some; any more would not be possible given the existing state of technology. Thus, the entire output is just large enough to maintain the means of production and to feed the population.

Assume also that the tasks required for the production of the annual output are divided among "specialties." This implies that no individual can produce all the commodities which he or she requires for survival. Instead, each person is dependent on the productive contributions of others. The commodities not produced must therefore be acquired through exchange.

The prices at which exchange takes place in a nonsurplus economy must be fixed at a predetermined level if continued survival is to be insured. Any deviation of prices from this level would mean that some producers would be obtaining too much of the other commodities being produced.

To see this, assume that only two commodities are required for survival: iron and wheat. Further assume that the technical requirements of production can be represented as

(1) $\quad$ 2,240 bu. wheat $+$ 12 t. iron $\rightarrow$ 3,200 bu. wheat
$\quad\quad\quad$ 960 bu. wheat $+$ $\;\;$8 t. iron $\rightarrow$ $\;\;$20 t. iron

Of the 3,200 bushels of wheat produced, 2,240 bushels are required to feed the people in the wheat sector and 960 bushels are required in the iron sector. No wheat is left over. Similarly, of the 20 tons of iron produced, 12 tons are needed to produce the wheat and 8 tons are needed to produce the iron. Thus, no extra iron is produced.

If iron workers and wheat farmers exchange commodities, and if each is to receive the required amount, then 1 ton of iron must exchange for 80 bushels of wheat. The wheat farmers will have exactly 960 bushels of wheat left over after they have deducted the amount which they need themselves; iron workers will have 12 tons of iron left over. The 12 tons will exchange for 960 bushels, or 1 ton must exchange for 80 bushels. This is how we obtain the necessary exchange ratio.[2] If exchange takes place at any other ratio then each sector will be unable to produce the necessary quantities in the next period. Using post-Keynesian/Marxian terminology, we say that the system as a whole will be unable to *reproduce* itself in the next period.

The significance of this simple model is that the interdependencies among producers are strictly determined by *economic necessity* when a surplus output is *incapable* of being produced. This economic necessity is defined by the technological requirements of subsistence production. Any attempt by one group to acquire more iron or wheat than that amount specified above would in the long run be self-defeating.

Non-surplus-producing societies are quite rare in modern history, however. It is therefore important to explore the full significance of surplus-producing potential. Briefly stated, the ability to produce surplus permits society to break away from strict economic necessity as it is defined above. The technical requirements of production and of survival no longer dictate economic interdependencies among people, and considerable flexibility is now introduced.

To see this, suppose the wheat farmers discover a new way of organizing production so that the same quantity of wheat and iron input results in a 10% greater (320 bushels) quantity of wheat output. Suppose further that the wheat farmers insist on keeping the new surplus output, calling it a "necessary" requirement for continued wheat production. The previous input requirements were 2,240 bushels wheat plus 12 tons iron. The new input proportions would now be 2,560 bushels wheat and 12 tons iron.

The input proportions in the wheat sector have changed, but not because of technical necessity. Instead, the proportions have changed because of a social and moral consideration. If the iron workers agree to this, we can readily obtain the new wheat–iron exchange ratio by solving the following equations:

(2)   2,560 bu. wheat + 12 t. iron → 3,520 bu. wheat
           960 bu. wheat + 8 t. iron → 20 t. iron

The exchange ratio would remain at 1:80 because the same quantity of wheat is being exchanged for the same quantity of iron. Thus, none of the newly produced surplus has been transferred between sectors.

If, on the other hand, another social and moral consideration results in the surplus's accruing entirely to the iron workers, the wheat equation would remain as written in (1), while the input side of the iron equation would be credited with an additional 320 bushels of wheat. Thus, solving the following two equations results in a new exchange ratio:

(3)   2,240 bu. wheat + 12 t. iron → 3,520 bu. wheat
           1,280 bu. wheat + 8 t. iron → 20 t. iron

The new ratio is now 1 ton of iron for 107 bushels of wheat. The ratio is different because the wheat sector's surplus has been transferred to the iron sector. More wheat is exchanged for 1 ton of iron.

These two ratios represent the two extreme cases, one in which the wheat farmers get all of the surplus (1:80), the other in which the iron workers get all of the surplus (1:107). The implication is, quite simply, that only the extremes are defined by technical and economic necessity. Where between these two extremes the actual price will settle is another matter. Since the fundamental production requirements remain unaltered and can be met at any price between the extremes, the actual price which will be settled upon must in consequence depend on social and moral considerations.

Expanding the two-sector example to a multi-sector model of an industrially advanced society clearly points out the enormous number of possibilities which exist for using the surplus potential. The surplus can be used for further economic expansion and growth. Projects such as highway construction, communication systems, and research and development all contribute to the growth in society's surplus-producing potential. The surplus could also be used to improve the life-styles of the people. It could be employed in the construction of ceremonial and religious projects such as monuments and churches; it could be used to provide for cultural amenities such as museums and theaters; or it could be used to reduce the workday. Moreover, the benefits derived from differing uses of the economic surplus may accrue to the whole of society, or they may accrue to a small privileged class.

These are all possible choices. They are choices that are made every day in our own society. Sometimes they are made as a result of conscious planning; sometimes they are made by default. In either case, the ultimate uses to which society's surplus is put are the result of human decisions, not the result of mystical powers or invisible hands. The uses of surplus are not rigidly prescribed.

The final significance of surplus production lies, then, in the fact that the capability to produce surplus gives society the flexibility for changing the way things are done. It provides society with the resources with which to solve social problems, or even to change the status quo. Whether this flexibility can be used to its full advantge depends in large part on historical, political, and social factors, as well as on the general attitudes of people. If everyone is rigidly set in his or her ways, existing social problems might be deplored while regarded as "necessary evils" about which little can be done. Separating those areas of flexibility from those of economic necessity is one of the major tasks of economic study. It is the surplus concept which comes forth as the strongest intellectual tool that can aid in our attempt to isolate economic necessity from economic freedom.

5.3 The economic surplus concept historically considered

The historical development of the surplus concept is closely associated with the development of value theory. Both of these concepts are, in turn, directly related to the broader question of wealth and its origins. The question of what causes material wealth has been a recurrent one among scholars throughout the ages, and continues to be a much discussed topic among economists. The following sections explore the various answers to the questions of how wealth originates. As we shall see, the post-Keynesian/Marxian answer to this question relies heavily on the concept of economic surplus.

5.3A The relative surplus in preclassical thought

Between the fifteenth and eighteenth centuries in Europe an increasing number of writings on economic topics began to appear. Most of these writings coincided directly with the latter phases of the "commercial revolution" which began in the Middle Ages. During this period, a growing commercial capitalist class came to set the tone of economic life, contributing to the ultimate decay of the old feudal social structure. The wealth accumulated by this rising class originated for the most part from the profits realized in commerce. These profits were in turn largely attributable to trade monopolies and other special economic privileges granted to the merchants by their respective governments. In certain areas of both northern and Mediterranean Europe, for example, spectacular fortunes were often made both in the luxury trade (silk, spices and jewelry, for example) as well as in the trade of raw materials (for example, Flemish and Swedish iron and steel).[3]

The writings of the new political economists of this period, generally referred to as mercantilists, reflected these profound social and economic changes. They wrote about what they witnessed: an extraordinary increase in monetary wealth brought about by the growth of domestic and foreign commerce. Much of the mercantilist writings were therefore directly concerned with the accumulation of wealth, and it seemed obvious to them that this wealth originated in the *exchange* of commodities. The works of such mercantilists as Thomas Mun (1571–1641) and Sir James Steuart (1712–1780) expressed the notion that the ultimate source of wealth was the margin of profit realized from selling. It is in this sense that we apply the term *relative* surplus because these profits were obtained mostly through the exploitation of buyers.

Accompanying the growth of commercial capitalism came significant changes in the way production was organized. At first the merchant classes accumulated profits by controlling the markets for commodities. They bought their goods from independent handicraftsmen and sold them to foreign and domestic buyers.

It was out of this economic arrangement that the *putting-out* system emerged. Merchants, in an effort to establish a competitive advantage in the marketplace, endeavored to gain control of the actual production process and hence production costs. This was a sphere of activity that had heretofore remained mostly within the province of independent producers. Control over production was accomplished by purchasing the inputs necessary for the production of a commodity and then contracting with independent handicraftsmen to produce the desired output. Previously, the commercial capitalists rarely applied their accumulated wealth directly to productive activity itself.

By the eighteenth century the putting-out system had evolved into a *factory system*, and the merchant capitalists evolved into industrial capitalists. The organization of production now permitted the capitalist to effectively control not only the inputs required and the output produced, but the laboring process as well. With the capitalists' wealth used to directly employ workers, control over the work process gradually came to be transferred from the independent handicraftsman to the capitalist employer. As a consequence, the independent handicraftsman eventually came to be entirely dependent on the capitalist class for employment.

The significance of this transition to a modern capitalist industrial system is that the focus of writers shifted from exchange to *production*. This new focus was reflected in the notion that wealth was thought to be made up of accumulated surplus output and that this surplus originated in the act of production, not in the act of exchange, as it was earlier believed.

5.3B The physical net surplus

5.3B(1) The Physiocrats. By the eighteenth century the question of the ultimate source of wealth had become a familiar one. The mercantilists attempted to provide an answer by pointing to the surplus generated in the sphere of exchange. But the development of capitalist industry made the mercantilist explanation appear superficial.

The inquiry into the origins of wealth was first redirected toward the sphere of production by the Physiocrats, a group of French political economists concerned with social reform. Unlike the English economy of the eighteenth century, that of France was still predominantly agrarian. The French economy was beset with major financial difficulties stemming from colonial wars and extravagant spending by the monarchy. Since the clergy and the nobility were exempt from taxation, the burden of paying for these financial extravagances fell mostly on those classes of people least able to bear it, the common landowner and peasant. This situation impeded economic growth, thereby significantly curtailing the economy's ability to expand the wealth of France.

The physiocratic solution to these difficulties consisted of tax reform measures intended to undermine feudal privileges in taxation and eliminate the severe restrictions on trade and commerce within France. Most importantly, these reform recommendations were based on a novel theoretical model, a model which for the first time took a general view of the whole economic process. This approach was a significant advance in the development of economics as a discipline. The model was fully developed by François Quesnay, a French physician whose name is most frequently associated with physiocracy. According to this approach, there are definite natural laws which govern how society produces its output and how it distributes that output. Compliance with these natural laws would insure that the welfare of society would be maximized. This is the meaning of the word "physiocracy": rule of nature.

Related to the notion of natural law was the physiocratic belief that "the earth is the mother of all our goods." The central focus of the physiocratic theoretical model was the production and reproduction of economic surplus. Since it was believed that nature was the source of all material wealth, it followed that an economic surplus is capable of being produced only in the agricultural sectors of the economy and not in the manufacturing sectors. This surplus was defined to be equal to gross agricultural output minus (1) the consumption requirements of those who worked the land, and (2) the expenses of maintaining the stock of fixed and circulating capital.[4] The economic surplus was, therefore, a *physical* concept. It was made up of material agricultural capital stock and the productive capabilities of the agricultural work force.

The economic surplus in Quesnay's model circulates among various classes in society. According to physiocratic doctrine, there are three classes who make up the social economy. The first class is the *proprietor class*, consisting of landowning individuals and institutions (e.g., the Church or the State). The land owned by these proprietors would be leased to a second class of individuals, the *cultivators*. The cultivators advanced their own capital and were responsible for hiring whatever wage labor was necessary. According to the Physiocrats, these cultivators were also the only productive class in society, because they were the only ones capable of producing an economic surplus. All others, including those working in nonagricultural pursuits, were nonproductive. These people comprised the third class, or the *sterile class*.

The proprietor class was the initial recipient of the economic surplus. The surplus was turned over to them by the cultivators as a rental payment. A portion of this surplus payment would then be kept by the proprietors for their own subsistence needs. Another portion of it would be exchanged for manufactured consumer goods. What remained after the surplus was deducted from total agricultural output would then go to replacing the fixed and circulating capital used up, and to paying wages. These wages included not only the payments to hired workers, but also payments to the cultivators who first advanced their capital. The latter payment was in fact profit, but the Physiocrats

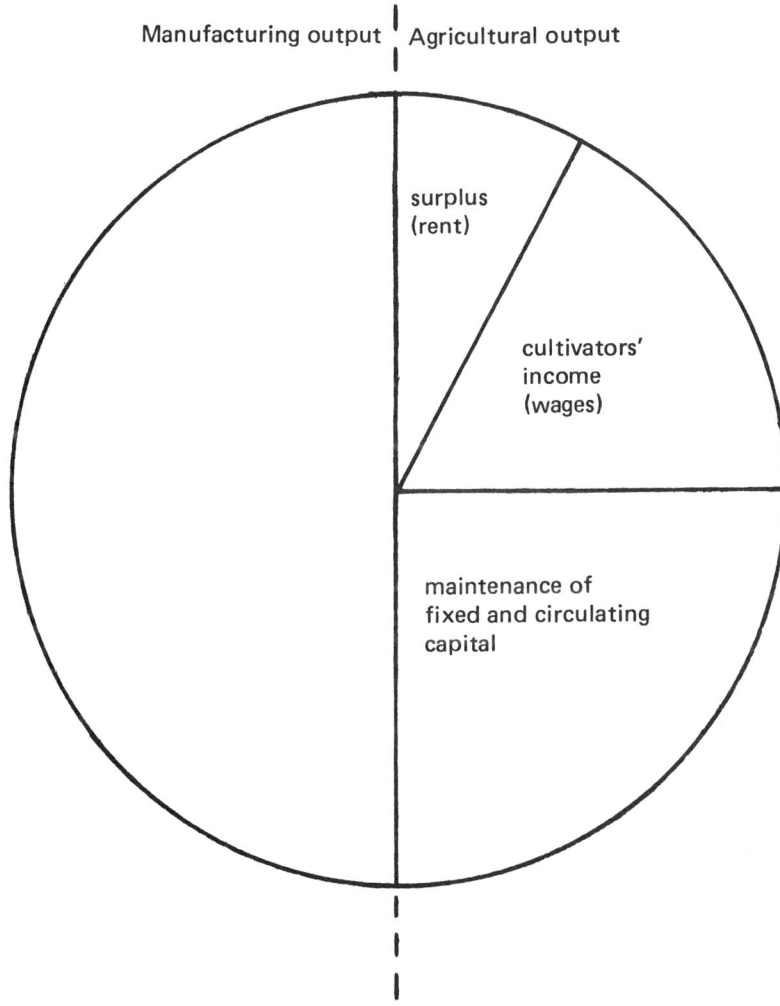

Figure 5.1

Physiocratic Surplus

tended to regard profits as the wages of management. This distributional scheme is illustrated in Figure 5.1.

The physiocratic notion of economic surplus, and the theoretical edifice constructed upon it, was a powerful stimulus to the later development of the labor theory and Marx's theory of surplus value. This is due to the fact that some consistent principle of measurement had to be developed in order to calculate the size of the surplus output. This problem was of small consequence in the physiocratic system because the surplus was restricted to agricultural output, which, in a very rudimentary and abstract way, may be regarded as homogeneous and hence easily aggregated. It was Adam Smith who was primarily responsible for extending the surplus concept to include manufactured goods. Thus the problem of measurement became critical because the surplus output now consisted of heterogeneous goods which could not be aggregated unless they were first reduced to some common denominator.

5.3B(2) Adam Smith. Smith attacked the physiocratic notion that nature was the source of all material wealth. By so doing he denied that the manufacturing sectors of an economy are sterile and incapable of producing surplus. Instead, both agricultural and manufacturing activities were productive because they were both capable of producing a net surplus. Therefore, by defining surplus output to include both agriculture and manufacturing, and by identifying labor as the agent primarily responsible for its production in both areas, Smith cast a different light on the nature of the capitalist system.

Smith's main interest, however, was in identifying the sources of material well-being and in explaining how these worked to increase the welfare of everyone in society. Smith believed that economic growth simultaneously increased the standard of living of both the capitalist class and the working class. Since Smith believed that consumption was the end of all production, this standard of living could best be represented by per capita consumption, or that amount available to *all* classes for subsistence and for their own "conveniences and amusements."

Smith's notion of surplus, then, differed from the Physiocratic version in a number of ways. Instead of using the surplus concept devised by the Physiocrats (agricultural output minus the expenses of maintaining the capital stock and the work force), Smith used the concept of net revenue (or, net output). This is the amount of output left over after deducting only the expenses of maintaining society's fixed and circulating capital from total output, or gross revenue. Thus, wages, as well as profits and rents, were included in net revenue.[5] The difference between net revenue and physiocratic surplus is that Smith (1) included the output of the manufacturing sectors and (2) regarded wages to be part of the surplus along with profits and rent. Smith's version is shown in Figure 5.2.

5.3B(3) David Ricardo. Ricardo was the next classical economist to construct a theoretical framework based on the surplus concept. His is

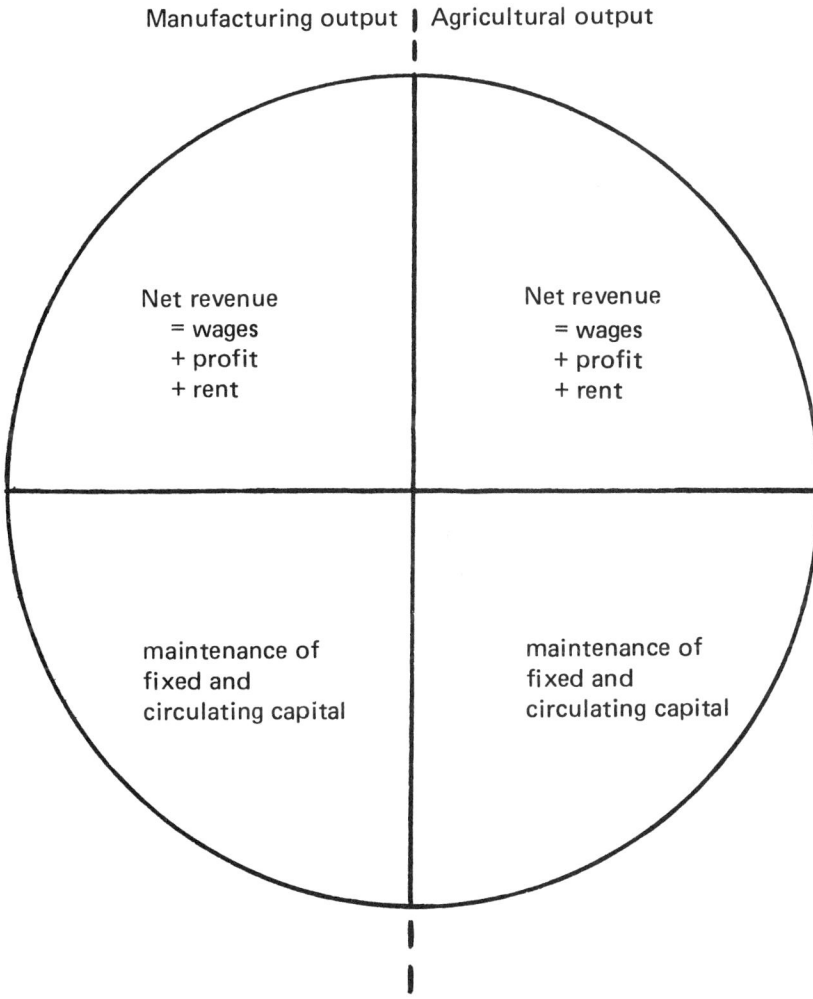

Figure 5.2

Smith's Surplus

similar in spirit to the physiocratic and Smithian concepts, although a bit more awkward. To Ricardo, a physical surplus also arises in both agriculture and manufacturing. This aspect he shared with Smith. However, unlike that of Smith, the surplus does not include labor's share, or wages. It only includes profits and rent. Wages are a necessary expense of production and are not to be regarded as a surplus. The level of wages, in turn, is determined by the level of subsistence. According to Ricardo, wages would always tend toward this subsistence level because of population pressures, an idea which he shared with Malthus.

Ricardo's surplus gets distributed to landowners in the form of rent and to capitalists in the form of profits. The portion of agricultural output going to rent, the only sector of the economy in which rents were paid, depended on the fertility of the soil. Given the market price of agricultural commodities, land of differing fertility would continue to be used as long as the revenues from agricultural sales were greater or equal to the costs of production. Thus, the costs of production on the worst land in use would just be covered and the land would yield no rent. Revenues on superior quality lands would, of course, be greater than the costs of production. The excess represents a rent which accrues to the landowners.

In Ricardo's model, the capitalist farmer leases the land from the landowner and operates in much the same way as a capitalist manufacturer. As population pressures place greater and greater demands upon the use of agricultural land, less and less fertile land would be brought into cultivation by farmers. Lands which had heretofore earned little or no rent would now begin to earn more rent.

According to Ricardo, the prices of homogeneous agricultural commodities produced on qualitatively different lands still have to be uniform. The price of corn produced on prime land has to be the same as the price of identical corn produced on second-grade land, and the price of corn on second-grade land has to be the same as the price on third-grade land, etc. Thus, it is ultimately the conditions of production on the worst land which determines the price of agricultural commodities in general.

According to Ricardo, then, the price of agricultural goods is determined by production conditions on the worst, no-rent land. Therefore, after the deduction of all rent payments from total agricultural output, the output remaining would go to the capitalist farmer's profits and the agricultural worker's wages. The rate of profit in agriculture would then depend on the workers' productivity and subsistence needs. Finally, once the rate of profit in agriculture is determined, the rate of profit in manufacturing will also be determined. This is true because, according to Ricardo, the manufacturing profit rate would adjust to the agricultural profit rate.

Ricardo's rather awkward model is represented in Figure 5.3. As in the previous diagrams, the area of the circle represents total agricultural and manufacturing output. Agricultural rent is first skimmed off the

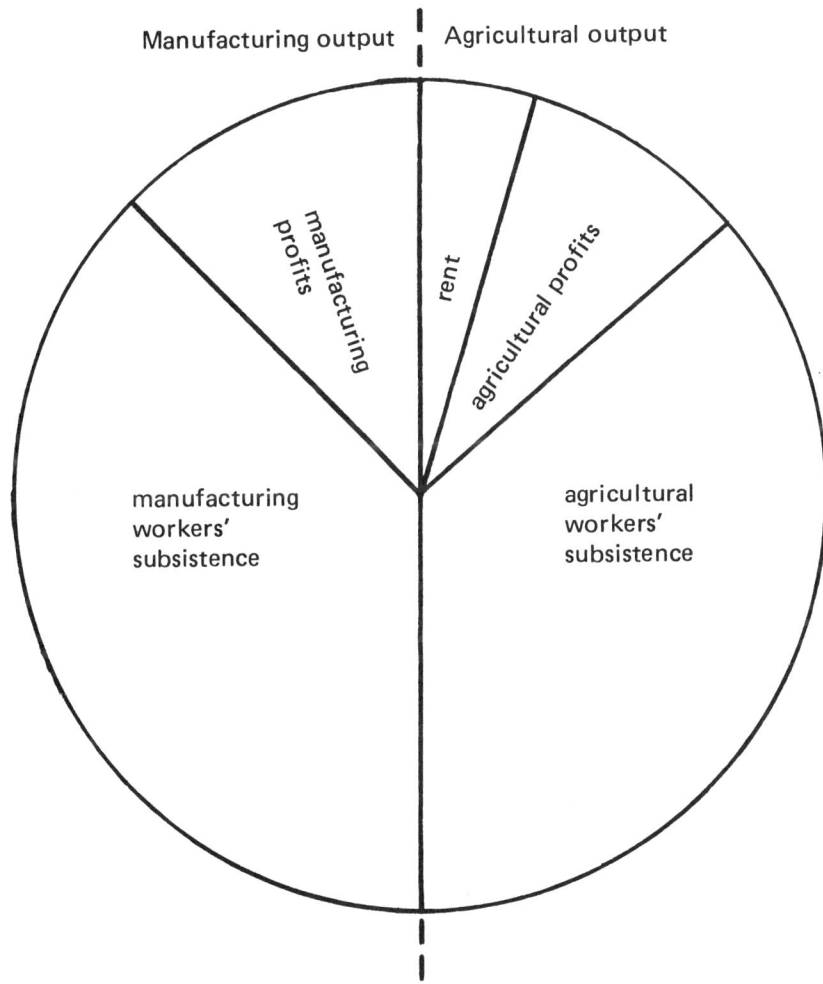

Figure 5.3

Ricardian Surplus

top, as shown. The amount left over goes to agricultural wages and profits. The rate of profit in agriculture in turn determines the rate of profits in manufacturing. Note, however, that Ricardo does *not* deduct a portion of output for the maintenance of fixed and circulating capital in either the agricultural sector or the manufacturing sector, as both Smith and the physiocrats did. Profit is defined simply as total output minus rent minus wages. What about the costs of maintaining capital? It is not clear what Ricardo actually had in mind here, but this is a critical and strange omission, one which was the basis of Marx's criticism of Ricardo.

5.3B(4) Karl Marx. Marx's concept of surplus was central to his entire analysis of society. According to Marx, a certain amount of output, both agricultural and manufactured, must be produced in order to (1) replace the means of production used up in production (fixed and circulating capital), and to (2) provide for the subsistence needs of the producing class. The amount of labor necessary to produce this much output is called *necessary labor*. If producers produce more than this amount, this excess is called *social surplus product*. The extra work done in order to make this surplus possible is called *surplus labor*. Thus the total work performed consists of necessary and surplus labor.

In class societies, however, the producers (i.e., workers in capitalist societies) are usually "forced" to contribute surplus labor. Under what conditions will producers be "forced" to contribute surplus labor? According to Marx,

> Wherever a part of society possesses a monoploy of the means of production, the labourer, free or not free, must add to the working-time necessary in order to produce the means of subsistence for the owners of the means of production . . . [6]

Thus, any class society, capitalist or otherwise, is one in which some "extra" labor must be performed by one class in order to sustain another class. Societies differ from one another on the basis of how the social surplus product produced by surplus labor is extracted from the actual producers.[7]

In a capitalist society this surplus is appropriated by the capitalist class. Because the latter own the means of production and the working class does not, the capitalists have the ability to set the workday beyond what is minimally necessary to reproduce the used-up means of production and to sustain the working class. It is therefore the capitalist–worker relationship, acting through the free labor market, which accounts for the production of a surplus product.

A given amount of output produced in a capitalist system consists of both agricultural and manufactured commodities. A portion of this output is called *constant capital*. Another portion of this output goes to wages and is called *variable capital*.[8] It only reimburses the working class for the necessary labor time which they contribute. The third and final portion of total output is *surplus value*, or that portion of output appropriated by the capitalist class and produced by labor during surplus labor time (i.e., unpaid labor).

This division of the total output is shown in Figure 5.4. The capitalist class advances a certain amount of variable and constant capital at the beginning of a production period and receives in return this amount

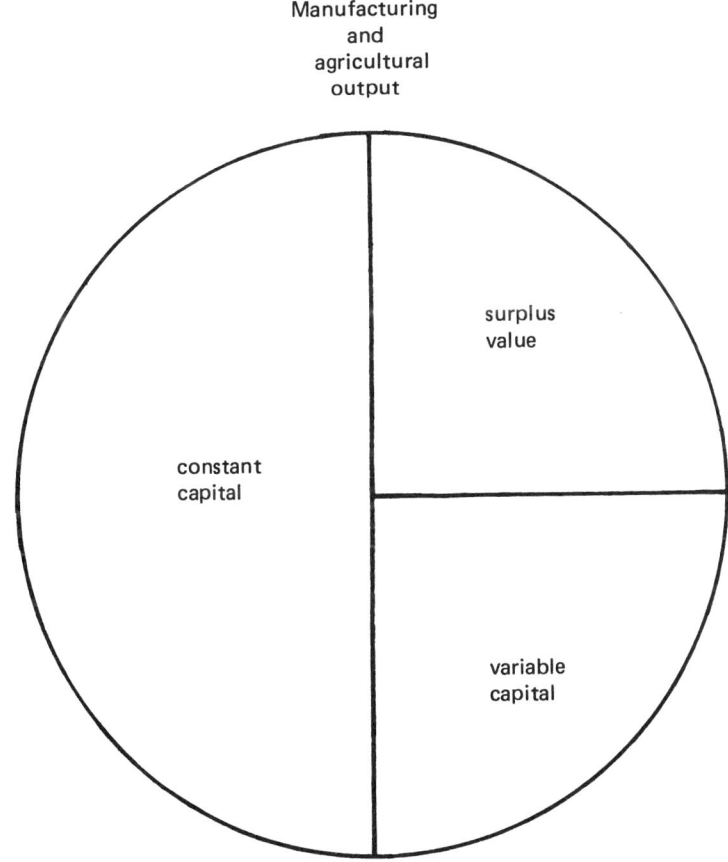

Figure 5.4

Marxian Surplus Value

plus the surplus produced. But how should these quantities be measured?

We have already had a cursory introduction to Marx's labor theory of value. According to this theory, the value of a commodity is determined by the amount of socially necessary labor time devoted to its production. Thus, in Figure 5.4, the value of the total output and its components can, conceptually at least, be measured in labor time. Using this value accounting procedure, we see that the value of the variable capital portion is determined by the amount of labor required to produce the worker's subsistence needs. This labor requirement in turn determines the price of the labor commodity, or the wage rate. The surplus value is determined by the labor necessary to produce the surplus product, which in turn is determined by the length of the workday. Finally, the value of the constant capital equals the labor required to produce the means of production consumed in production.

Before concluding this section, we must note the uses to which the surplus value is put. Marx enumerated in his writings four basic uses of the surplus. The *first* use is for new investment. New investment means that some of the surplus value is used by the capitalist class to acquire additional means of production (fixed and circulating) as well as additional labor. These added inputs serve to expand the capitalist's capacity to produce more output in the future and, perhaps, more profits. The *second* use of the surplus is for consumption of luxury goods by the capitalist class. *Thirdly*, a portion of the surplus goes to the payment of interest and rent. *Fourthly*, a portion of the surplus is used to pay for the services of "unproductive" labor. The term "unproductive" refers to those kinds of labor which do not produce new value but rather provide certain services which are unrelated to the production of commodities (e.g., the labor of menial servants).

5.4 The theoretical significance of economic surplus

If we accept the idea that an economy can produce a surplus, then we are forced into a position of having to answer a very crucial question.

Simply put, if labor is responsible for producing all of society's value, and if a portion of that value is a surplus, then who should get this surplus? Who should have control over its disposition? In capitalist society the surplus partially accrues to the capitalists and landowners. The share going to these groups is not determined by the extent to which they may have actually contributed to the production of output, but rather by the amount of resources which they own. This is a fundamental issue, one already noted earlier in this book.

The reader should note well that, if we employ a subjective theory of value, the above questions do not even arise. One is always capable of saying that the portions accruing to capitalists and landowners are rewards for their subjective contributions to the production of value (abstinence, risk, waiting, etc.). This notion is examined in Chapter 6.

Contemporary surplus concepts

6

Thus, there is always a sort of gap between total utility and total market dollar value. This gap is in the nature of a surplus, which we consumers get because we "receive more than we pay for."
Paul Samuelson

6.1 Neo-Marxian surplus

Marx based most of his theoretical analyses on the assumption of a competitive capitalist economy. Many contemporary followers of Marx, however, have suggested that, since today's reality of oligopoly and monopoly departs significantly from the competitive nature of capitalism in Marx's day, some adjustments have to be made to Marx's economic theory. One such adjustment has to do with defining economic surplus.

In the previous chapter we observed that Marx defined surplus value to be the *labor time* value (labor embodied) of the commodities produced during surplus labor time. In fact, the value of the subsistence commodities produced during necessary labor time, as well as the value of the means of production used up, was also equal to the labor time embodied in their production.

An alternative to this *value accounting* procedure is a *price accounting* procedure whereby all commodities produced, including the surplus, are valued using market prices rather than labor time. Now, these two methods of accounting are in fact related to one another. The value of a commodity will, according to Marx's theory, regulate the price of the commodity. Under certain restrictive conditions, the prices of commodities may even be directly proportional to the values of commodities. These conditions are: (1) a competitive economy exists in which firms are "price-takers" and (2) all industries must use labor and capital in the same proportions.[1]

Let us assume that these two conditions hold true. If it takes 50 hours of labor to produce a table which sells for a competitive price of $100, then a chair which requires 25 hours to produce would sell for a competitive price of $50. Whether we measure the value of the table and the chair in terms of values or prices does not really matter since the relative values would always be the same.

As we already know, prices in imperfectly competitive markets deviate significantly from competitive prices. One of the features of an imperfectly competitive market is that a firm can raise and maintain its price above the competitive level because of the market power which that firm possesses. This would be true even if the unit costs of producing a commodity in an imperfectly competitive market are identical to the unit costs which would exist if that market were perfectly competitive. Hence, if we drop the competitive assumption, prices would no longer be in proportion to labor time values, and price accounting would give different results from value accounting.

In the example above, if the table industry remains competitive, then tables will continue to be sold for $100. If, however, the chair industry becomes monopolized, the monopoly prices may go up to (say) $75, even if chairs still require 25 hours of labor to produce. Whereas in the previous case the table contained twice the labor of the chair (50 hours vs. 25 hours) *and* sold for twice the dollar price ($100 vs. $50), the table now still contains twice the labor of the chair but sells for *less* than twice the price ($100 vs. $75). Prices and values are no longer proportional.

One of the main features of neo-Marxism is the use of price accounting rather than value accounting. This choice does not necessarily imply a rejection of Marx's labor theory of value. It simply implies that, because of the concentrated nature of our modern economy, prices are more suitable than values for empirical and theoretical research. Moreover, government statistics are not collected on the basis of labor values, but rather on the basis of prices.

The implication of this change in emphasis is that the surplus concept is redefined in a way which departs from Marx's formulation. For example, consider the works of the prominent neo-Marxian economists Paul Baran and Paul Sweezy.[2] According to their formulations, the *actual* surplus produced in a modern monopoly-capitalist economy is the difference between *actual* total current output and *actual* current consumption. Note that the consumption of the capitalist class, the shares going to interest and rent, and the shares going to "unproductive" labor are *not* part of the surplus as Marx had suggested they should be. The surplus consists only of net investment (new additions to the capital stock). This definition is illustrated in Figure 6.1(a).

Part of the reason for this change in definition is that government

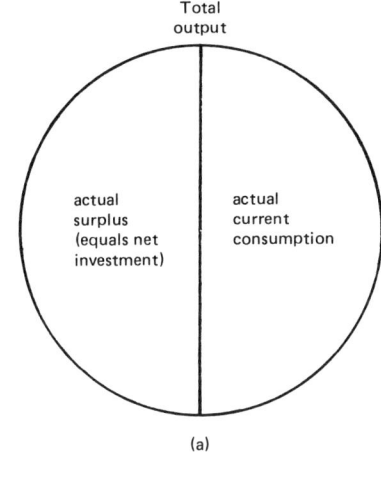

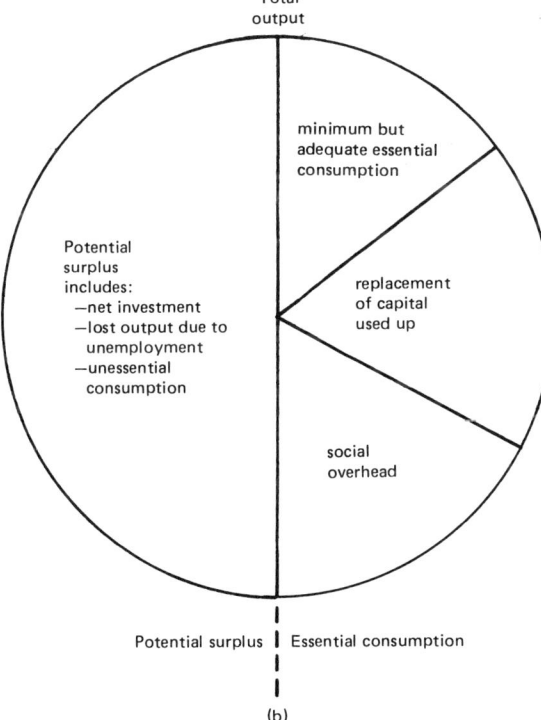

Figure 6.1

Neo-Marxian Surplus

data do not distinguish between "classes." Thus the "capitalists'" consumption is statistically indistinguishable from "workers'" consumption. The neo-Marxian surplus concept lends itself to statistical estimation whereas the Marxian notion of surplus value does not.

A more sophisticated and perhaps more interesting definition of surplus is *potential surplus*. This is defined to be equal to the difference between *potential* output and *essential* consumption.[3] Potential output is total actual output plus that amount that could have been produced if no unemployment and no excess plant capacity existed.

Essential consumption includes, first of all, that amount of output that would provide a "minimum but adequate" standard of living for everyone (capitalists and workers). Also included in essential consumption is that amount of output required to replace the capital used up in production. A third element, called "social overhead," is that amount of government expenditures at all levels necessary to maintain the viability of and productive capacity of business enterprise (e.g., education expenditures, highway maintenance, unemployment insurance, etc.). Any consumption above this total amount is "unessential" and must be included as part of the surplus. Figure 6.2 displays the trend of these three categories between 1929 and 1980.

6.2 Sraffa surplus

The last and final surplus concept originates with the works of Sraffa and modern post-Keynesians. This version serves as the basis for the theory of prices developed in Part IV. In spirit, Sraffa's surplus falls in the tradition of surplus analysis common to all post-Keynesian/Marxian economists, but technically it comes closest to Adam Smith.

It should be recalled that Smith's notion of surplus was expressed as net revenue. After he deducted from total output the amount necessary to replace the capital used up in production, the amount left over, the net revenue, was then available for distribution to wages, profits, and rent. In similar fashion, Sraffa's surplus is defined as the output left over after the means of production consumed in production are replaced. This surplus is then the fund out of which wages, profits, and rents are paid. This approach is illustrated in Figure 6.3 and elaborated fully in the next chapters.

6.3 The surplus in neoclassical economics

It is instructive to see how the concept of economic surplus is treated in neoclassical economics. First of all, the post-Keynesian/Marxian

CONTEMPORARY SURPLUS CONCEPTS

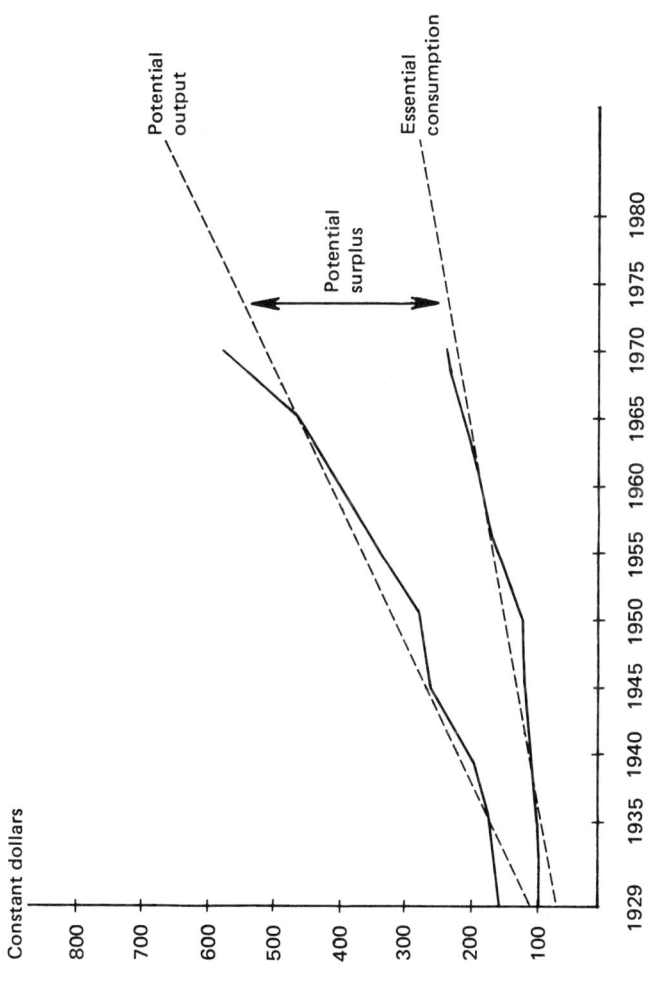

Source: Ron Stanfield, *The Economic Surplus and Neo-Marxism*, Lexington Books, Lexington, Mass., 1973, pp. 59, 80-81.

Figure 6.2
Potential Economic Surplus

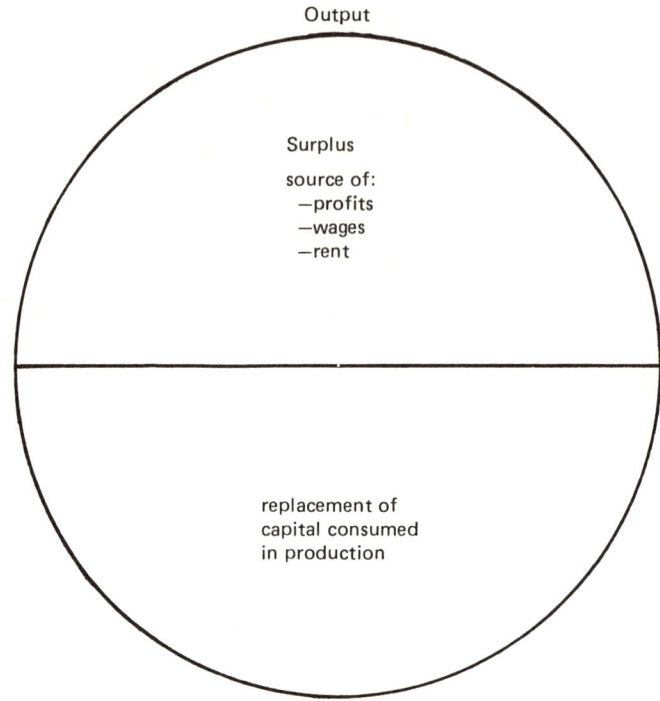

Figure 6.3

Sraffa's Surplus

notion that a *physical* surplus product remains after the minimal requirements of reproduction are met (however defined) is rejected by most neoclassical thought. The rejection is based on the idea that nonlabor inputs are also "productive" and are hence capable of making a contribution to total output independently of labor. Thus, the physical surplus product of post-Keynesian/Marxian economics is in fact produced by these nonlabor inputs. The surplus, according to neoclassical theory, does not exist. This view is clearly developed in the Clark-Wicksteed product exhaustion theorem discussed below.

A second point of departure between post-Keynesian/Marxian and neoclassical theory is that the latter, although rejecting the notion of a labor-produced physical surplus, does accept a *psychological* definition of surplus. This difference in definition is consistent with the observation that neoclassical economics is rooted in the "subjective" attributes of individual agents. This approach to surplus is also explored below.

6.3A Clark-Wicksteed product exhaustion theorem

The product exhaustion theorem is attributed to two pioneers of marginal productivity theory, John Bates Clark (1847–1983) and Philip Wicksteed (1844–1927). According to this theorem, if each factor of

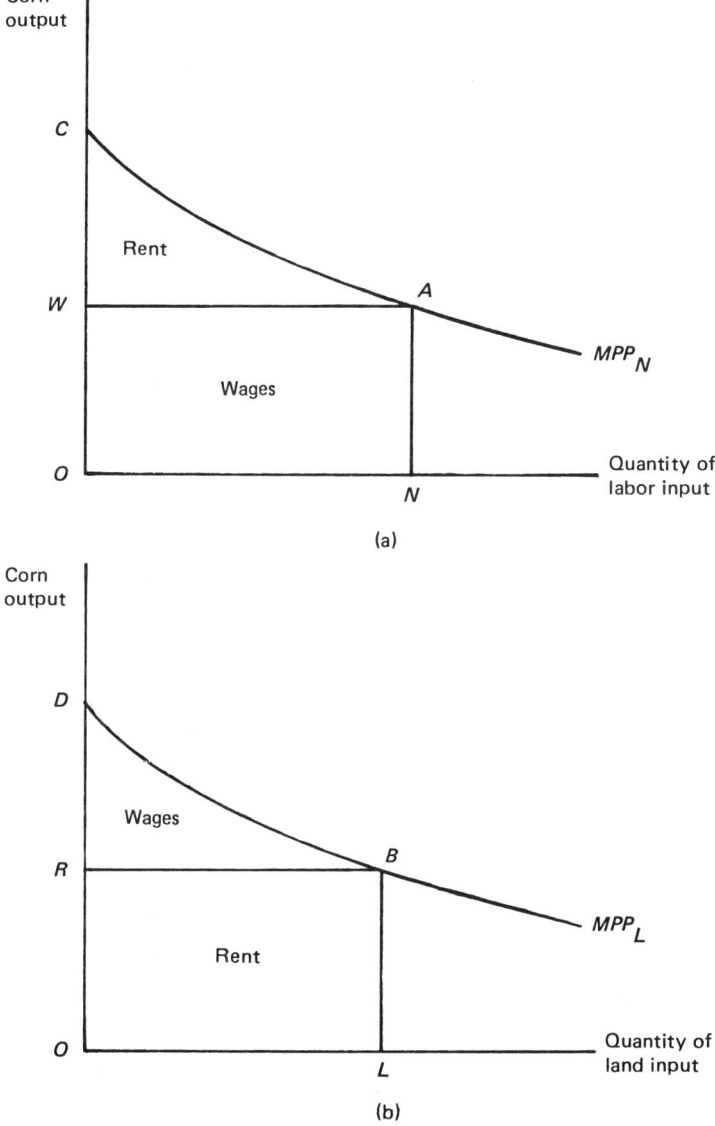

Figure 6.4

Clark-Wicksteed Product Exhaustion Theorem

production is paid according to its marginal physical product, then total physical output would be precisely exhausted in long-run competitive equilibrium. No physical surplus would remain.

To see how this works, assume a perfectly competitive economy in which corn is one of the outputs produced. Suppose, for simplicity, that corn is produced with only labor and land (no capital) and that all labor is alike and all land is of equal quality.

With a given amount of land, successive applications of labor will result in diminishing marginal productivity. This situation is described in Figure 6.4 (a). If *ON* is the amount of labor employed, then the real wage rate (in terms of corn) would be *OW*. Each laborer is paid in corn the marginal product of the last worker hired.

The total wage bill in terms of corn would be the area *OWAN*. However, total corn output equals the area beneath the *MPP* (marginal physical product) curve, or *OCAN*. The difference between total output (*OCAN*) and total wages (*OWAN*) is what remains for the payment of rent to the landlord, or the area *CWA*. But this amount is not, as we shall see, a surplus output appropriated by the landlord. Rather, it is looked upon as the land's net contribution to the total output.

According to the product exhaustion theorem, this same rent payment (*CWA*) is also based on the marginal physical product of the last unit of land employed together with the above supply of labor—*ON* in Figure 6.4 (a). To see this, refer to Figure 6.4 (b). Assume in this case that the above supply of labor (*ON*) is fixed,, and vary instead the amount of land used. Thus, one obtains the marginal physical product curve for land. If the same amount of land is employed as in the previous case, or *OL*, then the rent per unit of land in terms of corn would be *OR* and total rent would be the area *ORBL*.

As before, total corn output is *ODBL*. Total rent is *ORBL*. Therefore, the amount of corn left over after the payment of rent equals *RDB*. This is the reward which goes to labor. The point of the theorem is that total output is the same in both cases, because the same amount of labor and land is used in both cases.Hence, *OCAN* = *ODBL*. Moreover, the total wage bill in Figure 6.4 (a) is identical to the total wage bill in Figure 6.4 (b). Thus *OWAN* = *RBD*. Finally, and for the same reason, the rent payment in Figure 6.4 (a) is identical to the rental payment in Figure 6.4 (b). Thus *CWA* = *ORBL*. This relationship can also be extended to the case where there are more than two inputs (e.g., labor, land, and capital).

In conclusion, the theorem expresses the view that free competition will in the long run (1) return to labor what labor creates, (2) return to landowners what land creates, and (3) return to capitalists what capital creates. Nothing remains left over to distribute. Not only labor but nonlabor factors of production are capable of *creating* new output according to this view. The concept of a physical surplus or residual therefore becomes meaningless.

6.3B The psychological surplus

The neoclassical notion of psychological surplus is best expressed by Alfred Marshall (1842–1924):

> We have already seen that the price which a person pays for a thing can never exceed, and seldom comes up to that which he would be willing to pay rather than go without it: so that the satisfaction which he gets from its purchase generally exceeds that which he gives up in paying away its price. The excess of the price which he would be willing to pay rather than go without the thing, over that which he actually does pay, is the economic measure of this surplus satisfaction. It may be called *consumer's surplus*.[4]

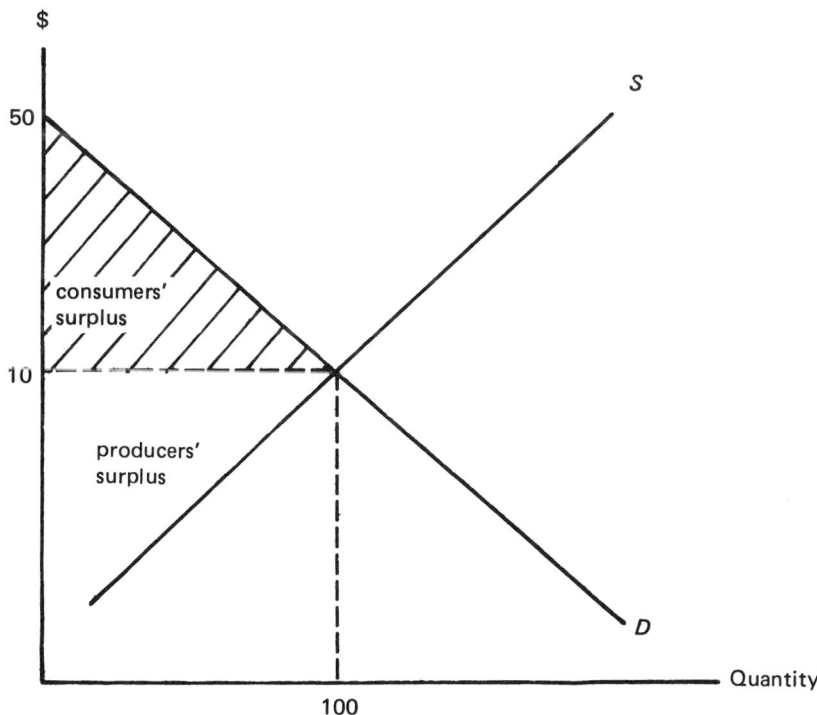

Figure 6.5

Psychological Surplus

Thus, in Figure 6.5, when consumers buy 100 units of commodity X at a a market price of $10 apiece, these same consumers would have been willing to pay more than this for the first 99 units. But they only had to pay $10. This "consumer's surplus," shown as the shaded area in Figure 6.5, measures the amount of satisfaction, or utility, received in excess of what is sacrificed to obtain a commodity in the marketplace.

The notion of consumer's surplus has also been applied to suppliers. In Figure 6.5, the suppliers of commodity X would have been willing to supply buyers at a price lower than $10 for the first 99 units of X. But the supplier in fact receives $10 apiece and therefore realizes a "producer's surplus." The amount of this surplus is equal to the area of the triangle immediately below the consumer's surplus triangle.

In conclusion, both consumers' and producers' surpluses are measures of psychological satisfaction received in excess of what is actually sacrificed to obtain or supply a commodity. The surplus notion is here limited to the subjective, or psychological attributes of market exchange.

6.4 Surplus and production: what lies ahead

A clear definition of economic surplus is the first step in constructing a model of capitalist production. Having now defined and examined the various points of view which have existed with respect to this concept, we are now in a better position to study the post-Keynesian and the Marxian production models. In both cases we see that the distribution of economic surplus among the various claimants, along with the technical requirements of production, helps to determine the prices of production. Thus, pricing and distribution function together in determining the dynamics of capitalism. Part IV looks at the post-Keynesian or Sraffaian model; Part V looks at the Marxian model.

Post-Keynesian theories of value and price

Part IV

The post-Keynesian (neo-Ricardian) theory of value and price

7

> *Profit is . . . income of those who struggle for it. Profit is not the income of those peaceful folk who bring something to the market for sale and wait quietly for what they may receive in exchange. Profit is the income of those who fight and love the battle. It is not the remuneration for the sale of something but the reward of victory.*
>
> Jean Marchal

7.1 Introduction

All post-Keynesian/Marxian theories of value and price rely upon some variant of the surplus concept. The direction which any particular post Keynesian/Marxian theory subsequently takes depends, however, on whether it follows more closely the methods of David Ricardo or the methods of Karl Marx. Because modern post-Keynesian theories of value, price, and distribution are largely derived from the methods of Ricardo, we also refer to this branch as neo-Ricardian.[1] The terms "neo-Ricardian" and "post-Keynesian" may therefore be thought of as equivalents.

Ricardo's theory of value and price represents a high point in the development of economic thought prior to Marx. The general principles of Ricardian theory are being rehabilitated today by many post-Keynesian economists. The most prominent figure in this movement, Piero Sraffa, presents his theory in his book *Production of Commodities by Means of Commodities*.[2] It is Sraffa's version which is examined in part IV.

The Marxian branch, on the other hand, begins of course with Karl Marx. Marx inherited the tools of economic analysis from his classical predecessors, in particular Ricardo, and most of his general theories of capitalism revolve around the labor theory of value. However, Marx did not accept these tools uncritically. Instead, he reworked them and transcended them in order to construct a general theory of society. This general theory was substantially larger in scope and more radical in content than any which came before him.

The Marxian approach to value and price theory is examined in Part V after we have developed the neo-Ricardian theory. Once having dealt with both traditions we will then be in a much better position to compare. Before we begin, however, let us summarize some of the basic principles which characterize all post-Keynesian/Marxian theory, in order to fully appreciate this approach to economics.

7.2 General principles of post-Keynesian/Marxian theory

7.2A Objective value

The starting point for economic analysis has always been value theory. Both post-Keynesian/Marxian as well as neoclassical economists observe that prices in a competitive market economy regulate the use of society's resources. What value theory sets out to do is explain the level toward which the prices of commodities will gravitate. According to neoclassical economics, these levels are strictly determined by subjective valuations made by buyers and sellers. This approach is the utility theory of value.

According to post-Keynesian/Marxian doctrine, the price level of any marketable commodity is governed by the technical conditions of production. These objective conditions of production include: the way production is organized within enterprises, the types of technology used, the productivity of the labor force, and the quality and availability of capital and natural resources. Hence the term "objective" has been chosen to describe this approach to value and price theory.

The objective theory of value therefore places the emphasis on production as a determining aspect of capitalist economic activity. Although the total complexity of a capitalist economy also includes market exchange (or, circulation) processes, it is the way in which production processes are organized that distinguishes capitalism from other social forms.

7.2B Class analysis

Unlike neoclassical theory, which uses the individual as its basic unit of analysis, the post-Keynesian/Marxian approach stresses the relationships between social classes. As a first approximation we view capitalism as a system based on the private ownership of the means of production in which the owning class (capitalist class), the landowning class (renter class), and the nonowning class (working class) are the basic units of analysis.[3]

The capitalist class, it should be remembered, accrues profit income and the landowning class accrues rent income. Both these forms of income are nonlabor income. The working class accrues wage or labor income. Savings come only out of current nonlabor income. These savings may be reinvested directly out of profits (i.e., undistributed profits) or indirectly by going through the capital funds markets. Workers, therefore, do not save in this model. They are outside the savings-investment nexus. This assumption is consistent with the original classical observation that wages always tend toward a subsistence level.

7.2C Economic surplus

Fundamental to the post-Keynesian/Marxian vision is the idea that a capitalist economy is a dynamic economy which requires for its survival the production of surplus. Generally speaking, surplus is defined as the amount of output produced in excess of what is necessary to sustain the working class at their customary standard of living and what is necessary to replace the means of production used up. Not only is the surplus output the source of economic growth; it is also the source of nonlabor income and hence of conflict between social classes. The surplus concept was explored in greater depth in the preceding chapter.

7.2D Reproduction

A central feature of the post-Keynesian/Marxian view is the notion that a large portion of the productive activities of enterprises in an economy is devoted to replacing what is used up in a given period of time. A certain amount of steel output, for example, must go to replace the steel used up in the production of trucks, and a certain number of trucks must be produced in order to replace the ones worn out in the steel industry. Similarly, a certain amount of agricultural commodities must be produced to feed the producers of both steel and trucks, and a certain amount of steel and trucks must also be produced to permit the continued production of agricultural commodities. These quantities of steel, trucks, and agricultural goods must be great enough to replace the quantities of these commodities used up in the three industries. If these amounts are produced, then production in all three industries may continue uninterrupted. The system is then said to be in a self-replacing, or reproducing, state.

Expanding this notion of reproduction to the entire economy, we see that a minimum amount of output of certain key commodities must be forthcoming in order to maintain the entire system in a self-replacing state. How large the output of each of these industries must be in order to sustain, or reproduce, the same levels of activity in all of these industries is largely a technical matter which will be explored later in this chapter. Any excess output above and beyond this minimum amount is a surplus.

By focusing on reproduction, then, the post-Keynesian/Marxian economists concern themselves with the structural attributes of a capitalist system. That is, they endeavor to examine and explain the technical relationships between industries and the pattern of interindustry flows.

There is, however, much more involved than just quantitative, technical interrelationships. If the economic system succeeds in smoothly reproducing itself from year to year, it will also and at the same time succeed in reproducing the class structure and social relationships of the system. The capitalists will continue as capitalists; the workers will continue as workers. *Technical reproduction*, then, goes hand in hand with *social reproduction* (i.e., the reproduction of social classes).[4]

Reproduction therefore ensures the continuance of the economic system and all the social relationships which make up that system. Reproduction is also the prerequisite for economic growth. This is the problematic of post-Keynesian/Marxian theory and is to be distinguished from the "scarcity" problematic of neoclassical theory. The latter possesses a linear view of production, according to which scarce factors are employed in the production of an end product destined for consumption. Post-Keynesian/Marxian theory possesses a circular view of production in which commodities are used to produce each other.

7.2E Competition

The concept of competition has become so ingrained in our culture that many people find it difficult to imagine how society could operate without it. In fact, in capitalism people *must* be competitive in order to survive and earn a living. There is therefore little opportunity to behave in any other way. As obvious as this may seem, the word "competition" has taken on a variety of meanings and is potentially ambiguous for students of post-Keynesian/Marxian economics.

It must be kept in mind that competition as a way of social and economic life did not become prevalent until the sixteenth and seventeenth centuries in Europe. Once competition became well entrenched as the dominant mode of economic intercourse it was quickly reflected in the writings of the early classical economists, including Marx. Later on, as we well know, the neoclassical perspective began to emerge and ultimately came to dominate economic thinking.

The word "competition" in post-Keynesian/Marxian economics simply means rivalry between two or more firms. More simply, competition implies the absence of monopoly and usually describes all kinds of industries, including those dominated by large corporate enterprises. In addition, competition in this economic tradition is the primary means by which the rate of return is equalized across industries.

Most economists today regard Adam Smith to be the "prophet of competition." Although competition was a well-known phenomenon well before Smith, it was he who first made the concept the central organizing principle for the entire economics discipline. Some even argue that Smith's idea of the "invisible hand" was a prototype for today's notion of perfect competition.[5] But there are still some basic differences between the way Smith and his followers used the term and the way it is used in neoclassical economics.[6]

Competition in post-Keynesian/Marxian economics is a kind of *business behavior*. It includes such actions as price undercutting by sellers and the bidding up of prices by buyers. Price is therefore seen as an important variable used by businesses to gain a competitive advantage in the marketplace. Just as important, however, is the type of investments carried out and the timing of these investments. Additionally, product development and advertising strategies are essential activities in obtaining a competitive edge.

Another feature of competition is that it forces market prices to their natural levels. The natural price of a commodity, it should be recalled, is that price about which the market price will fluctuate. It is the measure of a commodity's value and is governed by the technical and social conditions of the commodity's production. If the market price exceeds the natural price, excessive profits would be made. Excessive profits are profits which exceed the supply price of capital and entrepreneurship. New competitors enter the market and the increased competition bids down the market price until it equals the natural price. At this point excessive profits would be eliminated. Only those profits would remain which are just sufficient to prevent capitalists from leaving the industry to seek other opportunities. If natural price exceeds the market price then deficits would occur and the adjustment process will work in the opposite direction.

Finally, in competitive markets capital would flow freely from sector to sector in search of profits. According to post-Keynesian/Marxian economics, it follows that the single most important attribute of a competitive economy is that the rate of profit would tend to be equalized among industries. If the rate of profit in one or more branches of the economy were higher than in others, then capital would flow out of the lower profit branches into the higher profit branches. This process would continue until the profit rate in the latter branches was lowered and brought into line with the other branches.

Very little else had to be said about competition in post-Keynesian/Marxian analysis. Competition was a rather obvious mode of business behavior in capitalist economies and its characteristic features were almost always implicitly assumed. The concept was never as rigorously formulated as it is today in orthodox theory and the conditions for the existence of competition never as clearly spelled out. Beginning in the 1870s, however, the marginal revolution of neoclassical economics began. With this revolution came two significant changes in the way competition was treated.

The first development was the analytical refinement of the term competition. This refinement is generally associated with the increased use of mathematics in economic theory. As early as 1838, Augustin Cournot (1801–1877) introduced the use of mathematics to economic analysis.[7] He was the first to rigorously formulate the marginal conditions for profit maximization (i.e., profits are maximized when marginal revenue equals marginal cost).

Although Cournot initiated the mathematical approach to economic modeling, the use of mathematics in economics did not begin to be popular until the late 1800s. Such neoclassical economists as Jevons, Edgeworth, Walras, and Clark were not only economists but competent mathematicians as well. Accompanying the mathematical approach to economic theory was the requirement that competition itself be explicitly defined and the conditions for its existence be clearly stated. This was essential if a competitive economy was to be described in mathematical terms. These requirements ultimately led to the construction of a separate category of analysis called "perfect competition."

A second and related development was the association of the term "competition" with the structure of a market instead of with a type of business behavior. By market structure is meant the number of firms competing in a market, their market shares, and the types of barriers to new entry. In neoclassical economics a perfectly competitive market is one which contains a large number of firms, each producing identical products. There are also no barriers to entry in perfectly competitive markets. Any market which deviates from this basic description is called "imperfectly" competitive.

In classical economics no distinction is made between perfect and imperfect competition on the basis of the number of firms constituting a market.[8] In fact, a market consisting of any number of firms could be called competitive, since competition describes what firms do to gain profits. Competition is a mode of behavior, a type of activity, and not a description of a market structure. It is this post-Keynesian/Marxian concept which business people typically have in mind when they speak of competition. The neoclassical economist, however, usually has something quite different in mind—a type of market structure rather than a mode of business behavior. It is crucial that we be sure as we proceed of the meaning given to the term "competition" by post-Keynesian/ Marxist economists.

7.3 The rudiments of neo-Ricardian theory

In this section we begin to develop a neo-Ricardian model, based directly on the one presented by Sraffa in his book. We start with an extremely simple situation and gradually build up to more complex situations.

The primary feature of this model is that it does not consider the long-run aspects of social and technological growth. Specifically, a *given state* in the long-run process of development of a capitalist economy is examined. To do this, the total quantity of output produced, and its composition, are taken as given. Also taken as given are the techniques of production. These techniques are rooted in the history of society and embody all of society's past achievements.

In this regard the analysis is a *static analysis*. Insofar as we will be comparing alternative static states, our analysis may also be termed *comparative statics*. This implies that we ignore the time sequence of events which, like a motion picture, takes us forward in time, showing how the economy grows and changes. Such an analysis would be a *dynamic analysis*.

7.3A A subsistence economy

Assume a very primitive noncapitalist society which produces no surplus. That is, it produces exactly enough to replace the commodities used up, and no more. The amount which is produced is the minimal requirement for continued survival. It is further assumed that there are only three industries which, respectively, produce 400 bushels of corn, 20 tons of iron, and 40 goats. Each of these three commodities directly enters into the production of the other two. We choose a three-commodity model because with less than three commodities there is no need for money, and with less than two commodities there is no basis for exchange.

The commodities are produced during the course of a year and, at the end of that year, exchanged for the other commodities required for the next year's production. These commodity inputs are used both as means of production *and* a subsistence goods for the producers. It is finally assumed that no fixed capital is employed and that each industry produces only a single output.[8]

In the corn industry, 260 bushels of corn, 10 tons of iron, and 20 goats are necessary to produce 400 bushels of corn. Remember that these inputs are used *both* as means of production *and* as subsistence goods for the workers. Similarly, in the iron industry, 100 bushels of corn, 8 tons of iron, and 10 goats are required to produce 20 tons of iron. Finally, in the goat industry, 40 bushels of corn, 2 tons of iron, and 10 goats are needed to produce 40 goats.

The relationship between the three sectors of this simple economy can be described in the following way:

(1)
$$\begin{aligned}
260 \text{ bu. corn} + 10 \text{ t. iron} + 20 \text{ goats} &\rightarrow 400 \text{ bu. corn} \\
100 \text{ bu. corn} + 8 \text{ t. iron} + 10 \text{ goats} &\rightarrow 20 \text{ t. iron} \\
\underline{40 \text{ bu. corn}} + \underline{2 \text{ t. iron}} + \underline{10} \text{ goats} &\rightarrow 40 \text{ goats} \\
400 \text{ bu. corn}   20 \text{ t. iron} 40 \text{ goats}
\end{aligned}$$

Note well that the total output produced of each commodity is just equal to the amount required in all three industries. Thus, vertically adding the corn input requirements gives 400 bushels, the amount actually produced in the corn industry. The same holds true in the other two industries.

Since the survival of this simple society hinges on the continued reproduction of corn, iron, and goats, it is essential that the exchanges which occur among the producers enable them to obtain the correct quantities. If the correct quantities cannot be obtained in one of the three sectors, then output will decrease in that sector. If this happens, then there will not be enough available for the other two remaining sectors. Total output will then fall short of subsistence requirements, and starvation will set in.

In the above example, there is only one set of exchange ratios (relative prices) that will permit reproduction to occur. If reproduction takes place, therefore, then exchanges of commodities will ipso facto occur at these ratios. These exchange ratios are called *prices of production*.

As we know by now, prices of production should not be confused with actual market prices. Prices of production are the prices toward which actual market prices will tend in a capitalist economy. Actual prices are determined by the market forces of supply and demand. Prices of production, on the other hand, are determined by the objective conditions of production (input requirements, costs, technical change, etc.).

The actual prices of commodities produced in an economy which is in a self-reproducing state will tend to be brought into equality with prices of production. Otherwise, the economy will be unable to reproduce itself from one period to the next. The mechanisms which work to bring this equality about are explored later in this chapter. For the time being we simply assume that actual prices are always equal to prices of production.

Let us now introduce prices of production into our system of equations. Arbitrarily choosing iron to be the *numeraire*, or standard of price measurement, we denote the relative price of corn in terms of iron by p_c and the price of goats in terms of iron by p_g. The price of iron, p_i, will of course equal unity because it is the numeraire.

Rewriting the above equations, we obtain

(2)
$$260p_c + 10p_i + 20p_g = 400p_c$$
$$100p_c + 8p_i + 10p_g = 20p_i$$
$$40p_c + 2p_i + 10p_g = 40p_g$$

With $p_i = 1$, the solutions for p_c and p_g can be readily determined to be 0.10 and 0.20, respectively.[10] This means that 1 ton of iron *must* exchange for 0.10 bushels of corn and 0.20 goats if the simple economy is to maintain itself in a self-replacing state. If the objective conditions of production change, as with a change in technology, then so too will the input requirements in each industry, as will the price of production of each of the commodities. If actual prices deviate from these prices of production, reproduction cannot occur.

7.3B A surplus-producing economy

Suppose, now, that a technological change has occurred which permits each industry to produce more output with the same amount of input. The extra output is a surplus because it is in excess of what is required for reproduction at a subsistence level. In this case it is also assumed that the workers in each industry receive the entire surplus output produced in their respective industries.

If the surplus output is 100 bushels of corn, 10 tons of iron, and 20 goats, then the set of equations (1) in the above section may be rewritten as

(3)
$$360 \text{ bu. corn} + 10 \text{ t. iron} + 20 \text{ goats} \to 500 \text{ bu. corn}$$
$$100 \text{ bu. corn} + 18 \text{ t. iron} + 10 \text{ goats} \to 30 \text{ t. iron}$$
$$40 \text{ bu. corn} + 2 \text{ t. iron} + 30 \text{ goats} \to 60 \text{ goats}$$

In the corn industry, the corn input requirement has increased from 260 bushels to 360 bushels because the workers in that sector must, by assumption, receive the extra 100 bushels of surplus corn. No other changes appear in that equation except, of course, on the output side. Similarly, the iron input requirement in the second equation has increased by the amount of surplus iron output, or from 8 tons to 18 tons. The goat input requirement in the third equation has, for the same reason, increased from 10 goats to 30 goats.

If the surplus output remains in each industry and is distributed only to the workers in that industry, what will the new prices have to be to insure smooth reproduction? Still using iron as the standard (i.e., $p_i = 1$), we convert the above set of equations to price equations as follows:

(4)
$$360p_c + 10p_i + 20p_g = 500p_c$$
$$100p_c + 18p_i + 10p_g = 30p_i$$
$$40p_c + 2p_i + 30p_g = 60p_g$$

Solving these equations yields $p_c = 0.10$ and $p_g = 0.20$. With $p_i = 1$, the prices of production are identical to those obtained in the previous section. This is not at all surprising, for the *inter-industry exchanges that have to take place remain the same as before.* The corn producers do not share in the surplus iron and goats. They receive the same 10 tons of iron and 20 goats as before. The iron producers also do not share in the surplus corn and goats, receiving the same 100 bushels of corn and 10 goats as before. Finally, the goat producers do not share in the corn and iron surplus, obtaining the same 40 bushels of corn and 2 tons of iron as before. Since the quantities required by each sector from the other two remain unchanged, the exchange ratios will also remain unchanged.

7.3C Another surplus-producing economy

In the situation next to be considered, the above model is modified by assuming that all workers, in all three industries, share equally in the total surplus product. Suppose there are 40 workers in the corn industry and 30 workers in both the iron and goat industries. Each of the 100 workers then receives an extra 1 bushel of corn, 1/10 ton of iron, and 1/5 goat. Together, the 40 workers in the corn industry must now receive an extra 40 bushels of corn, 4 tons of iron, and 8 goats; the 30 workers in both the iron and goat industry must now receive an extra 30 bushels of corn, 3 tons or iron, and 6 goats. Adding these increments to the original amounts shown in the system of equations (1), we obtain

(5)
$$300 \text{ bu. corn} + 14 \text{ t. iron} + 28 \text{ goats} \rightarrow 500 \text{ bu. corn}$$
$$130 \text{ bu. corn} + 11 \text{ t. iron} + 16 \text{ goats} \rightarrow 30 \text{ t. iron}$$
$$70 \text{ bu. corn} + 5 \text{ t. iron} + 16 \text{ goats} \rightarrow 60 \text{ goats}$$

Since each industry now receives a share of the industries' surplus, the prices must change. With $p_i = 1$, it should be intuitively clear that the prices of both corn and goats must change in order for the corn, iron, and goat producers to get (i.e., command) more of the other commodities. These new prices can be found by solving the following three price equations for p_c and p_g

(6)
$$300p_c + 14p_i + 28p_g = 500p_c$$
$$130p_c + 11p_i + 16p_g = 30p_i$$
$$70p_c + 5p_i + 16p_g = 60p_g$$

With the p_i set equal to unity, $p_c = 0.11$ and $p_g = 0.29$. This confirms the observation that corn and goat prices will change.

7.3D A surplus-producing capitalist economy

Assume that a capitalist class now emerges and, by virtue of its ownership of the means of production, manages to appropriate the entire surplus output. The workers would then sink back to the subsistence standard of living implied in the first model of 7.3A.

Suppose, moreover, that the capitalists in each industry obtain only the surplus produced in their own industry. This situation is identical to that described in 7.3B where the workers received only the surplus produced in their own industries. The only difference here is that the claimants of the surplus are the capitalists rather than the workers.

Since it is customary to refer to the capitalists' share of the surplus as "profit," and since profit is normally expressed as a percentage of the cost of the means of production invested, we may write our system of equations in price terms as

(7)
$$(260p_c + 10p_i + 20pg)(1 + r_1) = 500p_c$$
$$(100p_c + 8p_i + 10pg)(1 + r_2) = 30p_i$$
$$(40p_c + 2p_i + 10pg)(1 + r_3) = 60p_g$$

where r_1, r_2, r_3 are the rates of profit (markup) in each sector.[11]

Setting the model up in this way suggests that only material inputs, used in advance of production, earn a return. This is an important assumption which underlies the Sraffa model and makes it less general than it might be.

In any case, since the surplus generated in each industry remains in that industry, the interindustry exchange ratios would be identical to those obtained in 7.3A and 7.3B. Thus, $p_c = 0.10$ and $p_g = 0.20$.

Looking first at the corn industry, we see that the value of the means of production invested ($260p_c + 10p_i + 20p_g$) is 40, using the prices of production just obtained. As before, this amount is also assumed to provide for workers' subsistence, which in this instance is the original level of 7.3A. The value of corn output is $500p_c$ or 50 (500×0.10). The surplus output (10 bushels, or 50 minus 40) represents a 25% return, or rate of profit. Hence, r_1 in (7) above equals 0.25. Similarly, the profit rate in the iron and goat industry can both be found to be 50%. Hence, $r_2 = 0.50$ and $r_3 = 0.50$.

7.3E A competitive capitalist economy

If there is competition among the capitalists within each industry, and if capital is free to flow from one industry to another, then it would be reasonable to expect that the rate of profit would in time be the same in each industry. Since the model described in (7) above assumes that two different profit rates coexist, a slight modification is called for.

If the capitalist class still receives the entire surplus, and if we let r stand for the *equalized* rate of profit, then

(8)
$$(260p_c + 10p_i + 20pg)(1 + r) = 500p_c$$
$$(100p_c + 8p_i + 10pg)(1 + r) = 30p_i$$
$$(40p_c + 2p_i + 10pg)(1 + r) = 60p_g$$

Since the surplus of each industry is now shared among the capitalists in all three industries, the inter-industry exchange ratios will change somewhat. Solving the above equations gives $p_c = 0.12$, $p_g = 0.20$, and $r = 0.34$.[12] Note that p_i is still equal to unity.

The reason for these price changes is fairly obvious. The corn price, for example, is now slightly higher than before (0.12 as compared to 0.10). But with the assumption of competition and the resulting equalized profit rate, the corn industry will receive a surplus equivalent to a 34% return. This is higher than the 25% received before. If the corn capitalists are to receive a greater percentage rate of profit, then the corn price must rise relative to iron and goats. With this higher corn price, and with the price of iron and goats the same as before, the additional iron and goats that must now be given up to obtain a bushel of corn will in this case be just enough to reduce the 50% profit rate to 34%.

7.4 The general case: preliminary summary

A general principle begins to emerge from the above illustrations. These illustrations are summarized in Table 7.1. *Whenever the distribution of the surplus product changes between industries, the price ratios will also change.* What these prices will finally be depends, then, on how the surplus is distributed, as well as on the objective conditions of production. These conditions will, in turn, consist of both technical conditions as well as social conditions (e.g., class relations). We shall return to this point later. In the meantime, the model derived in the above section will be generalized from the three-industry case to the k-industry case.

Let the letters $A_a, B_a, \ldots, K_a$ be the quantities of commodities a, $b, \ldots, k$ necessary to produce A; $A_b, B_b, \ldots, K_b$ be the quantities of commodities $a, b, \ldots, k$ necessary to produce B; and so on. With r representing the equalized rate of profit, and $p_a, p_b, \ldots p_k$ the prices of production of the k commodities, we may write:

Table 7.1

Summary of Models

Models	Prices of Production			Profits		
	p_i	p_c	p_g	iron	corn	goats
1. no surplus	1.0	0.10	0.20	n.d.	n.d.	n.d.
2. surplus-producing noncapitalist economy; surplus remains in industries	1.0	0.10	0.20	n.d.	n.d.	n.d.
3. surplus-producing noncapitalist economy; surplus distributed among industries on per worker basis	1.0	0.11	0.29	n.d.	n.d.	n.d.
4. surplus-producing capitalist economy; all surplus goes to capitalist class; surplus stays within industry	1.0	0.10	0.20	50%	25%	50%
5. surplus-producing capitalist economy, but with equalized profit rate; surplus shared with other industries	1.0	0.12	0.20	34%	34%	34%

(9)
$$(A_a p_a + B_a p_b + \ldots + K_a p_k)(1 + r) = A p_a$$
$$(A_b p_a + B_b p_b + \ldots + K_b p_k)(1 + r) = B p_b$$
$$\ldots\ldots\ldots\ldots\ldots\ldots\ldots\ldots\ldots\ldots\ldots\ldots\ldots\ldots$$
$$(A_k p_a + B_k p_b + \ldots + K_k p_k)(1 + r) = K p_k$$

There are k independent equations in the above system. If we continue to set one of the k prices equal to unity, this leaves $(k - 1)$ prices to be determined. Adding the unknown profit rate r to the $(k - 1)$ unknown prices gives us k unknowns. With k equations, the system can be solved.

Wages, profits, and prices

8

> *It should be fairly clear . . . that a system which determines distribution in terms of exchange and its emergent prices must, in one way or another, with possibility of varying emphasis, be cast in terms of supply and demand; but* au contraire *the Ricardian system, which explains exchange in terms of distribution, and distribution itself in terms of productivity and conditions of production in one industry or sector (given the real wage), has no place for the relations of supply and demand—at least until it comes to* movements *in relative prices, and in particular of Smithian market prices.*
>
> Maurice Dobb

8.1 Income distribution and price determination

The models developed in Chapter 7 gave little attention to labor as an explicit input to production. It was simply noted that a portion of the commodity input requirements in each industry went to meet the workers' subsistence needs. Nothing was said about how much this amount exactly was. Total workers' income, then, was this unspecified amount plus whatever was left of the surplus after profits were paid. Until this problem is clarified, little more can be said about income distribution and price determination.

8.1A Wages as a share of surplus

It is assumed for simplicity that the labor force is homogeneous and that the wage rate is the same in all industries. It is further assumed that the *entire* wage income, as with profit income, is paid out of the surplus product. This clearly differs from the previous treatment of workers' income.[1] This also causes some difficulties when no surplus exists, since workers' income would theoretically be equal to zero. But as long as we continue to deal with surplus-producing economies, which would be more realistic to do anyway, this causes no difficulties.

The implication of the last assumption is that the capitalist class and the working class must in some way come to an agreement about how to divide the surplus. We make no assumption about how this is accomplished, leaving the problem open-ended. It should nevertheless be clear that the solution to the problem would to a large degree depend on the relative strengths of the two classes and on other sociological and institutional factors.

8.1B Wages and profits as shares of surplus

One final change must now be made. If we were to continue with our practice of selecting one industry's output as the standard of price measurement, then the prices of all other commodities would be expressed in terms of that industry's output. Since the share of the surplus going to the working class, represented by w, is also a variable price in the system, it too would be expressed as some multiple of this standard of measurement. Thus, in our example, the wage rate w would be expressed in terms of iron, where $p_i = 1$. Similarly, the prices of corn and goats would continue to be expressed in terms of iron.

However, it would be a great deal more convenient to express wage rates in terms of the total system surplus rather than in terms of iron because it was just assumed that the whole wage comes out of that surplus.

Moreover, the standard of measure need only be redefined. Any commodity can serve as a standard. *In fact, any combination of commodities can serve as a standard.* Thus, rather than let iron serve as a standard, let the standard be the value of the entire surplus output. Instead of measuring w in terms of iron, it will be measured in terms of the aggregate surplus. If for instance w equals 0.5, this now means that the share going to labor is 50% of the surplus. This means, of course, that the prices of corn, iron, and goats will now be measured in terms of this same surplus bundle.

Taking the entire surplus output in the model of the previous section, multiply the corn, iron, and goat components of that total surplus by their respective prices. The surplus components must be multiplied by their respective prices because this is the only way to add heterogeneous commodities. The physical commodities themselves are thus reduced to "value" terms and it is the aggregate value of the surplus which we set equal to unity.

We obtain as our new standard a "composite" commodity. Setting the value of this composite commodity (i. e., total surplus) equal to unity, we obtain

(1) $\quad [500 - (260 + 100 + 40)] p_c + [30 - (10 + 8 + 2)] p_i +$
$\quad\quad [60 - (20 + 10 + 10)] p_g = 1$

Each of the three terms in brackets on the left represents the value of the surplus output produced in the corn, iron, and goat industries, respectively. Simplifying (1), we obtain

(2) $$100p_c + 10p_i + 20p_g = 1$$

The entire model of the previous section may now be written as

(3)
$$(260p_c + 10p_i + 20p_g)(1 + r) + 0.4w = 500p_c$$
$$(100p_c + 8p_i + 10p_g)(1 + r) + 0.3w = 30p_i$$
$$(40p_c + 2p_i + 10p_g)(1 + r) + 0.3w = 60p_g$$
$$100p_c + 10p_i + 20p_g = 1$$

The coefficients of w (0.4, 0.3, and 0.3) represent the fraction of the total labor force allocated to each sector. Since there is a total of 100 workers, with 40 in the corn sector and 30 each in the iron and goat sectors, the values for these fractions are readily obtained. Thus, the first equation states that the total wage bill in the corn industry (0.4w) plus the total cost of the means of production ($260p_c + 10p_i + 20p_g$), plus the $r\%$ profit markup on these latter costs equals the total value of corn output ($500p_c$). The same interpretation applies to the iron and goat industry equations.

Letting $L_a, L_b, \ldots, L_k$ stand for the fraction of the total labor force allocated to the k sectors of the economy, we see that the generalized model of Chapter 7 now becomes

(4)
$$(A_a p_a + B_a p_b + \ldots + K_a p_k)(1 + r) + L_a w = Ap_a$$
$$(A_b p_a + B_b p_b + \ldots + K_b p_k)(1 + r) + L_b w = Bp_b$$
$$\ldots\ldots\ldots\ldots\ldots\ldots\ldots\ldots\ldots\ldots\ldots\ldots\ldots\ldots\ldots\ldots\ldots$$
$$(A_k p_a + B_k p_b + \ldots + K_k p_k)(1 + r) + L_k w = Kp_k$$
$$[A - (A_a + A_b + \ldots + A_k)]p_a + [B - (B_a + B_b + \ldots + B_k)]p_b +$$
$$\ldots + [K - (K_a + K_b + \ldots + K_k)]p_k = 1$$

Including the last equation, there is now a total of $k + 1$ independent equations. There are also the following unknowns: k prices, r, and w. This totals $k + 2$ unknowns. Because the number of unknowns is greater than the number of equations, the system cannot be determined until either the rate of profit or wage rate is first specified. In other words, once the distribution of income between the capitalist class and the working class is stated, the prices may then be determined. These prices will insure that each sector receives enough of all the other commodity inputs so that the system can (1) replace the means of production used up, and (2) provide a surplus payment that is sufficient to provide for profits and wages at the specified rates.

It should be clearly noted that this approach to income distribution differs significantly from the neoclassical approach. In neoclassical economics the income received by each of the three "factors of production" (land, labor, and capital) depends on the prices of these factors *as determined in their* respective factor markets. Income distribution, then, is determined in the marketplace according to the same principles which determine the prices of all other commodities.

The neo-Ricardian approach, on the other hand, sees a given income distribution as an outcome of a quite different social process, the basis of which is conflict over the surplus that is annually produced. The distribution of income betwen labor, capital, and land is, in the aggregate, *not* determined by marketplace relationships; it has little to do with the processes which determine relative commodity prices. Instead, the distribution of the surplus depends on a rather large number of sociological and institutional factors, very few of them having to do with the marginalist principles of neoclassical theory. Union membership, financial and political power of employers and unions, degree of competition, unity of employers, race and ethnic relations, and the like are what ultimately determine the wage-profit relation.[2]

8.2 The wage-profit relationship

It is evident from the previous discussion that there exists an inverse relationship between the wage rate and the rate of profits. If we specify a relatively low wage share, then the share (of the surplus) going to profits will be relatively large. If we specify a relatively high wage share, then there will be a correspondingly low rate of profits.

To obtain a clear picture of the nature of this relationship, we shall use our three-sector example summarized in equations (3). Selecting various wage shares ranging from 0% of the surplus to 100% of the surplus, we see that the corresponding rates of profit can be solved together with the unknown prices. The wage rate, profit rate, and price data are shown in Table 8.1.

When wage rates are zero, the entire surplus goes to profits. This amount, when expressed as a uniform percentage of the means of production employed in each industry, represents a profit rate of 34%. This is the maximum obtainable rate of profit. Similarly, when the entire surplus goes to wages ($w = 100\%$), the profit rate is zero.

Two things should be noted about this wage-profit relation. The first is that it is a negative relation. This is due to the fact that less surplus is available for profits as the wage rate rises. This implies a decline in the rate of profits, for reasons considered above.

The second feature of the wage-profit relation is its nonlinearity. This is explained by the fact that the proportions in which labor and means of

Table 8.1

Wage, Profit Rate, and Price Data

Wage Rate (% of surplus)	Profit Rate (%)	Price of Corn (X 10⁻³)	Price of Iron (X 10⁻³)	Price of Goats (X 10⁻³)
0	34.0	4.69	37.90	7.58
10	30.5	4.63	37.83	7.93
20	27.0	4.57	37.76	8.28
30	23.5	4.51	37.69	8.63
40	20.0	4.44	37.63	8.97
50	16.4	4.38	37.56	9.30
60	12.8	4.32	37.49	9.64
70	9.2	4.27	37.42	9.96
80	5.6	4.21	37.36	10.29
90	2.0	4.15	37.29	10.61
100	0	4.09	37.23	10.93

Note: Once again the method of successive approximations was used to find the solutions. See footnote 12 in Chapter 7.

production are combined differ from industry to industry. To see this, imagine a situation in which each industry employed labor and means of production in identical proportions. Suppose also that the entire surplus goes to wages. Now, if wages are reduced from 100% to (say) 80%, surplus will then be released and made available for the payment of higher profits. With the labor/means-of-production proportions remaining identical, just enough surplus will be released from wages in each industry to enable the payment of profits at the new, higher uniform rate. Because of this, no adjustments would need to be made in the flow of commodities between industries, and prices of production would therefore remain unchanged. Additionally, every time wage rates are reduced by a given amount, the profit rate would increase in direct proportion to this amount. Any given change in w would always result in a proportional change in r. Since the slope of the wage–profit relation is equal to the change in profits divided by the change in wages ($\Delta w/\Delta r$), the wage–profit relation would therefore be linear as in Figure 8.1.

If the proportions of labor to means of production differ among industries, then the above conclusions would *not* be obtained. A wage reduction from 100% to 80% would then mean that some industries would have an insufficient amount of surplus released for the payment of a uniform rate of profit, and others will have too much. How much is released depends on how much labor is employed, and how much is

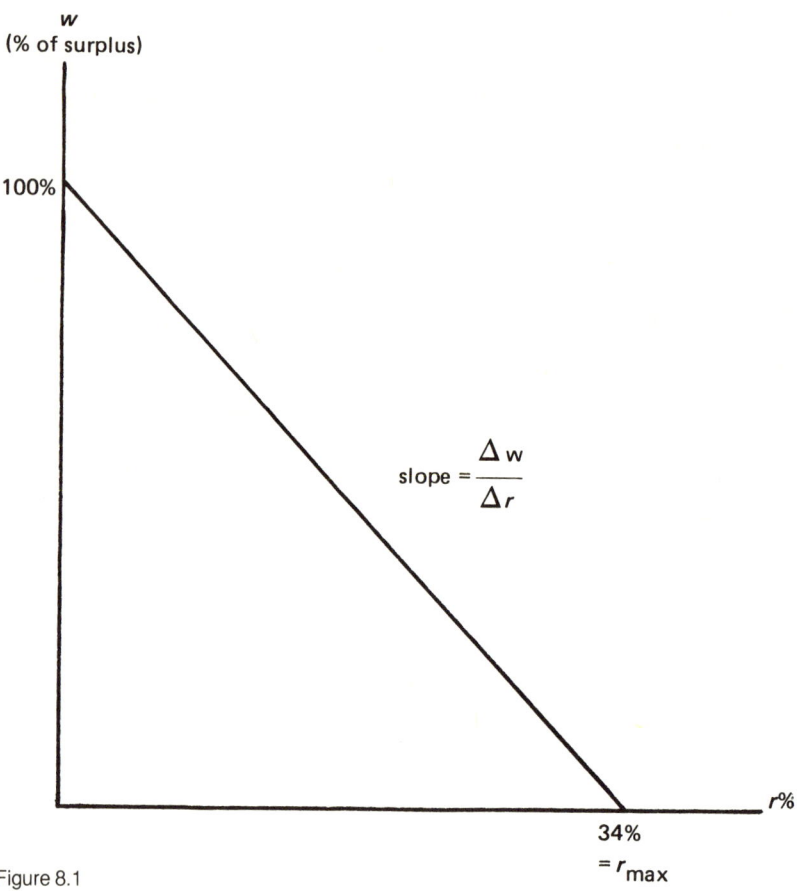

Figure 8.1

A Linear Wage-Profit Relation

needed depends on the aggregate value of the means of production used.

In order to redress these imbalances and maintain a uniform profit rate, relative prices will have to change. Examination of the last three columns of Table 8.1 reveals that the prices of corn and iron gradually fall whereas the price of goats increases. These price movements reflect differing proportions of labor to means of production in the three industries and serve to adjust the inter-industry flow of commodities. Thus, as the wage rate falls gradually from 100% to 0% the rate of profits will increase from 0% to 34%. However, the corresponding changes in profit rates would *not* be in direct proportion to the changes in wages as is the case when labor/means-of-production proportions are identical in all industries. This of course implies that the wage–profit relation is nonlinear. The exact shape of the curve would normally be too difficult to determine, but it would probably look like Figure 8.2(a).

The direction in which prices will have to change as a result of an alteration in the distribution of surplus therefore depends on the overall structure of production. The structure of production is characterized by the composition of commodity inputs, the proportions in which these inputs are combined with labor, and the size and composition of the resulting output. Moreover, the ability of the system to avoid major crises depends on the behavior of the capitalists who set commodity prices and their responses to wage demands. If, for example, wage increases are granted by capitalists, profit rates will have to fall. However, some capitalists may refuse to relinquish their share of the surplus to labor. They may in a subsequent time period attempt to recoup past

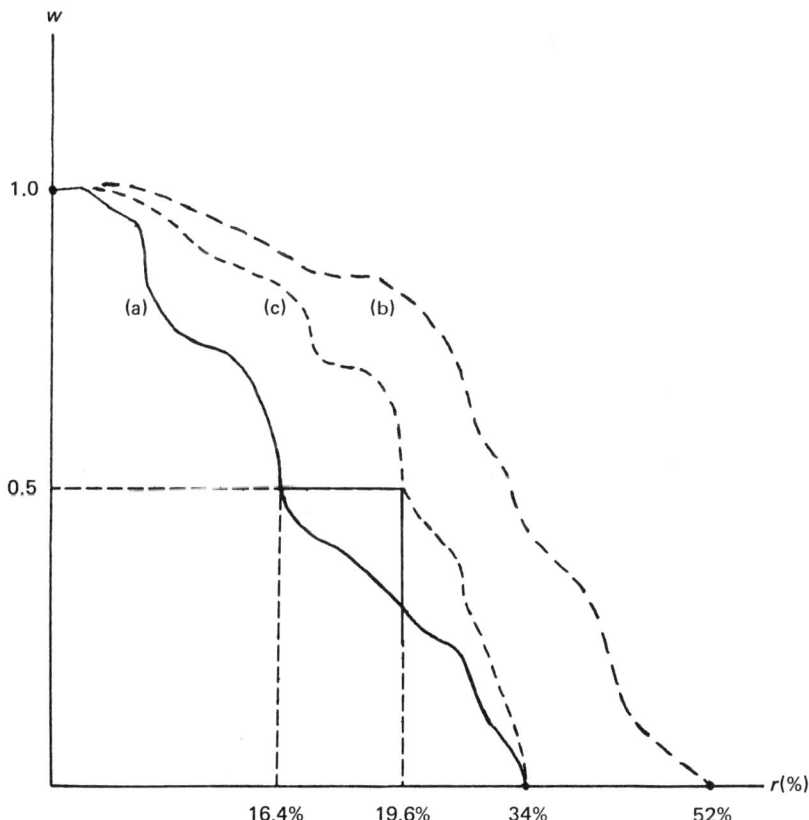

Figure 8.2

A Nonlinear Wage-Profit Relation

losses in profits by raising prices above the levels required to maintain inter-industry balance. An economic crisis may ensue, resulting in bottlenecks, inflation, and unemployment.[3]

8.3 The structure of production

The shape and position of the wage–profit relation depends on the structure of production in each industry. In order to demonstrate this we consider two cases. In the first case a change in the structure of iron production is considered. It is assumed that a technological change has occurred which now enables iron producers to produce twice as much iron with the same amount of inputs. In the second case it is assumed that the initial level of iron output can be produced with the same commodity inputs but with half the labor input. This implies a change in the proportion of labor to means of production.

8.3A An increase in iron output

With a doubling in iron output, 60 tons of iron are now being produced instead of 30. The new system of equations becomes

(5)
$$(260p_c + 10p_i + 20p_g)(1 + r) + 0.4w = 500p_c$$
$$(100p_c + 8p_i + 10p_g)(1 + r) + 0.3w = 60p_i$$
$$(40p_c + 2p_i + 10p_g)(1 + r) + 0.3w = 60p_g$$
$$100p_c + 40p_i + 20p_g = 1$$

Since all other input requirements remain unchanged, the added iron output (30 tons) means an increase in total surplus output. The right-hand side of the iron equation increased from $30p_i$ to $60p_i$, and the iron surplus in the fourth equation increases by $30p_i$ as well. Everything else remains the same.

The wage–profit relation also shifts outward from its initial position (a) to its new position (b) in Figure 8.2. Solving equations (5) for varying values of w yields a maximum profit rate of 52% when $w = 0$. Likewise the profit rate is higher at every wage rate greater than or equal to zero and less than 100%. When the wage rate is 100%, the profit rate is zero.

8.3B A reduction in labor requirements

If the amount of labor necessary to produce iron falls from 30% of the labor force to 15%, the system of equations now becomes:

(6)
$$(260p_c + 10p_i + 20p_g)(1 + r) + 0.4w = 500p_c$$
$$(100p_c + 8p_i + 10p_g)(1 + r) + 0.15w = 30p_i$$
$$(40p_c + 2p_i + 10p_g)(1 + r) + 0.3w = 60p_g$$
$$100p_c + 10p_i + 20p_g = 1$$

We assume that the released workers in the iron industry are not used to produce more corn, iron, or goats. The amount and composition of output therefore remains the same as before, and the size of the surplus remains unchanged. The only change in the industry equations appears in the iron sector, in which case the labor requirement is now shown to be $0.15w$ instead of its previous level of $0.3w$.

Solving (6) for profit rates and prices at alternative wage levels yields a wage–profit relation that intersects both axes at the same point. This is shown in graph (c) of Figure 8.2. When wages are zero, the entire surplus goes to profits. At this point it does not matter how many workers are needed; capitalists get all the surplus and the rate of profits remains at 34%. When $w = 100\%$, the entire surplus is earmarked for wages and the profit rate is zero. But 15% of the work force is unemployed and receives no wage income. Thus, at every wage rate between 0% and 100% the profit rate can now be higher than before because labor's share of the surplus does not get entirely distributed (since unemployed workers do not get paid). Thus, if 50% of the surplus is earmarked for wages ($w = 50\%$), only 42.5% gets distributed [0.4 (0.50) + 0.15 (0.50) + 0.3 (0.50)]. The remaining 7.5% can be added back to the capitalists' profit share or taxed away. If it is added back to profits the profit rate will increase from 16.4% to 19.6% (when $w = 0.50$), shown in Figure 8.2.

To generalize, the above two cases suggest that whenever a technological change occurs the distributional opportunities change as well. This is due to the fact that new technologies alter the surplus-producing capacity of the system. How these distributional opportunities change depends on how the new technologies are used. If the previously existing level of resource employment remains the same, the wage-profit relation rotates counterclockwise about the wage axis at $w = 1$. If the new surplus-producing capacity of the system is used to release labor from employment (i.e., labor-saving technology) the w and r intercepts remain the same but the shape of the curve changes. How this shape changes depends not only on the production coefficients but also on what happens to the surplus share that originally accrued to the workers who lost their jobs.

8.4 Basic and nonbasic commodities

The earlier classical economists typically assumed that wages were fixed at the subsistence level. This is quite different from our assumption that wages can be above this level, sharing in the annual surplus. Because the commodities consumed by the working class provided only for subsistence, the early classical economists referred to these as "necessaries." Those commodities which were not essential to subsistence were termed "luxuries" and were consumed largely by the capitalist classes.

According to the early classical analysis, if the costs of producing necessaries changed, then the wages of all labor would also have to change. The entire system of relative prices would therefore be influenced, since wages are an expense incurred by all industries. If, on the other hand, the costs of producing luxuries changed, then only the prices of those luxuries would change. This would be true because luxuries do not enter into the production of anything else.[4]

According to the early classical economists, whether or not a change in the conditions of production of a commodity would occasion a general change in all relative prices depends entirely on where that commodity fits into *consumption*. It depends ultimately on the working class's consumptive habits and hence on how the concept of subsistence is defined. Thus, if the price of a luxury item increases, then there would be no effect on other prices. If that commodity is a necessity, then just the opposite would result.

The approach taken by modern neo-Ricardians departs somewhat from this necessary–luxury distinction. It adopts instead a distinction which is more general in nature. To see this, consider the general system of equations described in section 8.1B:

$$
\begin{aligned}
(A_a p_a + B_a p_b + \ldots + K_a p_k)(1 + r) + L_a w &= A p_a \\
(A_b p_a + B_b p_b + \ldots + K_b p_k)(1 + r) + L_b w &= B p_b \\
&\ldots \\
(A_k p_a + B_k p_b + \ldots + K_k p_k)(1 + r) + L_k w &= K p_k \\
[A - (A_a + A_b + \ldots + A_k)] p_a + [B - (B_a + B_b + \ldots + B_k)] p_b + \\
\ldots + [K - (K_a + K_b + \ldots + K_k)] p_k &= 1
\end{aligned}
\tag{7}
$$

Suppose that a portion of the surplus output in all k industries is allocated to the production of a new commodity X. Further suppose that, even though each of the k commodities is essential to the production of X, none of the X produced is needed for the production of any of the k commodities. With $A_x, B_x, \ldots, K_x$ representing the amounts of A, $B, \ldots, K$ used in X production, and L_x the fraction of society's labor going to this new sector, we add the following industry equation to (7) above:

$$(8) \quad (A_x p_a + B_x p_b + \ldots + K_x p_k + X_x p_x)(1 + r) + L_x w = X p_x$$

where $X_x p_x$ is the value of X used to produce X. This latter term would, of course, be zero since X is assumed not to enter into the production of *anything* else (i. e., $X_x = 0$).

The entire system may then be written as

(9)
$$(A_a p_a + B_a p_b + \ldots + K_a p_k + X_a p_x)(1 + r) + L_a w = A p_a$$
$$(A_b p_a + B_b p_b + \ldots + K_b p_k + X_b p_x)(1 + r) + L_b w = B p_b$$
$$\ldots$$
$$(A_k p_a + B_k p_b + \ldots + K_k p_k + X_k p_x)(1 + r) + L_k w = K p_k$$
$$(A_x p_a + B_x p_b + \ldots + K_x p_k + X_x p_x)(1 + r) + L_x w = X p_x$$
$$[A - (A_a + A_b + \ldots + A_k + A_x)]p_a +$$
$$[B - (B_a + B_b + \ldots + B_k + B_x)]p_b +$$
$$\ldots + [K - (K_a + K_b + \ldots + K_k + K_x)]p_k +$$
$$[X - (X_a + X_b + \ldots + X_k + X_x)]p_x = 1$$

Note well that because X is a final product which does not enter any other process, all of the terms $X_a, \ldots, X_k, X_x$ are equal to zero. We can therefore eliminate the entire column of X entries in the above equations. Since the term $(X_a + X_b + \ldots + X_k + X_x)$ in the last equation is also zero for the same reason, we are left with only the total X output in the numeraire equation. This is a constant number which is simply added to the surplus. Since the prices bear the same relationship to one another no matter what standard of measure is used, we can easily eliminate the X from the standard composite commodity equation without affecting relative prices.

The entire system may be rewritten therefore as

(10)
$$(A_a p_a + B_a p_b + \ldots + K_a p_k)(1 + r) + L_a w = A p_a$$
$$(A_b p_a + B_b p_b + \ldots + K_b p_k)(1 + r) + L_b w = B p_b$$
$$\ldots$$
$$(A_k p_a + B_k p_b + \ldots + K_k p_k)(1 + r) + L_k w = K p_k$$
$$(A_x p_a + B_x p_b + \ldots + K_x p_k)(1 + r) + L_x w = X p_x$$
$$[A - (A_a + A_b + \ldots + A_k)]p_a + [B - (B_a + B_b + \ldots + B_k)]p_b +$$
$$\ldots + [K - (K_a + K_b + \ldots + K_k)]p_k = 1$$

The above $k + 2$ equations will, if the wage rate is given, provide solutions for the $k + 1$ commodity prices $(p_a, p_b, \ldots, p_k, p_x)$ and the rate of profit r.

Now suppose that subsequent to the determination of these solutions the conditions of production in (say) industry A change such that the quantities of inputs required to produce the same amount of A are different. What impact will this have on relative prices? Since commodity A is used in all sectors, including X, one would expect that all prices would be affected, depending on the relative amounts of A used.

If, instead, the conditions of production in the new X industry changed, what would happen to relative prices? Since X is not used anywhere else, the impact would only be felt in the X industry. Thus, the price of X will change, but all other prices will stay the same.

Generally speaking, it is said that when a commodity is directly or indirectly required to produce all other commodities, then this commodity is a "basic." In our three-sector corn–iron–goat model, each of the three commodities is a basic since each enters into the production of all three. Any commodity which does not meet this criterion is termed a "nonbasic." Commodity X is a nonbasic in the above model.

Additionally, any system of equations which describes an entire economy contains basics and nonbasics. However, as we have seen, the nonbasic equations can be eliminated and the remaining basic system can be independently solved for all basic prices.

The modern distinction between basics and nonbasics differs from the older classical distinction between necessaries and luxuries, although both could be synthesized by assuming that labor earns both a subsistence wage and a share of the surplus (for luxury goods). Also, the distinction between basics and nonbasics is valid only with a given technique of production. Technological changes may result in basics' becoming nonbasics, and nonbasics' becoming basics.

8.5 The Cambridge debates

The Sraffa model has been presented as an example of the neo-Ricardian or post-Keynesian approach to modern economics. Because many neo-Ricardians reside in Cambridge, England, they are sometimes referred to collectively as the Cambridge School. This group places emphasis on the objective conditions of production, class antagonisms, economic surplus, and reproduction. Its concepts also convey the notion that income distribution bears a unique relationship to exchange and production. This is expressed by what might be called "Sraffa's Theorem":

> *The real wage and the conditions of production, when specified in terms of actual physical quantities, are sufficient to determine prices of production and the rate of profit. No demand theory is necessary.*

In spite of the logical consistency of the Sraffa model, however, an enormous controversy has surrounded it. For example, modern economists, writing in the neoclassical tradition, have generally taken exception to the idea that prices can be determined without considering consumer demand.[5] They argue that only in the very special case of perfect competition with constant returns to scale will changes in consumer demand have no impact on the long-run equilibrium price. In any other case, market prices will be determined not only by supply considerations, but by demand considerations as well.

Cambridge economists (neo-Ricardians) have responded in several ways. One response reminds the critics that the prices used in these models are not market prices, but prices of production. Prices of production are really the centers of gravity around which market prices fluctuate. Because neoclassical economists subscribe to a subjective value theory, and because they have no theory of production, they cannot accept a production price that is determined solely by objective circumstances. They therefore do not believe that there is such a center of gravity.

A second response appeals to empirical observation, noting that prices of commodities, especially basic commodities produced in heavily concentrated industries, are not set by supply and demand. Instead, management fixes a markup on prime costs which will cover the total costs of production and which will be consistent with the long-run growth of the corporation. Included in this markup will be a net profit allowance which depends on the bargaining strengths of labor, stockholders, and management. If market demand increases or decreases, as it may be expected to do during the course of a business cycle, these firms will not adjust their prices accordingly. They will instead stick to their long-run pricing plans, which frequently extend well beyond a given business cycle.[6] This also suggests a vast difference between the conventional, neoclassical theory of supply and that of post-Keynesian theory.[7]

A third response would suggest that demand is not unimportant at all. To the contrary, demand is quite essential. The difference lies in the way in which demand enters into the general theoretical framework. Neoclassical theory suggests that demand determines price and price determines income distribution. The post-Keynesian, or neo-Ricardian, model suggests that distribution is indeterminate in the sense that income shares are arrived at outside the price-production model. That is, demand enters the post-Keynesian, or neo-Ricardian model as "aggregate demand" which in turn is partially determined by the savings (consumption) and investment decisions made by capitalists. As we saw in Chapter 2, (section 2.3) the distribution of income is determined by aggregate demand and hence by decisions made by the capitalist class. In neoclassical theory, distribution is determined within the general equilibrium pricing model.

A fourth, and final, response is a variation of the previous one: demand functions to determine the *scale of the whole system* and not the proportions into which it is divided. Unlike neoclassical economics, the classical analysis makes no assumption about the existence of a fixed quantity of scarce resources that must be allocated to alternative lines of production. It is this assumption of given resources that fixes the scale of the neoclassical system. Because the neo-Ricardian approach examines only the question of proportionality, no such assumption is required.

As we will see, Sraffa's approach is also the center of controversy among Marxian economists. Some argue that Sraffa is inherently at odds with Marxism and cannot be incorporated into the general Marxian framework of analysis without causing serious damage. Specifically, it is argued that Sraffa's model conceals the basic nature of capitalism by failing to reveal the exploitive use of labor. Sraffa depicts the working class and capitalist class as "sharing" the surplus output, and, by so doing, the model neglects to point out that the surplus output is a result of the exploitation of labor in the first place.

Other Marxian economists claim that Sraffa's approach is not inconsistent with Marx, that it does not necessarily exclude an exploitation theory of surplus. More generally, it is believed that Sraffa's model is not a general theory of society, but rather a specific theory which deals with only one aspect of society. It would therefore be unjustified to compare Marx with Sraffa at all.

The Ricardian value problem: the invariable measure 9

> *When commodities varied in relative value it would be desirable to have the means of ascertaining which of them fell and which rose in real value, and this could be effected only by comparing them one after another with some invariable standard measure of value, which should itself be subject to none of the fluctuations to which other commodities are exposed. Of such a measure it is impossible to be possessed, because there is no commodity which is not itself exposed to the same variations as the things the value of which is to be ascertained. . . .*
>
> *David Ricardo*

9.1 Introduction

The most basic of post-Keynesian/Marxian themes is the production and distribution of social wealth. Social wealth is simply the accumulated output of society. A portion of this output is necessary to replace the commodities used up in that year's productive activities and a portion is necessary to maintain the population (e.g., food, clothing, housing, etc.). Whatever remains after these requirements are met is a surplus. This surplus, or net output, is then available for reinvestment and/or for advancing the standard of living for some or all of the population. Post-Keynesian/Marxian economics endeavors to describe how the production of social wealth occurs, how it grows, and how it is distributed among various classes in society.

It should be clear that, before any economic theory of production, growth, and distribution can be devised, some method of measuring the social wealth has to be devised. Otherwise, not much can be said about its size. Now, this would not be a problem if the social wealth consisted only of one kind of commodity, such as corn. The measuring device, or unit of measurement, would simply be *physical* bushels of corn. The production and distribution of corn could then be discussed solely in terms of physical units.

The difficulty is that the social wealth consists of millions of heterogeneous commodities. It is therefore not possible to speak of "the" social wealth in physical terms as we did when only corn was produced. In order to speak of the social wealth in terms of a single bundle of disparate commodities, some standard has to be used in terms of which each of the constituent commodities can be measured. Such a standard represents a unit of *value*, much like an "inch" is a standard which represents a unit of *length*. The values thus attached to all commodities may then be aggregated in order to determine the size of the social wealth.

This chapter concerns itself with the search for such a standard of value. Ideally, a standard of value should not be subject to any of the forces which normally affect the commodities being measured. This is the most essential requirement of a standard of value. If it is not met, then it would be impossible to have a clear picture of what is happening to social wealth. For the same reason, an inch must always represent the same length.

Ricardo was the first to clearly articulate the problem of finding an invariable standard of value. We shall therefore refer to this problem as the *Ricardian value problem*. Ricardo was unable to find an invariable standard of value, however, as the chapter quotation attests. The solution was left to Piero Sraffa, about which this chapter is mostly concerned. Before we describe Sraffa's solution, we first explain why the search for an invariable standard is problematical.

9.2 The Ricardian value problem

The most accurate unit of measure is, of course, *price*. But which price? Price of production? Market price? *Market price*, it should be recalled, is the day-to-day price of a commodity. It is determined by market supply and market demand. The natural price, or *price of production*, is determined by the objective conditions of production. It is a sort of equilibrium price, or center of gravity, about which market prices naturally fluctuate. In fact, the forces of supply and demand would always work to drive market prices toward their respective prices of production. If market price exceeds the price of production, then an above-average profit is being made in that industry. New firms, attracted by this high profit rate, would enter to compete with existing firms. Supply would increase and price would fall to its natural level. The reverse would occur if natural price exceeds market price.

Returning to the initial question of selecting a price for measurement, the classical economists chose to measure and explain social wealth on the basis of price of production, or natural prices. These were the prices used in Chapter 8. But now what determined these prices? Here too the classical response was unanimous: *labor*. It was believed that, by measuring social wealth on the basis of labor-determined prices of production, you would in fact be measuring the true cost to society for the labor sacrificed. Market price, however, could deviate from this level, so it was not as useful as prices of production were.

Smith, as we know, was among the first to point to labor as the basis for natural price. Smith believed that, in that "early and rude state of society" when there were no capital goods, labor was the only true cost of production. Natural prices would therefore be strictly proportional to labor embodied. Thus, if two commodities, A and B, required the same amount of labor for their production, then their natural price would be identical.

Smith soon realized, however, that the introduction of capital goods destroyed the strict proportionality between labor embodied and price. If commodities A and B required identical quantities of homogeneous labor, the wage costs of each would be the same. But if A required $1,000 worth of capital goods and B required $2,000, then total profits paid out in each industry would be unequal even if the *rate* of profit were equal. If the rate of profit were 5%, then profits in A would be $50 and in B $100. Treating profit as a cost of production, we see that the costs of producing A and B would now be different, even though the same amount of labor was being used in both. Therefore, the natural price of these two commodities would no longer be proportional to labor embodied. *Only if the proportion of capital to labor in each industry is the same would prices be proportional to labor embodied.*

Smith never resolved this difficulty. Neither did Ricardo. The problem of differing capital-to-labor ratios became more acute in Ricardo's work, however, because his focus was more on the distribution of national output than on its growth and development.

Ricardo's immediate theoretical problem was to discover the laws which worked to distribute a *fixed* national output between wages and profits. Ricardo employed a labor-embodied approach to natural price in order to add up the value of heterogeneous commodities. He vastly improved the sophistication of this theory, however, by including not only present labor in the value calculations, but past labor as well. The past labor was embodied in the capital and raw materials currently used to produce the commodities in question. It is labor expended in the past to produce the capital used in the present.

Ricardo discovered, however, that, if you measure the national output in this way, the size of that output will change as the distribution of it changes. This would be like dividing an apple pie between you and a friend. Every time you give yourself less, and your friend more, the size of the pie changes! When you want to discuss distribution, you want the quantity to be distributed to remain the same irrespective of who gets what share. But why would such a problem emerge in the first place? The answer lies with the unequal capital-to-labor proportions that exist among industries.

9.2A Capital, profit, and value

Ricardo's labor theory of value distinguishes between present and past labor. Present labor is the amount of labor currently employed in the production of a commodity. Past labor is the amount of labor that has been employed in previous years in the production of the capital which is currently used to produce the commodity in question. The sum of present and past labor is the total labor value of a commodity.

It is a basic feature of capitalist production that capitalists are entitled to receive a profit for every year that their capital is tied up. Thus, if a capitalist has $1,000 tied up for two consecutive years, and if the going rate of profit is 10%, then that sum will be worth $1,100 after the first year and $1,210 after the second year (the $1,100 of the first year plus 10%).

Imagine two production processes. One process produces one unit of commodity A and the other produces one unit of commodity B. The production of A requires the application of 100 hours of present labor. The capital that is required to produce A has itself been produced by past labor. In this case we assume that 400 hours of labor has been uniformly applied over a four-year period in order to produce that capital. The process is shown in Figure 9.1.

Process B also requires a total of 500 hours of labor, although only 100 hours is past labor embodied in capital. This 100 hours is uniformly spread over a two-year period. The remaining 400 hours is all present labor.

Now, because the capitalists' funds have been tied up for four years in order to produce A, the labor value of that tied up capital has to be compounded annually at the going rate of profit. The same holds true for the capitalists who produce B. If the wage rate is $1 per hour, and if the profit rate is 25%, then the price of A and B can be calculated as in Table 9.1(a). Note that the price of A is almost twice the price of B, even though they both require 500 hours of labor to produce. The reason the prices deviate from labor-embodied value is that the capital–labor compositions of A and B are different.

Let us now change the distribution of income, so that wages go up to $2 per hour and the profit rate falls to 10%. The price calculations are

THE RICARDIAN VALUE PROBLEM 121

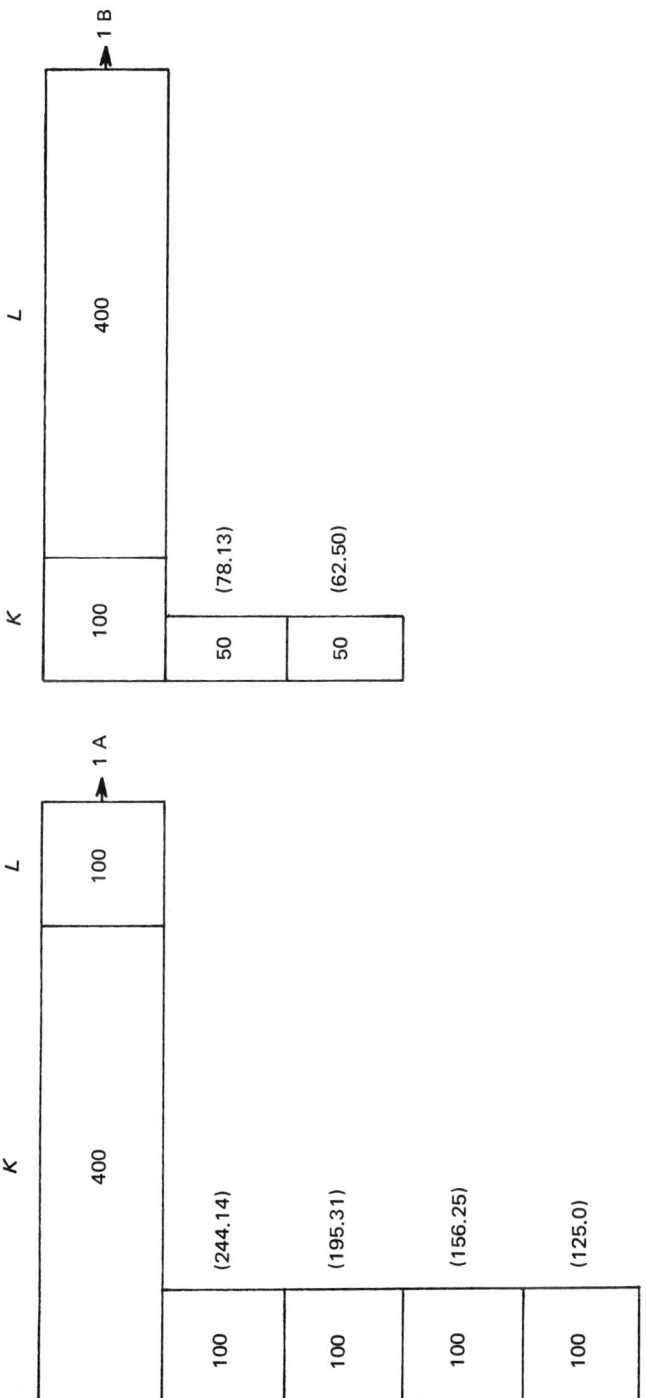

Figure 9.1
Production Over Time with Differing Capital and Labor Applications

Table 9.1

Pricing and Capital–Labor Applications Over Time: An Illustration

(a)

If $w = \$1$ per hour and $r = 25\%$

Commodity	Cost of Labor	Cost of Capital	Cost of Profit on Capital	Price
A	$100	$720.70	$180.18	$1,000.88
B	$400	$140.63	$ 35.16	$ 575.79

(b)

If $w = \$2$ per hour and $r = 10\%$

Commodity	Cost of Labor	Cost of Capital	Cost of Profit on Capital	Price
A	$200	$1,021.02	$102.10	$1,323.12
B	$800	$ 231.00	$ 23.10	$1,054.10

made in Table 9.1(b). Note that the price of A is much closer to the price of B; profits have become a less significant cost factor. In fact, as the profit rate drops toward zero, the two prices converge. They will become equal when the profit rate drops to zero. When profits are zero, prices will be exactly proportional to labor embodied. This corresponds to Smith's "early and rude state."

This example illustrates the nature of the value problem. It is the payment of profit which causes prices to diverge from their labor values. Because capital-labor ratios differ among industries, changes in the wage-profit distribution will also change prices. And as prices change, the size of the pie (social wealth) changes too! Thus, the size of the aggregate output would reflect not only the quantity of commodities actually produced, but the distribution of income as well.

9.2B Ricardo's tentative solution

In order to resolve the Ricardian value problem, a commodity would have to be found whose price would *not* change as the profit rate (and hence distribution) changed. All other commodities could then be measured in terms of this special standard commodity. Aggregate output would then only reflect actual quantities produced and not income distribution.

Ricardo felt that, if some commodity could be found which was produced under "average" conditions, then such a commodity could serve as a standard. By average conditions it was meant that the capital-labor ratio would be an average of all the ratios in the economic system. If all lines of production employed capital and labor in identical proportions then prices would always be proportioned to labor embodied. The value problem would not arise in this case. Similarly, if all commodities had differing ratios, then deviations above the average would exactly cancel deviations below the average. The average commodity itself would therefore always have a price that is proportional to labor embodied.

Ricardo was unable to discover such a commodity. He assumed that gold would be a suitable standard, but he knew all along that none could really be found. Sraffa's solution, which follows this section, is based on the idea that a standard can be artificially constructed. By blending together certain quantities of basic commodities, one can construct a standard which resembles Ricardo's "average commodity."

9.3 Sraffa's standard system

9.3A Unbalanced industries

It was shown in Chapter 8 that changes in relative prices of production can be caused by two factors. The first is a change in the technology of production, given a certain distribution of the surplus between wages and profits. Such a change would alter the input coefficients in one or more of the industry equations. The consequence would be a different set of equilibrium prices.

The second factor which would cause a change in relative prices is a change in the distribution of the surplus, given a certain technology of production. The precise manner in which such a change in distribution influences relative prices depends on the inequality of the proportions in which labor and means of production are employed in the various basic industries.

When, for instance, wages fall in the basic economy, surplus will be released in each industry. But this surplus will have to go to profits. Whether the amount of surplus released because of the decline in wages is just sufficient to pay the extra profits at the now higher uniform rate depends on the relative amounts of labor and means of production used. If the former amount does not equal the latter amount, an *imbalance* will exist in the industry.

Only in the very unusual case in which each industry employs labor and means of production in identical proportions would there be no need for a change in prices subsequent to a change in distribution. When inequalities in these proportions exist, however, prices will have to change in order to redress imbalances.

Because we are not immediately concerned with changes in technology (the first factor mentioned above), we look only at the effects of changes in surplus distribution on relative prices. The technology of production is therefore assumed to be constant.

In order to illustrate the effect which unequal proportions of labor to means of production have on prices when distribution changes, consider the following two-commodity model:

(1)
$$(4p_i + 8p_c)(1 + r) + 0.5w = 12p_i$$
$$(6p_i + 10p_c)(1 + r) + 0.5w = 24p_c$$

In this simple example the labor force is equally distributed between two sectors, an iron sector and a corn sector. We assume that these are the only two basic commodities. All nonbasic industries using iron and corn as inputs have been eliminated, because nonbasic industries have no influence on the prices of basic commodities.

Following the convention of using the basic system surplus as the numeraire, we now add the following equation to the above two:

(2)
$$2p_i + 6p_c = 1$$

The surplus consists of 2 tons iron (12 tons output minus 10 tons used up in both industries) and 6 bushels wheat (24 bushels output minus 18 used up in both industries). The prices of production of iron and corn are now expressed as a fraction of this surplus value, which in turn is set equal to one. Specifying a value for w, we can now determine the values for p_i, p_c, and r.

Assume initially that the entire surplus goes to wages, so that $w = 1$. The resulting prices would be $p_i = 0.172$ and $p_c = 0.109$. The rate of profit would, of course, be zero because the entire surplus goes to wages.

Suppose now that we reduce the wage rate from 100% of the surplus to 50% (from $w = 1$ to $w = 0.5$). This will release surplus for profits in each industry. Before the wage reduction, the iron industry was paying 0.5 surplus units to labor (0.5 × 1). After the wage reduction, the iron industry pays only 0.25 surplus units to labor (0.5 × 0.5). This represents a surplus savings of 0.25 units. Since the corn sector employs the same amount of labor and pays each worker the same wage, it too will realize a savings of 0.25 units. Will these savings be sufficient to pay profits at the new, higher, uniform rate?

The profit rate which governed when wages were at 100% was 0%. The rate which now governs when wages are at 50% is 13.8%. Using the above prices to estimate the value of the means of production employed in each industry, we can calculate how much must now go to profits.

In the iron industry, the value of the means of production is 1.56 units. At 13.8% this would require 0.215 surplus unit for profit. But 0.25 unit of surplus was released because of the wage reduction. Thus, in the iron industry, more surplus is released than is required. This industry is therefore said to be "positively" unbalanced.

In the corn industry, the value of the means of production is 2.122 units. At 13.8%, this would require 0.293 surplus unit for profits. Since only 0.25 unit was released, the corn industry will experience a deficit because not enough surplus has been released by the wage reduction. Such an industry is said to be "negatively" unbalanced.

In the absence of any price changes, these imbalances will persist. However, in order to achieve the specified distribution of the surplus and maintain a uniform profit rate, prices must change. In that way the imbalances can be corrected. In the model just presented, the new price solutions would be $p_i = 0.168$ and $p_c = 0.111$. That these prices will satisfy the above conditions can be confirmed by substituting them into the industry equations (1).

The only situation in which a price change would not be necessary is one where the amount of surplus released is just adequate to pay profits at the new higher rate. An industry that falls into this category is called a *balanced industry*. If such an industry existed, its price relative to the prices of the other commodities would remain unchanged no matter how the surplus is distributed.

9.3B Problems associated with unbalanced industries

In the above example it should have been clear that the amount of surplus released, subsequent to a wage decline, depends on the amount of labor employed in an industry. Similarly, the extra amount of surplus required to pay the new, higher, profit rate depends on the value of the means of production employed in that industry. The same principle also holds in the face of a wage increase.

Whether or not an industry is balanced depends, therefore, on the ratio of labor to means of production employed. Generally speaking, industries with the lowest ratios of labor to means of production experience surplus shortages if wages decline. Industries with the highest ratios realize surplus overages. The opposite is true when wages rise.

If each industry in the basic system uses labor and means of production in the same ratio, then the change in surplus released would always offset the change in the additional surplus required. Prices would then not have to change when distribution changes. When these labor-to-means proportions differ among industries, prices have to change, as we have already observed. But the *direction* in which prices have to change is very difficult to determine.

On the surface it would appear that, if wages fall, the prices of commodities produced in industries which release insufficient quantities of surplus would have to rise, while the prices of commodities produced in industries which release too much surplus would have to fall. A higher price, it would seem, would command more of the other commodities than before, thereby redressing a deficit. A lower price, it would seem, would command less of the other commodities than before, thereby redressing an overage.

Before we leap to these conclusions, we must first consider another factor. The means of production employed in any industry are themselves produced by other industries in previous time periods. These latter industries may be characterized by entirely different labor-to-means ratios from the industry currently under observation. Thus, the means of production in high-ratio industries may themselves be produced by industries with low ratios, and vice versa. The prices may therefore change in the *opposite* direction.

In order to ascertain the direction of price changes, each previous generation of production (or "layer of production") would have to be examined. Not only would we have to consider the labor-to means ratio of the previous generation, but also that of each of the generations prior to that one, going backward in time. The means used to produce the means, which produced the means, which produced the means, etc., may all be characterized by varying labor-to-means ratios. The pattern of price variations then may be extremely complex and irregular. All that we do know for certain is that prices would have to change in order to redress imbalances. Otherwise a uniform profit rate and the specified distribution cannot be maintained.

Another difficulty exists when industries are characterized by differing labor-to-means proportions. This difficulty has to do with the numeraire used to measure prices.

In our illustrations of basic commodity systems, prices were *relative* prices and not *absolute* prices. An absolute price is one which is expressed in terms of some *independent* third commodity. By independent it is meant that this third commodity, or measuring standard, is not itself part of the system. Therefore, its value is not influenced by the peculiarities of the commodities being measured. A relative price is one which is measured in terms of another commodity that is part of the system, or in terms of some combination of commodities that are parts of the system. Using the system surplus as numeraire, as we have been doing, results in relative prices and not absolute prices because the commodities which make up the surplus are themselves parts of the basic system. Hence, the composite commodity used as the measuring standard is influenced by the conditions which exist in the industries being measured.

Thus, if the prices of iron and corn change, it may be because of (1) a change in the technique of iron production; (2) a change in the technique of corn production; (3) a change in distribution; or (4) any combination of the above. Simple knowledge of the changes in relative prices will not reveal whether the peculiarities of the numeraire, or of the commodities being measured by the numeraire, have changed.

It turns out that the difficulties discussed in this section can be eliminated simply by devising another numeraire. This is done in the following sections.

9.3C Features of the unbalanced actual system

Before we actually construct a new standard measure, let us fully examine the four main features of the two-sector model of the previous section. These features are outlined in Table 9.2.

The first characteristic of this system is that the proportion in which iron and corn appear as inputs (1:1.8) is not the same as the proportion in which iron and corn appear as outputs (1:2). As a consequence of this difference in proportions, the surplus iron and corn produced is also proportioned differently (1:3).

Another feature of the system derives from the above irregularities of proportions. The rate of surplus product, or the amount by which each commodity output exceeds the amount used up, is different for each industry. In the iron sector, the rate of surplus product is 20%, whereas in the corn sector the rate of surplus product is 33% (2/10 and 6/18, respectively). It is only because iron and corn appear as inputs and outputs in different proportions that the rates of surplus product differ.

The third feature of this system involves two kinds of *aggregate* ratios. The first is the ratio of total labor to total means of production; the second is the ratio of total surplus to total means of production. The former ratio is calculated by dividing the total labor force employed,

Table 9.2

Features of the Unbalanced Actual System

Original system

					Ratio of iron output to corn output
4 t. iron +	8 bu. corn +	0.5L	→	12 t. iron	
6 t. iron +	10 bu. corn +	0.5L	→	24 bu. corn	1 : 2

Total input: 10 t. iron   18 bu. corn   1L

Ratio of iron input to corn input: 1 : 1.8

Surplus: 2 t. iron   6 bu. corn   *Surplus rates:*   20% iron   33% corn

Ratio of iron surplus to corn surplus: 1 : 3

Aggregate ratios

(1) $\dfrac{\text{Total labor}}{\text{Value of total means}} = \dfrac{1}{3.7 \text{ units}} = 27\%$

(2) $\dfrac{\text{Value of total surplus}}{\text{Value of total means}} = \dfrac{1 \text{ unit}}{3.7 \text{ units}} = 27\% = R$

which in our case is set equal to one, by the value of the total means of production. Now, in order to calculate the value of the means of production, we must resort to prices, and these depend on how the surplus is distributed. It turns out, however, that the value of the aggregate means is always the same no matter what the prices are. In our example, it equals 3.7 surplus units, where one surplus unit is the whole of the actual surplus produced ($2p_i + 6p_c = 1$). The first ratio is therefore approximately 27%, or 1/3.7.

The second ratio is also 27%. The value of the surplus is set equal to one because the surplus serves as the numeraire. Therefore, the ratio of value of surplus to value of aggregate means of production is also 27%.

The fourth feature of the system also stems from the disproportional manner in which iron and corn are combined. This feature has already been observed. The iron industry, in the face of a reduction in wages, releases more surplus than what is required to pay a higher uniform profit rate. The corn industry, on the other hand, releases less than what is required. These imbalances, as we have already observed, stem from the unequal combinations of labor and means employed in each industry. To see this, suppose that $w = 0.5$ and that $p_i = 0.168$ and $p_c = 0.111$. The value of the means used in the iron industry is 1.56; the value of the means employed in the corn industry is 2.12.

Since each industry is assumed to employ equal fractions of the labor force, the iron industry labor-to-means ratio is 0.5/1.56, or 32%; the corn ratio is 24%, or 0.5/2.12. Although the aggregate ratio is 27%, the two industries differ markedly. The iron industry is a high labor ratio industry; the corn industry is a low labor ratio industry.

9.3D The notion of a standard industry

It would be rare indeed to be able to discover a system, or even an industry, which is truly balanced. This is why Ricardo said that an invariable standard could never be found. Some industries would always release too much in the face of falling wages or not enough in the face of rising wages.

However, it is possible to imagine that any unbalanced system of basic industries has a center of gravity around which the individual industries of the system locate themselves. This center of gravity can be conceptually viewed as a single balanced industry. Some industries will have labor-to-means ratios smaller than this hypothetical balanced industry; others will have ratios that are larger. Due to its central place within the system, however, the sum of the deviations from the central focal point would cancel out. The imagined balanced industry is therefore an "average," a "focal point," or a "center of gravity" of the actual system, reflecting a notion similar to Ricardo's average industry.

Such an imaginary balanced industry would by definition of the word "balanced" always release just the right amount of surplus to pay higher wages or profits. Because of this, there would never be any need for the price of production of such a commodity to change relative to the other commodities used to produce it. Since there would never appear an imbalance, no price change would ever be called for (relative to other prices) when the distribution of the surplus changes.

The commodity produced by such a balanced industry would therefore be an ideal standard of measure. It could be used in place of the numeraire we have been using. By so doing we would always be sure that any observed change in prices brought about by a change in distribution would be due to the peculiarities of the commodities being measured and not due to the peculiarities of the standard itself, since the value of the standard commodity would always be unaffected by changes in distribution.

Although a balanced industry may not exist, one could always be artificially constructed. This can be done by creating a *mixture* of the basic commodities produced in the actual system. If there are two basic industries, then the mixture will contain a certain amount of each of the two basic commodities. If there are n basic industries, then the mixture will contain n basic commodities.

If there are two actual basic industries then, as we have seen, the standard of measure will be a mixture of the two commodities. In our illustration, the standard mixture will consist of a certain amount of iron and a certain amount of corn. The balanced industry, then, is really made up of two subindustries, one producing the correct portion of iron going into the mixture, the other the correct portion of corn going into the mixture. The balanced industry, therefore, is made up of as many subindustries as there are actual industries. The equations which describe these subindustries are called the *standard system*. This system is called "standard" because the mixture which results is used as the standard commodity measure.

How can such a balanced industry, comprised of two fictional subindustries, be constructed? It should first of all be remembered that the cause of a system's imbalances is the unequal proportions in which the commodities appear as inputs and outputs. If we can construct a balanced industry which uses the same commodities as does the actual system, but in different proportions, then our goal will have been met.

To construct a standard system, the rate at which surplus is generated from a given amount of means of production should be the same as in the actual system. Thus, if the actual system produced aggregate surplus at the rate of 27%, then so too must the standard system. An additional, and just as important, requirement is that the same amount of labor be employed in each of the two systems. When these two conditions are met, then the two systems will be of the same overall size. The only difference will be that the standard system will be characterized by different proportions.

The standard system can now be derived algebraically as follows. Let R be the rate of aggregate surplus production for the actual system as a whole. We want the standard system to produce at the same rate. We need to find two multipliers which, when multiplied times the actual equations, give us the desired proportionalized system. Let q_1 be the multiplier which we use for the iron industry and q_2 the multiplier used for the corn industry.

The object, then, is to find a q_1 and q_2 which could be multiplied as follows:

(3)
$$q_1[(4p_1 + 8p_2)(1 + r) + 0.5w] = [12p_1]q_1$$
$$q_2[(6p_1 + 10p_2)(1 + r) + 0.5w] = [24p_2]q_2$$

In order to find multipliers which would proportionalize the system, we must solve the following equations for q_1 and q_2:

(4)
$$(4q_1 + 6q_2)(1 + 0.27) = 12q_1$$
$$(8q_1 + 10q_2)(1 + 0.27) = 24q_2$$
$$0.5q_1 + 0.5q_2 = 1$$

The first equation states that the total iron input ($4q_1$ tons and $6q_2$ tons) will be generating the required 27% rate of surplus product, which will in turn be $12q_1$. The second equation states that the total corn input ($8q_1$ bu. and $10q_2$ bu.) will also be generating the required 27% rate of surplus, which will equal $24q_2$. The third equation states that the total labor force, however redivided between the two industries, will be fully employed.

Solving these equations, we obtain $q_1 = 1.05$ and $q_2 = 0.95$. Thus, we scale the iron industry up by 5% and the corn industry down by 5%. The resulting standard system, which ought to be considered as a single composite industry, is:

(5)
$$(4.2 \text{ t. iron} + 8.4 \text{ bu. corn}) + 0.53L \rightarrow 12.6 \text{ t. iron}$$
$$(0.57 \text{ t. iron} + 9.5 \text{ bu. corn}) + 0.47L \rightarrow 22.8 \text{ bu. corn}$$

The surplus output consists of 2.7 tons of iron and 4.9 bushels of corn. It should be remembered that this is a fictionalized system, a purely theoretical construct which provides a standard of measure which is invariable in value to changes in distribution.

9.3E Features of the balanced standard industry

The standard equations are summarized in Table 9.3. The first thing to be observed is that iron and corn appear as inputs in the same proportions as they appear as output (1:1.81). Because of this, iron and corn appear in the surplus in the same proportions. Also because of these equalities, the rate of surplus production is identical in both sectors (27%).

Another interesting feature of this proportionalized system is that the

Table 9.3

Features of the Balanced Standard System

Standard system

					Ratio of iron output to corn output
	4.2 t. iron +	8.4 bu. corn +	0.53L →	12.6 t. iron	
					1 : 1.81
	5.7 t. iron +	9.5 bu. corn +	0.47L →	22.8 bu. corn	
Total output:	9.9 t. iron	17.9 bu. corn	1L		
Ratio of iron input to corn input:		1 : 1.81			
Surplus:	2.7 t. iron	4.9 bu. corn		Surplus rates:	27% iron 27% corn
Ratio of iron surplus to corn surplus:		1 : 1.81			

Aggregate ratios

(1) $\dfrac{\text{Total labor}}{\text{Aggregate physical means}} = \dfrac{1}{3.7 \text{ standard commodities}} = 27\%$

(2) $\dfrac{\text{Physical surplus}}{\text{Aggregate physical means}} = \dfrac{1 \text{ standard commodity}}{3.7 \text{ standard commodities}} = 27\% = R$

total iron and corn input is exactly 3.7 times the total iron and corn surplus. Thus, 3.7 × 2.7 equals 9.9 (total iron input) and 3.7 × 4.9 equals 17.9 (total corn input). We will therefore consider the surplus 2.7 tons of iron, together with the surplus 4.9 bushels of corn, as a *single commodity bundle*. There would therefore be 3.7 of such bundles used as aggregate means of production in the standard system.

Note also that the total iron and corn output is exactly 4.7 times the total iron and corn surplus. This is the same as saying that the output consists of 4.7 commodity bundles. The only reason it seems that we can add apples and pears, or iron and corn, in this way is that they are all made up in the same proportions.

Finally, the aggregate ratios in the standard system are identical to the ratios in the actual system (27%). We forced it to be that way when we calculated the multipliers in the previous section. The only difference between these standard ratios and the actual ratios is that the former are

THE RICARDIAN VALUE PROBLEM 133

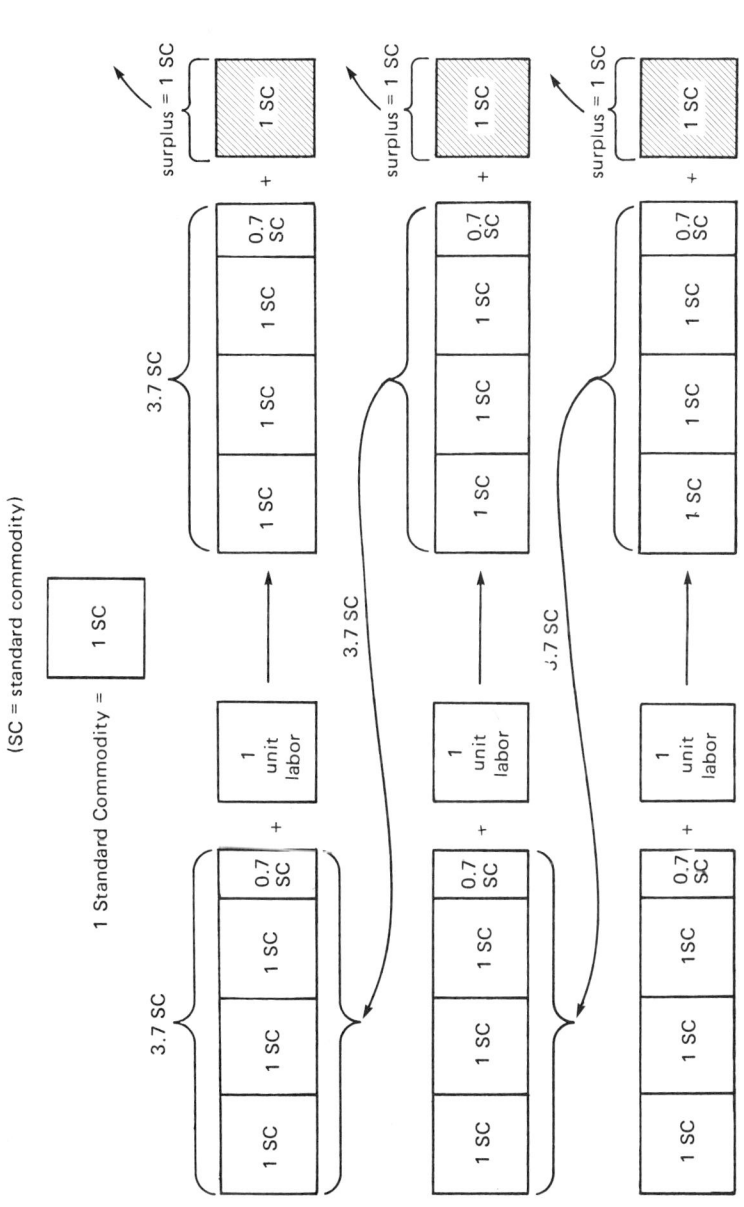

Table 9.4

The Balanced Industry

ratios of physical units (i.e., commodity bundles). The latter ratios are of values, or physical units times prices.

The complete picture of the balanced standard industry is shown in Table 9.4. The surplus of the standard system is referred to as the *standard commodity*. This is the commodity mixture referred to above, and *it is the value of this commodity mixture which remains invariable to changes in distribution*. Since both subindustries are treated as one, the table shows that 3.7 standard commodities (the aggregate input), plus 100% of the labor force, results in 3.7 standard commodities plus one standard commodity as surplus (a total of 4.7 standard commodities). Thus, standard commodities are used to produce standard commodities.[1]

The illustration also shows that the 3.7 units of means of production were themselves produced in the previous period of production by 3.7 units of means plus 100% of the labor force. We assume for simplicity that the surplus commodity is not reinvested in order to expand production. Thus, each generation of production is preceded by another generation which is characterized by the same proportions and by the same scale. It is in this sense that the ratios of Table 9.2 are said to recur period after period.

9.3F Linearity of the wage–profit relation

To see that the fictional standard system, viewed as a single industry, is fully balanced, let us observe what happens as we vary the distribution of the surplus.

We must recall from our previous discussion that the features of the standard industry can be described in physical terms because of the equality of proportions in that system. Thus, we need not make any reference to prices in discussing this industry.

The total means employed in the standard industry is 3.7 standard commodities. The total output is 4.7 standard commodities. Letting w stand for the wage rate as a fraction of the surplus, and r the rate of profit, we describe the standard industry as:

$$(3.7)(1 + r) + 1w = 4.7$$

The total surplus produced in this industry is 27% of 3.7, or 1 standard commodity. This surplus commodity is then divided between the fictional capitalists and workers in this industry.

If $w = 1$, then $r = 0$. If we reduce the wage to $w = 0.5$, then one half of the surplus commodity goes to wages and the remaining half to profits. *That is, one half of 27% goes to profits*. The new profit rate would then be 13.5% or one half of 27%. The surplus released as the wage falls just equals the extra surplus required for profits. The industry is balanced!

Because reductions in w are always in direct proportion to increases in the rate of profit, the relationship between w and r is linear. It can be described as:

(6) $$r = R(1 - w)$$

This relationship is illustrated in Figure 9.2. When wages are zero, the maximum rate of profit is $R\%$. When profits are zero, the entire standard commodity goes to wages and $w = 1$.

Not only will this linear relation apply to the standard industry, but it will apply to the actual system as well. This will be true only if we express

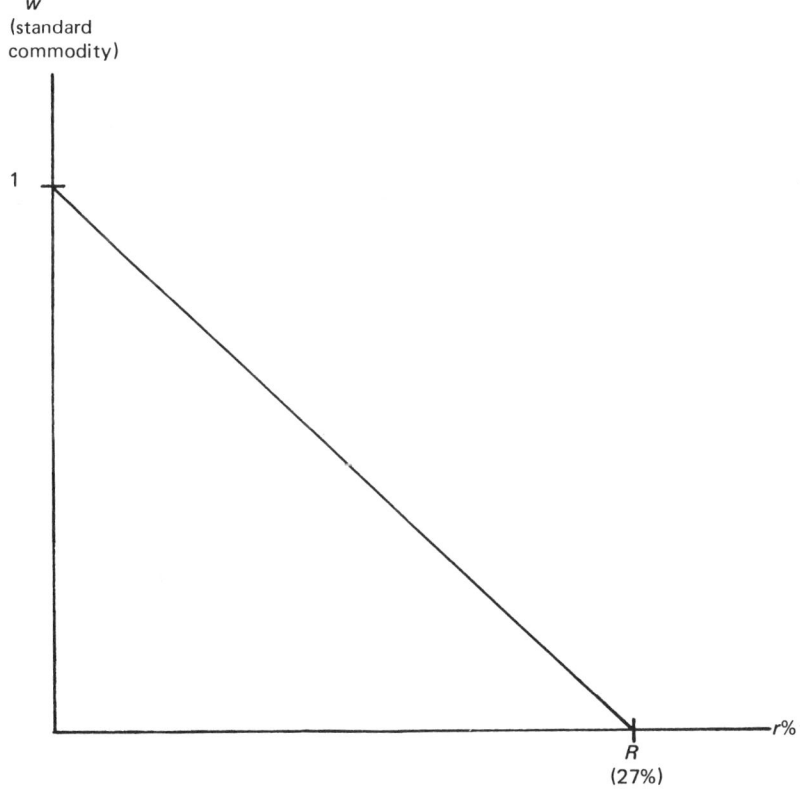

Figure 9.2

The Simplified Wage-Profit Relation

the actual wage rate and all actual commodity prices in terms of the fictional standard commodity. Thus, if we set $w = 0.5$ standard commodity in the *actual* system, then the other 0.5 standard commodity goes to pay *actual* profits. Since the actual system also produces at a 27% aggregate rate of surplus production, the uniform rate of profit must be 13.5%.

The linear relationship shown above between w and r therefore applies also to the actual system. This greatly simplifies the otherwise nonlinear relationship described in Figure 8.2, which obtains when the more conventional numeraire is used.

Because of this simplification, it now becomes possible to determine the rate of profit over the economy as a whole *without prior knowledge of prices*. All that is required is that R be determined (which can also be done independently of prices) and w specified. We were *not* able to do this in the model of Chapter 8. There, the rate of profit had to be solved simultaneously with prices.

The importance of this theoretical point is that it validates the cost-of-production theory of price advanced by Ricardo and later on by Marx. According to this theory, prices are determined by capitalists by adding together (1) labor costs (Lw); (2) capital costs ($A_a p_a + \ldots + K_a p_k$); and (3) a suitable profit markup of r%. These three factors therefore *determine* the prices of production in any industry.

The standard commodity device permits these calculations to be made by making the rate of profit depend only on the technical features of the system (represented by R) and the distribution of the surplus (set by fixing w).

Without the standard commodity, prices can still be mathematically determined. In fact, in the previous chapter, prices and profit rates were mathematically determined without the standard commodity. But the price and profit rate solutions had to be performed *simultaneously*. Because of the simultaneity of the solution, we could not say that the costs of production *determined* prices.

9.3G A final simplification

We know from the previous discussion that if we express all prices and wages in the actual system in terms of the fictional standard commodity, then the linear relationship between the actual w and r will hold. The opposite reasoning may also apply. That is, if we force the linear relationship to apply to the actual system then we will, ipso facto, express all prices and wages as fractions of the standard commodity. By following the latter procedure, we need not even calculate the q multipliers as we did before. Nor must we calculate the composition of the standard commodity. All this will be done implicitly by specifying that $r = R(1 - w)$.

In general form, we may now rewrite the system of equations of the previous chapter as follows:

$$
\begin{aligned}
(A_a p_a + B_a p_b + \ldots + K_a p_k)(1 + r) + L_a w &= A p_a \\
(A_b p_a + B_b p_b + \ldots + K_b p_k)(1 + r) + L_b w &= B p_b \\
&\cdots \\
(A_k p_a + B_k p_b + \ldots + K_k p_k)(1 + r) + L_k w &= K p_k
\end{aligned}
\tag{7}
$$

$$r = R(1-w)$$

This equation is identical to equation (4) of Chapter 8, except of course for the last equation.

There are $k + 2$ unknowns (k prices, w, and r) and $k + 1$ equations. The value for R can be determined independently of the system. Thus all we need to do is specify the distribution of the surplus between w and r. That is, once we set w (or r), all of the other variables can be determined.

Extensions of the basic model

10

> *To prevent [growth for the sake of growth] it is necessary to place a "life cost" on growth. This is done by looking through all forms of produced things, specifically the produced inputs or "means of production," recognizing in them the labor that at one time or another made them into means of production . . . . The technique for preventing an undue diversion of labor and other resources, the technique applicable to a highly complex social economy, is to put a life cost on growth by dating labor, counting not only what is currently used but how much has been diverted and for how long . . . .*
>
> George Zinke

10.1 Reduction to dated labor

One interesting theoretical extension of the Sraffa model is the examination of the effects of differing applications of labor over time, or the *time pattern of production.*

In the previous chapter we noted that a production process can be viewed as a sequence of generations, or layers of production processes. In each sequence, labor and means of production are combined to produce an output. These means of production, in turn, are themselves produced in a previous generation with labor and means of production; and these means of production were also produced in yet another previous generation with labor and means of production.

We begin by calling the labor currently employed in production *direct labor*. All of the past labor embodied in the currently employed means of production is called *indirect labor* (or past labor). The current value of the industry output is, as we already know, equal to the value of the means employed, which is represented by the amount of indirect labor employed times $(1 + r)$ plus the amount of direct labor times the wage w.

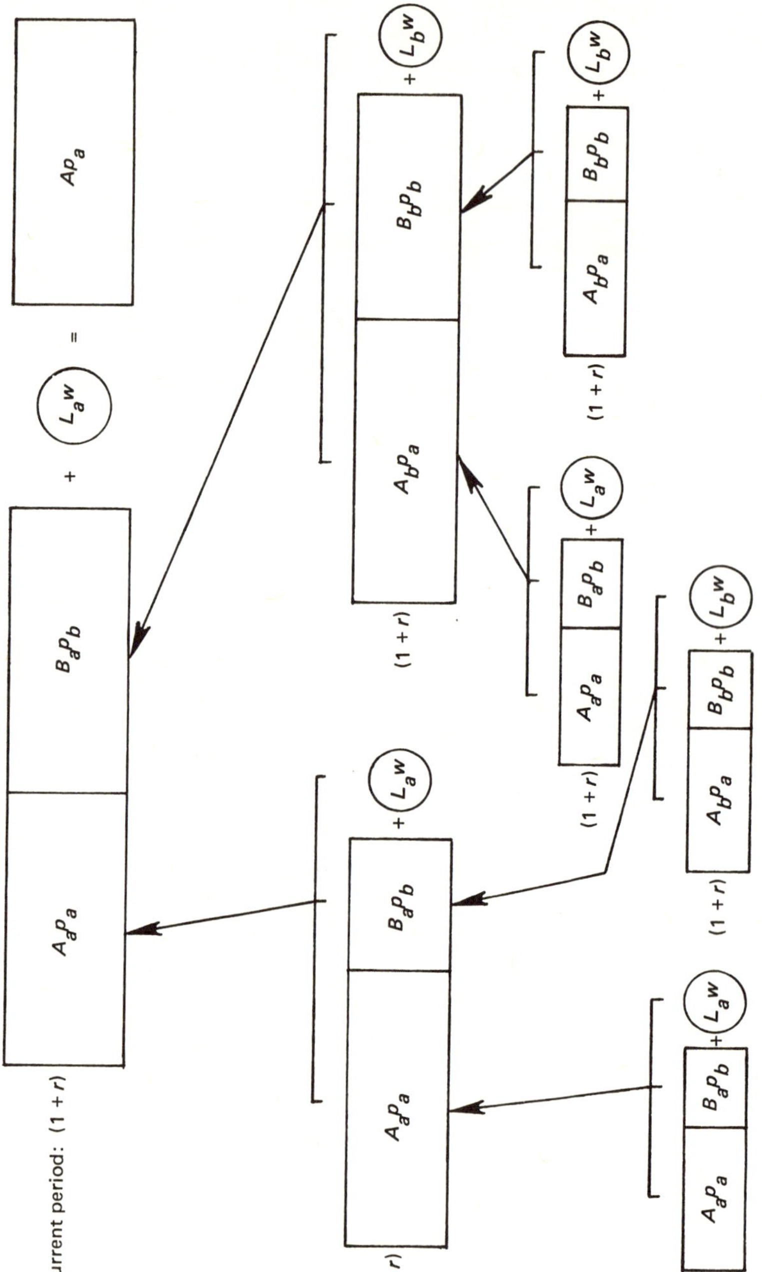

Figure 10.1
Generations of Production: Dated Labor

The value of the means of production in any period can be replaced by the value of the means of production in the previous period plus the direct labor used to produce it in that previous year. Thus, in Figure 10.1, the current period's means of production $(A_a p_a + B_a p_b)$ is replaced by (1) $(A_a p_a + B_a p_b)(1 + r) + L_a w$ and (2) $(A_b p_a + B_b p_b)(1 + r) + L_b w$. The current year's equation may thus be "reduced" to:

(1) $[(A_a p_a + B_a p_b)(1 + r) + L_a w + (A_b p_a + B_b p_b)(1 + r) + L_b w]$
$(1 + r) + L_a w = A p_a$

or

(2) $(A_a p_a + B_a p_b)(1 + r)^2 + (A_b p_a + B_b p_b)(1 + r)^2 + (L_a w + L_b w)$
$(1 + r) + L_a w = A p_a$

Thus, the means of production are replaced by the means of production of the previous period times $(1 + r)^2$, plus the direct labor of the previous period times $(1 + r)$.

Suppose that once again we replace these latter means of production by means of production of the next previous period and the direct labor of that previous period. The former would by multiplied by $(1 + r)^3$ and the latter by $(1 + r)^2$. This sum would then be added to the previously calculated sum.

If we were to carry this process out indefinitely we would quickly discover that the remaining means of production would eventually become infinitesimally small. Thus, if we add all of the direct labor employed in each of the n previous time periods, then this sum could replace $(A_a p_a + B_a p_b)(1 + r)$ in the current period. This collection of indirect labor, plus the current $L_a w$, equals the value of the current output, $A p_a$. Mathematically,

(3) $[L_a w (1 + r) + L_a w (1 + r)^2 + \ldots + L_a w (1 + r)^n + \ldots] +$
$L_a w = A p_a$

where the sum in brackets represents the total indirect labor embodied in the means of production in all of the previous layers of production.

Reducing the means of production to labor leads to some interesting conclusions. To understand these conclusions, let us modify equation (3) slightly. We know from the previous chapter that, if we measure prices and the wage rate in terms of the standard commodity, then $r = R(1 - w)$. Solving this equation for w, we obtain

(4) $$w = 1 - \frac{r}{R}$$

Substituting this expression for w into equation (3) results in

(5) $$L_a\left\{1 - \frac{r}{R}\right\} + L_a\left\{1 - \frac{r}{R}\right\}(1 + r) + L_a\left\{1 - \frac{r}{R}\right\}$$
$$(1 + r)^2 + \ldots + L_a\left\{1 - \frac{r}{R}\right\}(1 + r)^n + \ldots = Ap_a$$

Note well that as w increases (and r decreases) the term $[1 - (r/R)]$ gets *larger*, reaching a maximum of 1 when $r = 0$. However, when w increases, the term $(1 + r)^n$ gets *smaller*, reaching a minimum of 1 when $r = 0$. Each of the two terms therefore pulls in opposite directions. When $r = 0$ and $w = 1$, the value of the output A is simply the sum of the L's, because $[1 - (r/R)] = 1$ and $(1 + r)^n = 1$ in each term. At the other extreme, when r is equal to R (its maximum), the sum of the labor terms is zero. The reason is that $w = 0$ when $r = R$.

At intermediate distributions, when the surplus goes to both profits and wages, the value of any given labor term depends on its age, n. The value of any labor term is given by $L_a[1 - (r/R)] (1 + r)^n$ and will come to depend on the net outcome of the two opposing terms which are multiplied by one another, $[1 - (r/R)]$ and $(1 + r)^n$. As a result, the time pattern of labor terms, which in the aggregate equals the value of the industry's output, becomes quite complex.

To illustrate the time pattern of production, refer to Figure 10.2. We suppose that the maximum rate of profit R is 27% and that the industry under observation employs the entire labor force. This latter assumption is made only for ease of calculation. Of the n labor terms, we arbitrarily select four of these: L_0, L_{10}, L_{15}, and L_{20}. The amount of labor in each of these terms is assumed to be 1, 0.5, 0.2, and 0.1. The labor terms will then be:

(a) $1 \left\{1 - \frac{r}{0.27}\right\} (1 + r)^0$

(b) $0.5 \left\{1 - \frac{r}{0.27}\right\} (1 + r)^{10}$

(c) $0.2 \left\{1 - \frac{r}{0.27}\right\} (1 + r)^{15}$

(d) $0.1 \left\{1 - \frac{r}{0.27}\right\} (1 + r)^{20}$

In Figure 10.2 the value of each of these terms is shown as r varies from 0 to 27%. If the uniform rate of profit is 6%, then the first term equals 0.78; the second term equals 0.70; the third term equals 0.48; and the fourth term equals 0.25. It appears "as if the rate of profits, in its

EXTENSIONS OF THE BASIC MODEL 143

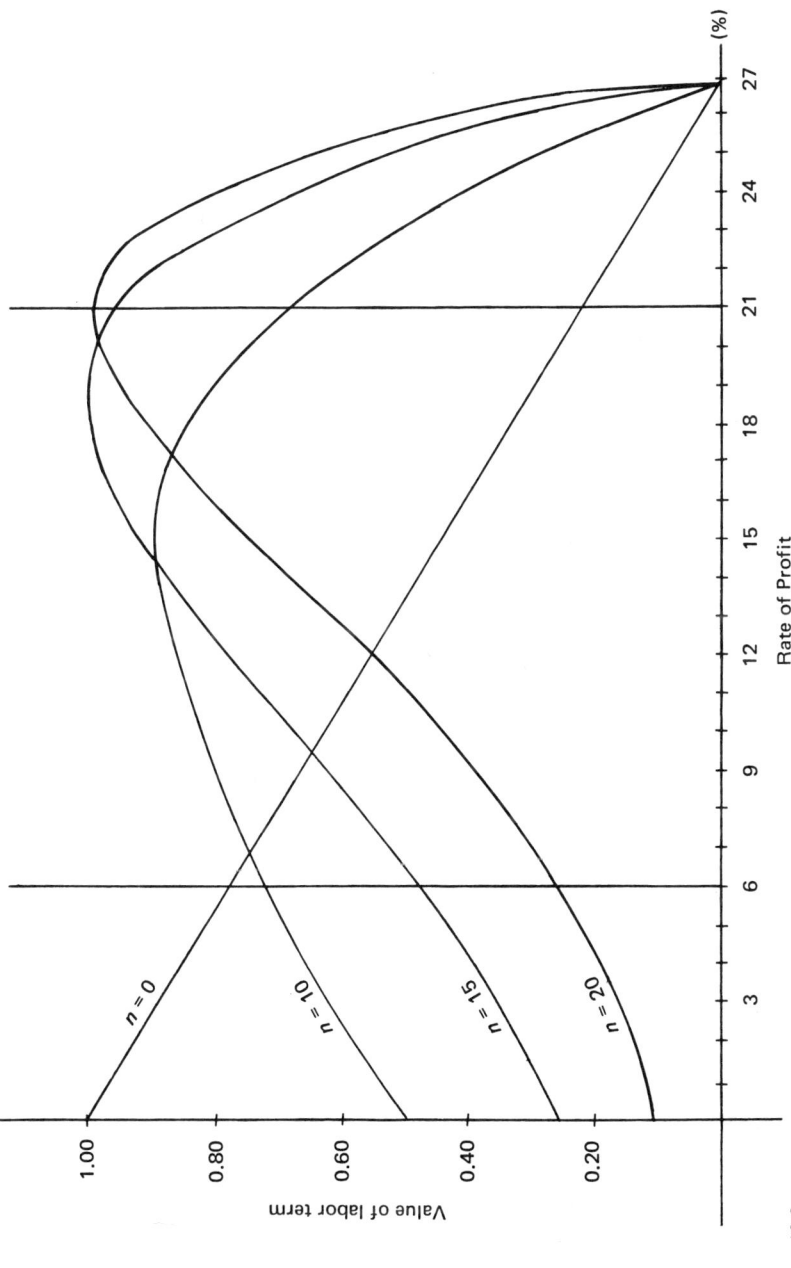

Figure 10.2

The Value of Dated Labor: An Illustration

movement from 0 to R, generated a wave along the row of labor terms the crest of which was formed by successive terms, as one after the other they reached their maximum value."[1] It can also be determined at what rate of profit any given labor term will reach a maximum. This can be given by the expression[2]

$$(6) \qquad r = R - \frac{1 + R}{n + 1}$$

Thus, when $n = 20$ and $R = 27\%$, the labor term $L_{20}[1-(r/R)]$ $(1 + r)^{20}$ will reach a maximum when $r = 21\%$.

The importance of this reduction to dated labor is that two commodities may be similar in the way they are *currently* produced, but dissimilar with respect to their time patterns of production. The two commodities may therefore have considerably different prices at certain values of r and quite similar prices at other values of r, as we saw in Section 9.2A.

A second observation is that the total amount of capital invested in an industry cannot be known unless the rate of profit is known first. Once the rate of profit is known [by setting the wage in $r = R(1 - w)$], prices can be determined. And once prices are known the different constituents of the total capital invested can be added. This does away with any attempt to measure quantities of capital before prices are determined as is done in neoclassical economics. Thus, if we don't know the prices of (say) machines and trucks, we cannot determine the aggregate value of machinery and trucks. And in order to know prices, the rate of profit must be known.

10.2 Fixed capital

The models employed thus far are incomplete because they assumed that all commodity inputs were entirely used up in the production period. Such commodities may be referred to as "circulating capital." Although expenditures by firms on circulating capital are universal, as are expenditures on labor, the analysis is nonetheless incomplete, because it excludes expenditures on *fixed capital*. In this section we shall incorporate fixed capital into the model.

The primary feature of fixed capital is that it lasts for more than one period of production. Typically, such capital goods have an ascertainable life expectancy and, in many cases, may even have some salvage value at the end. Although fixed capital usually becomes less efficient as it ages, we shall assume for simplicity that the efficiency of such capital is constant over its life. Additionally, we assume that it has no salvage value at the end of its life.

The model is unusual in its treatment of capital. For each period, a certain quantity of fixed capital, say machines, is combined with a certain quantity of labor and circulating capital. The output consists of (1) the commodity itself *and* (2) the same quantity of fixed capital, but one period older. Thus fixed capital is regarded as an input and an output. The fixed capital output is the fixed capital input, aged one period.

To simplify matters further, presume that there is only one kind of machine which is used by only one of the K industries in the previous model. Let us say it is industry G. Assume also that the machine lasts for three years, after which time it is worth nothing. In the first year, industry G capitalists purchase M_0 machines at a price of P_0. At the end of the first year (and the beginning of the second), the G capitalists will have the same number of machines, but they will be one year old. Let M_1 stand for the number of one-year-old machines, where the subscript denotes age. At the end of the second year there will be M_2 machines. At the end of the third year there will be M_3 machines.

Because the machines wear out, their value depreciates over time. The value of a new machine is P_0, or the purchase price. But at the end of the first year, its value P_1 will be less than that. And its value at the end of the second year P_2 will be even less. At the end of the third year the machine's value, P_3, will be zero, since we assumed the machine lasts only three years. Thus $P_0 > P_1 > P_2 > P_3 = 0$.

Let us now examine the structure of the G industry. In the first year of acquisition the cost of fixed capital is $M_0 P_0$. The cost of circulating capital is $(A_g P_a + B_g P_b + \ldots + K_g P_k)$ and the cost of labor is $L_g w$. If the general rate of profit on capital (fixed and circulating) is $r\%$, then we may write

(7) $M_0 P_0 (1 + r) + (A_g P_a + B_g P_b + \ldots + K_g P_k)(1 + r) + L_g w =$
    $GP_g + M_1 P_1$

The output consists of G and M_1 one-year-old machines valued at P_1.

In the second year, the G industry equation is

(8) $M_1 P_1 (1 + r) + (A_g P_a + B_g P_b + \ldots + K_g P_k)(1 + r) + L_g w =$
    $GP_g + M_2 P_2$

where the output is the same amount of G plus a two-year-old machine. In the third year the equation is

(9) $M_2 P_2 (1 + r) + (A_g P_a + B_g P_b + \ldots + K_g P_k)(1 + r) + L_g w =$
    GP_g

Note that, since $P_3 = 0$ (no salvage value), $M_3 P_0 = 0$.

Let us now multiply the first equation by $(1 + r)^2$, the second equation by $(1 + r)$, and the third equation by 1. Once this is done, add the equations together. This gives the following rather complicated result:

(10) $\quad M_0P_0(1 + r)^3 + M_1P_1(1 + r)^2 + M_2P_2(1 + r) +$
$(A_gP_a + B_gP_b + \ldots + K_gP_k)(1 + r)^3 +$
$(A_gP_a + B_gP_b + \ldots + K_gP_k)(1 + r)^2 +$
$(A_gP_a + B_gP_g + \ldots + K_gP_k)(1 + r) + L_gw(1 + r)^2 +$
$L_gw(1 + r) + L_gw(1 + r) = GP_g(1 + r)^2 + GP_g(1 + r) + GP_g +$
$M_1P_1(1 + r)^2 + M_2P_2(1 + r)$

Cancelling the M's where possible from both sides, and simplifying, we get

(11) $\quad M_0P_0(1 + r)^3 + [(A_gP_a + B_gP_b + \ldots + K_gP_k)(1 + r)]$
$[(1 + r)^2 + (1 + r) + 1] + L_gw[(1 + r)^2 + (1 + r) + 1] =$
$GP_g[(1 + r)^2 + (1 + r) + 1]$

The term $[(1 + r)^2 + (1 + r) + 1]$ is simply the total amount of an annuity of 1 unit received every period for three periods. This term may be rewritten as $[(1 + r)^3 - 1]/r$.[3] The above equation then reduces to:

(12) $\quad M_0P_0(1 + r)^3 +$
$\left\{(A_gP_a + B_gP_b + \ldots + K_gP_k)(1 + r) + L_gw\right\}\dfrac{(1 + r)^3 - 1}{r} =$
$GP_g\dfrac{(1 + r)^3 - 1}{r}$

Dividing both sides by $[(1 + r)^n - 1]/r$ we have

(13) $\quad M_0P_0\left\{\dfrac{r(1 + r)^3}{(1 + r)^3 - 1}\right\} + (A_gP_a + B_gP_b + \ldots + K_gP_k)$
$(1 + r) + L_gw = GP_g$

Generalizing for machines that last n years we have the following equation for industry G:

(14) $\quad M_0P_0\left\{\dfrac{r(1 + r)^n}{(1 + r)^n - 1}\right\} + (A_gP_a + B_gP_b + \ldots + K_gP_k)$
$(1 + r) + L_gw = GP_g$

Except for the first term on the left, the equation is identical to the ones we have been using. But what is the meaning of the first term on the left-hand side of this equation? The term indicates the amount by which the book value of the machine must be reduced each period so that $P_n = 0$. It is an amortization charge and gives an accurate estimate of the true cost of the machine.

To see how this works, suppose you buy a machine at P_0. Suppose further that the amortization charge is \$$C$ every year until the machine wears out in n years. According to the formula in footnote 3, after n years of \$$C$ per year, the total amount charged (S_n) is:

$$(15) \qquad S_n = C \frac{(1 + r)^n - 1}{r}$$

Now, the charge \$$C$ must be such that the value of S_n, discounted to the present, will equal the purchase cost P_0. In that way the entire P_0 will be exactly amortized after n years.

The present value of S_n at the end of n years is $S_n/(1 + r)^n$. This amount must equal P_0:

$$(16) \qquad P_0 = \frac{S_n}{(1 + r)^n}$$

Substituting equation (15) for S_n, we get

$$(17) \qquad P_0 = \frac{C[(1 + r)^n - 1]/r}{(1 + r)^n} = \frac{C[(1 + r)^n - C]/r}{(1 + r)^n}$$

or

$$(18) \qquad P_0 = \frac{C(1 + r)^n - C}{r(1 + r)^n} = C \left\{ \frac{(1 + r)^n - 1}{r(1 + r)^n} \right\}$$

Solving the above equation for C, the desired amortization change, yields

$$(19) \qquad C = \frac{P_0 r (1 + r)^n}{(1 + r)^n - 1}$$

which is the coefficient of M_0 in the G industry equation above—equation (14).

The system in its entirety may now be summarized as follows:

$$(A_a P_a + B_a P_b + \ldots + K_a P_k)(1 + r) + L_a w = A P_a$$
$$(A_b P_a + B_b P_b + \ldots + K_b P_k)(1 + r) + L_b w = B P_b$$
$$\cdots\cdots\cdots\cdots\cdots\cdots\cdots\cdots\cdots\cdots\cdots\cdots$$

$$M_0 P_0 \left\{ \frac{r(1 + r)^n}{(1 + r)^{n-1}} \right\} + (A_g P_a + B_g P_b + \ldots + K_g P_k)$$
$$(1 + r) + L_g w = G P_g$$
$$\cdots\cdots\cdots\cdots\cdots\cdots\cdots\cdots\cdots\cdots\cdots\cdots$$
$$(A_k P_a + B_k P_b + \ldots + K_k P_k)(1 + r) + L_k w = K P_k$$

} Circulating-capital basic industries

$$(A_m P_a + B_m P_b + \ldots + K_m P_k)(1 + r) + L_m w = M_0 P_0$$

} Fixed-capital basic industry

$$r = R(1 - w)$$

} Implicit numeraire

There are $k + 3$ unknowns: r, w, k prices, p_0. There are also $k + 2$ independent equations. Specifying the distribution of the surplus permits solutions for these unknowns to be found.

The only difference between this system and the previous generalized system is the appearance of fixed capital in industry G and the addition of an industry which produces that fixed capital. The model could easily be further generalized by permitting all industries to employ a variety of fixed capitals, but this would unnecessarily complicate our presentation. Some difficulties emerge, however, in attempting to define a standardized system. But a standard system can still be constructed as before.

10.3 Other special cases

The Sraffa model can be expanded to ever higher degrees of complexity. Developing the model any further would not, however, significantly add to our understanding of the Sraffaian theory of prices of production. Thus, we shall only briefly mention the extensions that are possible to carry out.

The first possible extension is to the general case in which all commodities appear as inputs and outputs in every industry (although some may have zero coefficients). This generalized model is called *joint production*. It is constructed in order to explain price relationships when there are multiproduct industries. However, the real interest of this model lies in its adaptation to fixed capital, which we have already done.

In our previous discussion we assumed that one industry employed fixed capital and that the same fixed capital, one year older, was jointly produced with the basic commodity G. The fully generalized multiproduct model simply represents all commodities as jointly produced commodities in each basic industry.

The only difficulty which arises in this expanded model is that the idea of a standard commodity becomes a bit more abstract, largely because nonbasic commodities may appear as joint products. The construction of a standard system may therefore require negative multipliers in order to get rid of the nonbasics.

Another extension is the inclusion of nonreproducible natural resources (i.e., land). Sraffa treats land as a nonproduced, nonbasic commodity. It may appear as an input into the production of basics, but not as an output. How land is incorporated into the model depends on what assumptions are made about differences in the quality of such resources and the number of different production processes which employ them.

Marxian theories of value and price

Part V

Marx's theory of value and price: an overview   11

> *Where labour is in common, relations between men in their social production are not represented as "value" of "things." Exchanges of products as commodities is a certain method of exchanging labour, and of the dependence of the labour of each upon the labour of the others, a certain mode of social labour or social production. In the first part of my work I have explained that it is characteristic of labour based on private exchange that the social character of the laborer is "represented" as a "property" of the things; and inversely, that a social relation appears as a relation of one thing to another.*
>
> *Karl Marx*

11.1 Introduction

In neoclassical economics, price means market price. This is the only price category which has significance to this school of thought. Concepts such as natural price, or price of production, are not to be found among the tools of neoclassical analysis.

The foundation of the neoclassical theory of market price is its individualistic methodology. According to this methodology market prices play a *social* role but are determined by *individual* decision making. This social role consists of coordinating society's human and nonhuman resources. In this context market prices serve as signals to buyers and sellers, telling them how to deploy the resources under their control.

The whole system of market prices thereby brings into harmony the *independent* activities of economic agents. It permits individuals to continue these activities while at the same time allowing them to partake in the fruits of the activities of others, also operating independently. Thus, the carpenter may continue doing carpentry work because the sale of his finished product provides him with the income with which to acquire the products of the baker. The carpenter and the baker thereby enter into a social relationship through the marketplace. The condition of this social interaction is the marketability, or price, of their respective products.

Price in neoclassical theory is thus a *social* phenomenon which is ultimately based on *individual psychological* behavior. Price is the result of the interaction of individual agents, each maximizing his or her personal satisfaction, each individually deciding how much to buy and how much to sell. Thus, as Medio observes, "it is possible to reduce all statements about social phenomena to a special class of statements about individual behavior."[1] Neoclassical price is therefore the quantitative outcome of a process of psychological valuation which economic agents engage in on an individual basis. It is this valuation process which determines market price.

Ricardian price theory, on the other hand, has a very different focus. It sustains the classical distinction between natural price, or prices of production, and market price, and builds a general theory which is based on the former and not the latter.

It will be recalled that prices of production in Ricardian theory are determined by the techniques of production in the various basic industries and the distribution of the surplus between social classes. This determination takes place through competition among capitalists and results in a uniform rate of profit. Prices of production serve as a sort of center of gravity toward which actual market prices will tend. The realization of these prices of production guarantees the continual reproduction of whatever social and economic relations happen to exist at the time.

In this setting, price is treated in a very classical way. It is not individualistic, but rather class related. It is not psychologically based, but rather objectively determined. Price, instead of being the outcome of individual decision making, is the outcome of a quite different social process involving class relations and technological know-how. It is the quantitative condition for continual economic and social reproduction.

The word "value," furthermore, is not equated with psychological use-value as it is in neoclassical theory. The value of a commodity is instead rooted in the objective circumstances of its production, specifically, the quantity of labor employed. However, in Ricardian theory, the labor value of a commodity is only important insofar as it can determine its price. The labor theory of value, therefore, is here primarily a theory of price determination.

In Sraffa's theory of price—a theory which we have called Ricardian because of its emphasis—the labor embodied in production actually becomes incidental to the whole process of price formation. Although costs of production can be reduced to dated labor, this is not essential to the analysis. For this reason the word "value" is frequently indistinguishable and indeed often synonymous with the word "price" in Sraffa's Ricardian theory.[2]

In Marx's theory, the word "value" takes on a very special meaning. This meaning is different from the other classical treatments of value and price and justifies the separation of the post-Keynesian/Marxian tradition into two distinct schools. Value, in Marx's theory, is a specific category of analysis which is intended to reveal the social connection that exists between (1) the exchange of commodities in capitalism and (2) the relations betwen producers and owners. More specifically, it is intended to explain the origin of profit as a social category.

Marx's value theory, therefore, attempts to describe the historically unique way in which human labor is used in a capitalist system. It is not primarily intended to explain price formation and price dynamics. Instead, it is intended to define what a price is in a capitalist market economy and how it reflects the human relationships prevailing in such an economy. Thus Marx's theory of value and price is a social theory, whereas Ricardian theory is more narrowly a theory of price information.

11.2 Marx's labor perspective

11.2A Appearance and reality

The key to understanding Marx's theory of value and price is his method of analysis. He employed an approach which distinguishes between *appearance* ("external form," "surface phenomenon") and *reality* ("content," "essence"). This duality, which characterizes most human and nonhuman affairs, is rooted in Greek philosophy.

Appearances refer to those activities, relations, and events which directly meet our eye. They are the surface phenomena which our senses meet first. Appearances are the external features of an observable reality, features which are immediately recognizable to us.

But as we all know, what we see "ain't always so." Reality, the outward appearances of which we initially perceive, may oftentimes be quite different. This could be the case because reality isn't always immediately observable. Much can lie beneath the surface, hidden from our view.

An excellent example of the appearance–reality dichotomy is the way we perceive the rotation of the planets in our solar system. Almost nineteen centuries ago Claudius Ptolemy (A.D.90–168) wrote that the earth was the center of the solar system. The sun, as well as the other planets, revolved around this stationary center. With the reawakening of scientific interest during the Renaissance, however, this viewpoint was challenged by Nicholas Copernicus (1473-1543). Copernicus advanced the "heliocentric hypothesis," according to which the sun is the center of our solar system.

Now, in the absence of any modern astronomical knowledge, and without the kind of scientific instrumentation available even to Copernicus, it would be quite reasonable to suggest that the sun orbits around the earth. That is, after all, what we actually see. While we stand still, it is the sun which moves across the sky. The reality is quite different, however. The reality, in order to be seen and understood, requires that we go beyond surface appearances. That is what "science" is all about—peeling away the surface appearances in an effort to obtain truth. It involves the application of reason, logic, and experimentation.

Let us consider another simple example of the appearance-reality dichotomy. Suppose that you are sitting in a rowboat and that you observe an oar partially submerged in the water. The oar will appear to be bent. How is it that you are not fooled by this *appearance*? How do you know that the oar is in fact straight? Clearly, you must have prior experiential knowledge of such events. Knowledge allows one to see through the surface appearance and understand the hidden reality.

It is important to note, finally, that the immediate appearances of social and physical phenomena are not always at odds with reality, as in the illustrations above. Moreover the essence of things may actually be quite translucent and easily understood without much "scientific" effort. Simple life experience, for example, together with some minimal knowledge about the refraction of light, resolves the paradox of the oar.

In other situations, however, smoke screens can arise to disguise the hidden reality, making it difficult to gain insight into the way things really work. These smoke screens can convince us either that the appearance is the reality, or that the reality is something other than what it in fact is. If I were able to convince you that the oar actually does bend when submerged in the water, then I would be creating a smoke screen to blind your perception of things. I would be doing the same thing if I could convince you that the oar doesn't really bend, but that God has instead made you imagine it that way. The most prevalent of such smoke screens are myths, propaganda, and, most importantly, ideology. They arise for reasons which we obviously cannot explore here. They may be consciously or unconsciously created, but in either case they stand in the way of human understanding and hence human development.

Marx had great faith in science and firmly believed that the methods of science could expose the hidden reality of capitalism. He was strongly influenced by developments in physiology, physics, and biology. The discovery of the cell as the basic unit of organic life and the discovery of the transformation of energy all significantly influenced Marx's thinking. Especially influential was Darwin's discovery of the laws of evolution. Both Marx and Engels held Darwin and his accomplishments in high esteem. They believed that the Marxian theory of historical development did for the study of society what Darwin's theory of evolution did for the study of the natural environment. Engels even claimed at Marx's funeral that "[j]ust as Darwin discovered the law of development of organic nature, so Marx discovered the law of development of human history."[3]

Both Marx and Engels strongly felt that these scientific achievements were indicative of the potentially revolutionary force of science and that if these scientific methods were applied to the study of society then similar revolutionary changes could occur. By uncovering the laws of human history in general, and of capitalism in particular Marx believed that we could change the dismal and inhumane circumstances of our existence. Peeling away the surface appearances and understanding the underlying reality were for Marx revolutionary activities. And this is what his theory of value was intended to do. It was intended to dispel the myths generated by "vulgar" economists who claimed that the price system was the "invisible" mechanism which made capitalism a harmonious and just system. It was supposed to enable one to peel away the appearances of harmony and justice which characterized capitalism and to expose its inner exploitive essence.

11.2B Appearance and reality: alienated labor

As we have seen, the distinction between appearance and reality has a central place in Marx's theory of value. According to Marx, there are certain universal features of human existence. These features constitute the reality, or essence, of life. But, they can take on a variety of forms. Two of these features are critical to a proper understanding of Marx's theory of value. We shall consider these before we examine the forms which they can take.

The first universal feature consists of the simple observation that people must continuously transform the material environment in order to survive. In so doing people create themselves. This process of transforming nature is called "labor." Labor is the very expression of human life. It is an aspect of our humanity. The necessity to labor is what defines the human race as a distinct species. The very existence of human beings requires the continual expenditure of mental and physical energy. The expenditure of this energy is creative, because with it human beings create themselves developmentally. And, what is more, humans have an infinite capacity for this free, creative, and spontaneous labor.

The second universal feature is that human labor is never undertaken in isolation. Labor always takes place in the context of some social setting. As human beings we are social beings. The image of Robinson Crusoe, stranded alone on an island, has little meaning in Marx's concept of human labor. It has meaning only to those theoretical systems which rely on an individualistic perspective (such as neoclassical economics).

According to Marx, these universal features make up the reality of human existence. This reality is the reality of *social labor*. However, it takes on different forms in different societies. These forms, or appearances, can sometimes reveal quite easily the reality which lies beneath. Sometimes, however, the reality remains submerged, obscured by the kind of smoke screens discussed earlier.

In precapitalist societies, for instance, the expenditure of labor by individuals occurs in an explicit, and oftentimes authoritative, coordinated way. In feudal societies, for example, the family unit is the center of laboring activities. The labor performed by an individual family member directly affects the physical and mental well-being of all family members. The nature of the work done, and the allocation of tasks to individuals, is based partly on ability and partly on custom and tradition. Individual labor therefore becomes social labor because the activities of all are interdependent.

Moreover, the continued reproduction of such social arrangements from year to year, and from generation to generation, requires that certain kinds of tasks be done, not only within families, but among families. Certain proportions of society's labor must be directed to certain activities if the means of subsistence are to be regularly reproduced. And the maintenance of those classes who do not participate in production at all (the nobility and the clergy in Medieval Europe, for example) also depends on the ability of those who do produce to coordinate their labor effectively.

Social labor, therefore, is individual labor that has been inducted into the service of the community (family, feudal manor, commune, etc.). It is the reality of all human existence. In most precapitalist societies this social labor is consciously regulated and the social interdependencies (e.g., master/slave, father/mother, landowner/serf, etc.) among people are clear and obvious.

According to Marx's analysis, however, the reality of social labor is hidden from view in capitalist societies. Capitalism is characterized by *commodity production*. That is, the products of labor are not destined to be used by the producers themselves or by the members of the group to which they belong, but rather by other independent economic agents. Production is not for use. Instead, production is for sale on markets. Whenever the motive for producing a good is salability, that good is defined to be a *commodity*.

A distinguishing feature of capitalism is that the power to labor also becomes a commodity sold in a market, unlike the situation in precapitalist societies. Thus, it is no longer an explicit and obvious force which draws labor into social service. Labor is no longer consciously regulated. Instead, the impersonal forces of the market make individual labor social. The "invisible hand" regulates the allocation of human labor in society and draws that labor into definite social relationships. However, labor can become social only if the product of that labor is successfully sold on the market. For this reason, one's place in the social economic order is sometimes tentative and uncertain.

Because the marketplace coordinates the allocation of labor, the social interdependencies which in fact must still exist are obscured. That is, the *precise* way in which each individual depends on the labor of all other individuals is no longer clearly visible. The forces which regulate the allocation of labor, and hence direct the activities of people, are no longer personal. They are no longer consciously regulated and part of an individual's immediate experience. As a result, it is difficult to see and understand one's place in a coherent world. It is hard to appreciate the extent to which a person's economic contribution to society is affected by the contributions of others. Thus, one cannot expect the auto worker to directly experience the activities of the steelworker and to see how the latter's productive contribution affects his or her own.

On the surface, therefore, it *appears* as if the production of commodities stems from the activities of individuals. It seems as if labor is private, independent, and free. But in *reality*, labor is still social. It is just that the social interconnections are hidden from view. Although these connections really exist, they seem to be incidental to the life process. The creative, social aspects of labor, aspects which define people as human beings, are lost from view. All we see and experience instead are individuals interacting through impersonal markets.

Furthermore, labor in capitalism is alienated labor. Work becomes a necessary and coercive evil rather than a means of self-actualization. Work becomes, in fact, quite secondary to the human life process because the entire environment in which that work takes place is determined by people other than the workers themselves. In addition, the product of that labor belongs to someone else, as do the very instruments of production.[4,5]

The consequence of alienated labor is that creative enjoyment and self-fulfillment can only be found off the job. Leisure time thus takes on a new significance in capitalism, and labor becomes the necessary and uncreative means for sustaining leisure activities. As Marx observes,

> The worker, therefore, feels at ease only outside his work, and during work he is outside himself. He is at home when he is not working and when he is working he is not at home. His work, therefore, is not voluntary, but coerced, *forced* labor. It is not the satisfaction of a need but only a *means* to satisfy other needs . . . that in work he does not belong to himself but to someone else.[6]

In conclusion, the appearance of capitalism suggests that labor is freely exchanged in markets, that labor is individual and independent, and that occupations are freely selected on the basis of individual ability and personal motivation. The reality or essence of capitalism, however, suggests that labor is social and hence interdependent. It is not individual; it only seems that way. And because labor in capitalism is also exploitive and coercive instead of self-actualizing, inner-directed, and spontaneous, it is alienated. Peeling away the appearances of capitalism and exposing the hidden reality is the primary function of Marx's labor theory of value.

11.3 Value, price, and labor

11.3A Abstract labor and value

The word "value" in Marx's theory refers to the amount of labor represented by a commodity. Value is an attribute of things and represents certain social relationships between people. The commodity, to Marx, represents expended social labor. It is labor that has been expended in a certain way. However, it is also labor which is considered apart from its specific, concrete qualities. That is, we disregard the many different forms which human labor can take (e.g., carpentry, weaving, plumbing) and consider only human labor in general. Says Marx,

> Tailoring and weaving, though qualitatively different productive activities, are each a productive expenditure of human brains, nerves and muscles, and in this sense are human labor.[7]

Marx calls human labor "in general" *abstract labor*, whereas labor considered only in the context of its specific qualities is called *concrete labor*.

Although the idea of abstract labor is largely a mental thought construct, it is nevertheless rooted in the real world. As we saw in the previous section, labor becomes social only insofar as the commodities which it produces can be sold on the market at certain prices. Since the sellers are concerned only with receiving money in exchange, and because buyers are only concerned with the features of the commodities themselves, the actual concrete work done is in fact a matter of indifference. How often, for example, do we think of the California farm worker and his family when we purchase oranges in a New York supermarket? Only the characteristics of the oranges themselves are important. Similarly, when a person buys a new automobile, he or she is most likely entirely unaware of, and unconcerned about, the many different kinds of skills that went into the production of that automobile. The buyers of commodities therefore do not directly experience or observe the labor process itself. Only the attributes of the commodities are considered relevant.[8] It is this which explains the meaning of abstract labor in Marx.

Value, then, is defined as the amount of abstract (alienated) labor represented by a commodity, measured in hours. However, it only includes the amount of labor *socially necessary* to produce that commodity. This means that we measure only the average quantity of abstract labor time; less efficient workers who require more time, or unusually efficient workers who require less time, are registered as having spent only the average time. Thus, value is a category peculiar to capitalist commodity production and arises from the special way in which market relations (the invisible hand) make labor social labor. Value is a feature of commodities and represents the amount of society's labor that has been allocated to the production of commodities.

11.3B Value and exchange

The market mechanism works to coordinate the activities of many individuals. It makes the labor of these individuals social by drawing them into an interdependent relationship with all other individuals. The greater the division of labor in society, the greater the interdependencies which must exist, the more the logic of the marketplace governs human activity. The extent to which individual labor becomes social labor, however, depends on the success with which the products of labor—commodities—are sold in the market.

Commodities exchange in the marketplace and thereby circulate from one location to another. Insofar as commodities are the product of social labor, the exchange and circulation of commodities results also in a certain allocation of labor to different activities in the economy. In fact, the exchange and circulation of commodities occurs simultaneously with the exchange and circulation of labor. And the conditions under which commodities exchange and circulate reflect, in a definite quantitative way, the conditions under which labor exchanges and circulates.

When commodities exchange in markets, they do so at very definite ratios. These ratios measure the exchangeability of one commodity for another. They are *exchange values*. These exchange values appear as properties of *things*. But things have exchange value only because labor has been expended on them in the first place. They are the products of labor, the "depositories" of human effort. So value, the quantitative measure of the amount of social labor expended in *production*, takes the form of *exchange* value when these things enter the sphere of *circulation*. When money is used as the universal medium of exchange value it is money *price* which then becomes the relevant category. Price and exchange value are, therefore, synonymous in capitalism. They are the forms which value takes when commodities leave the sphere of production and enter the sphere of circulation.

In order to clearly see the manner in which value "takes the form of" exchange value, or price, let us approach the problem from the following angle. Exchange value, as we know, means the ability of one commodity to exchange for another. This ability is measured by money price. A price, therefore, symbolizes a relationship between things.

The process of exchange is one in which a certain quantity of a commodity is brought into equivalence with a certain quantity of another commodity. The two commodities are made commensurable with one another through exchange. If they could not be made commensurable, they would not be exchanged in the first place.

Consider this example. Suppose that we weigh coffee and sugar on a balance scale and observe that

$$3 \text{ pounds coffee } = 3 \text{ pounds of sugar}$$

There is only one sense in which coffee and sugar are commensurable: they both weigh the same. On a balance scale these two commodities are equal to one another, and *weight* is the characteristic which makes them that way.

Consider this example now. Suppose coffee and sugar exchange on the market in the following ratio:

3 pounds coffee = $5 = 10 pounds of sugar

The only thing which can now make coffee and sugar commensurable is the fact that 3 pounds of coffee has the same exchange value as 10 pounds of sugar. In the first case it was weight which made both coffee and sugar commensurable; in the second case it is exchange value.

But what is weight? It is simply a measure of mass. In order to have the same weight, coffee and sugar must have the same mass. Thus, mass manifests itself—is given expression by—the weight of objects. In the first example above, both coffee and sugar contain the same mass and this is reflected in the form of identical weight.

What renders coffee and sugar commensurable in the second example? What is it that exchange value measures? Only two possibilities exist. Either coffee and sugar both provide each of the trading partners with the same quantity of utility, or both commodities contain the same amount of social labor. Utility and labor are the only two possible characteristics which can be contained in coffee and sugar *in the same degree*. Marx (as well as his classical predecessors) opted for the labor value approach; neoclassical economics opted for the utility value approach. To Marx value takes the form of exchange value and price, just as mass takes the form of weight.

11.3C Price theory and value theory

There are two levels of analysis in Marx's theory. On the surface level we see the circulation of commodities. These commodities (including labor power) are sold *freely* in markets at certain prices. Prices are determined by capitalists by adding a certain profit markup to the costs of production. The size of this markup depends on the degree of competition. The capitalist's costs of production depend on the techniques of production employed and hence on the quantities and prices of the human and nonhuman resources bought.

The sphere of circulation is one which is indeed characterized by freedom and voluntary choice. Individual and independent buyers of commodities are free to choose how much of what to purchase; individual and independent sellers are free to choose how much to supply. No one forces buyers and sellers to enter into exchange agreements. Similarly, labor is free in the sense that choice of occupation is unconstrained, and the amount of labor the workers wish to sell is voluntarily decided upon.

However, if we stop at this surface level all we will ever see is freedom and voluntary choice. It will appear to us as if this is what capitalism is all about. It will seem as if capitalism can be explained solely on the basis of the fact that independent and egoistic individuals freely interact in markets and thereby, by consensus, determine the allocation of society's resources. But accepting this interpretation would be the same as accepting the thesis that the submerged oar is indeed bent.

According to Marx, there is a second level of analysis which underlies and defines the surface phenomena described above. Marx's value theory forces us to see beyond the surface phenomena.

In so doing he exposes what in reality are the alienating and exploitive social relations of capitalism. It is on this second and more basic level that we speak of value. Whereas the first level is the realm of *price theory*, the second level is the realm of *value theory*.

Price theory deals with the quantitative relationship between commodities which are bought and sold freely on markets. Price is the form which value takes. Value defines what a price is. It is a precondition for price. Sraffa's model is the most sophisticated treatment of price from a classical perspective, superior in many ways to Marx's treatment of price. But it operates only on the first level. Neoclassical theory also operates solely on this level.

Marx's value theory, however, is a theory which describes the inner structure and social relations of capitalism. It too is a quantitative theory. But it is a theory of the exploitation of labor. It is also a theory which explains the source of profits. Value is a measure of the output produced by labor under certain specific social conditions.

As we shall see, when viewing the operation of a capitalist system from this perspective one no longer sees free labor and voluntary choice. Thus, for example, when the assembly line worker sells his labor to the automobile manufacturer at a certain wage, it clearly seems to be a voluntary exchange which enhances the welfare of both parties. Without the job the worker starves and without the worker the capitalist cannot make profits. The exchange is free and mutually advantageous. But at the second level we see labor producing value and the capitalist appropriating a portion of this value by virtue of the fact that the capitalist owns the means of production. The worker has no choice but to work for a capitalist. The alternative is starvation, which is not a choice at all.

In summary, the realm of price theory is exchange and circulation. It is the realm of freedom and voluntarism. Exchange is always mutually advantageous to all participants. Therefore, this realm is also characterized by social harmony.

The realm of value theory is the sphere of production. It is a realm which is characterized by a particular set of social relations. Instead of harmony, one sees conflict. The quantitative relationships which exist on this level allow the relationships which operate on the surface level to exist as well. Moreover, the exchange and circulation of commodities already produced is necessary for *reproduction* to occur. Therefore, value and price are not separate phenomena. Instead, they are two aspects of the same phenomenon.

11.4 Value analysis

11.4A The value of labor power

The value analysis begins with the observation that in capitalism the capacity to labor—labor power—becomes a commodity. It is bought and sold on markets, at certain prices. Because labor power is a commodity, it has value. The value of this unique commodity is defined in the same way as that of any other commodity. It is equal to the amount of socially necessary labor time required to produce the commodity *labor power*.

What is meant by "producing labor power?" Quite simply, it means that certain quantities of society's resources must be devoted to the maintenance of the labor force. These resources are used to produce the commodities which labor needs for subsistence: food, clothing, shelter, and whatever else is necessary for survival. The amounts of such commodities, and their characteristics, vary over time. Subsistence is therefore a historical concept. These subsistence commodities are called *means of subsistence* and are themselves produced by labor.

Producing labor means making the laboring classes available for work on a regular and reliable basis. The amount of labor necessary to produce the commodity "labor power" is simply the amount of labor which is necessary to produce labor's means of subsistence. All those industries which actually produce the means of subsistence belong to what we call Department II. (Department I stands for the capital-producing industries, which we get to later.)

When capitalists buy labor power, they pay a wage. The wage is a money price like any other money price. It is the money form which the value of labor power takes in the marketplace, just as with any other commodity. The value of the labor power purchased is, as we have already said, determined by the amount of socially necessary (abstract) labor required to produce the labor commodity. It is equal to the value of the means of subsistence used up by laborers. The capitalist pays out the equivalent of this amount of value.

Once labor power is purchased, the capitalist can make the worker create more value than the labor power costs the capitalist. Capitalists can do this because, as a class, they own the means of production and can therefore set the length of the work day. Thus, capitalist employers receive more value from the worker than the worker costs the capitalists. Otherwise, they would earn no profit.

The value of the commodities produced in excess of what is required to replace the means of subsistence is called *surplus value*. Surplus value is *newly created value*; it is value that has been created above and beyond the value of the labor input itself.

For example, suppose that, on the average, it requires four hours of labor to produce what the worker needs for subsistence. A capitalist then pays that worker a wage proportional to four hours of labor. But once labor power is purchased, the worker will be required to work for longer than four hours.

Say that eight hours of work are required. The commodities produced during the first four hours—"necessary labor time"—are equal in value to the cost to the capitalist of the labor power initially purchased. The second four hours—"surplus labor time"—is used to produce additional value. The amount of value produced during this time is the surplus value referred to above.

11.4B The value of the means of production

The means of production, like labor power, are commodities sold on markets. They include machinery, facilities, raw materials, and all other nonlabor inputs. The value of these ingredients, as with all other commodities, is determined by the amount of socially necessary labor time required for their production.

The value of the means of production, according to Marx, gets *transferred* to the final product. For example, when a screw which requires one hour of labor to produce is driven into a new bookcase, the value of that bookcase increases by one hour. In this case, the means of production (the screw) is entirely used up and its value is entirely transferred to the product (the bookcase). No more than this amount can be added or created.

Suppose, however, that a power screwdriver is used to drive the screw. The value of this screwdriver must also be taken into account. Because the screwdriver can drive hundreds of thousands of screws, and lasts several years, only a small fraction of its value gets transferred to the bookcase.

Unlike labor, the means of production can transfer no more value to the product than what is actually contained in those means. This is a critical assumption because, with labor, more value can be created than what the labor commodity itself contains. For this reason, the acquisition of means of production by the capitalist is an acquisition of *constant capital*. It is constant in the sense that the total amount of value represented by the means of production remains constant; it just gets transferred to the products which it helps produce. The acquisition of labor, however, is an acquisition of *variable capital*. It is variable because the total amount of value represented by that labor reproduces an equivalent amount of value (represented by the value of the means of subsistence used up) plus a surplus value.

11.4C The circuits of capital

Capitalist production according to Marx takes place in the following way. The capitalist begins with a certain sum of money, $\$M$, which is used to buy means of production, symbolized by mp, and labor power, symbolized by lp. Both of these categories of inputs are commodities and their aggregate value is denoted by CC.

Labor power and means of production are then combined in a production process (symbolized by P). The end result, or output, of this production process is a mass of produced commodities which bear no physical resemblance to the commodity inputs. Also, the value of this mass of commodities, symbolized by CC', is larger than the value of the commodity inputs (CC) paid for by the capitalist. The difference is surplus value. We call it $\Delta CC\ (= CC' - CC)$.

The mass of commodity outputs is then entered into the sphere of circulation. That is, the commodity outputs are sold on markets. Once this is done, no further value is added to the commodities. Value is *produced* by social labor. Exchange cannot alter the value of commodities. The activities involved in circulation (transportation, advertising, wholesaling, etc.) do not augment the value of the commodities already produced. They simply help the capitalists to sell the commodities.

Depending on the money price received for these commodities, the capitalist will receive a sum of money in exchange, $\$M'$. The difference between the original sum advanced, $\$M$, and the amount realized, $\$M'$, is the capitalist's money profits. We call the sum of money profits $\Delta \$M$.

The entire process of production and circulation can be described symbolically as follows:

(1) $\$M \ldots CC <^{lp}_{mp} \ldots P \ldots CC' (= CC + \Delta C) \ldots$
    $\$M' (= \$M + \Delta \$M)$

In this way, value undergoes a continuous series of transformations.

Marx calls it a "metamorphosis." We begin with a certain sum of value in the form of money, then transform it into commodity form (the inputs), then into another commodity form (the outputs), and then once again into the money form. The prices at which the commodities exchange determine the magnitude of $\$M$ and $\$M'$. *It really doesn't matter, however, what these prices are because they do not affect the magnitude of the value already created in production.*

From values to prices

12

Aside from the fact that the price of a certain product . . . differs from its value . . . the same fact applies also to those commodities which form the constant part of its capital, and which indirectly, as necessities of life for the labourers, form its variable part. . . . Under capitalist production, the general law of value enforces itself merely as the prevailing tendency, in a very complicated and approximate manner, as a never ascertainable average of ceaseless fluctuations.

Karl Marx

12.1 Value, price, and profit

In this chapter we explore the connection between value and money price. The connection is systematic, even though value and money price are distinct concepts. Value originates in production; money price originates in circulation. The connection between value and money price is therefore the connection between the spheres of production and circulation.

12.1A Value of output and value added

When the capitalist initiates production, the means of production (constant capital) and labor power (variable capital) must be purchased. The value of the constant capital bought we denote by C. The value of the variable capital bought is denoted by V. Therefore, the capitalist's cost of production, in value terms, is $C + V$.

The value of the output which results from production will be larger than the value of the inputs. It must be larger, or else there would be no profit. This difference is the surplus value, which we call S. It is the value of the extra commodities which labor produces during surplus labor time. It represents the value added by labor in production.

The value of the constant and variable capital is $C + V$. The value of the surplus is S. The total value W of the commodities produced in a given period of time may thus be written as

(1) $$C + V + S = W$$

12.1B Some fundamental ratios

There are three ratios which are important in Marx's theory. The first is the *organic composition* of capital. The second is the *rate of exploitation*. The third is the *value rate of profit,* or rate of surplus value.

12.1B(1) The organic composition of capital. The organic composition of capital is simply the ratio of constant capital to variable capital: C/V. The total capital advanced by the capitalist is $C + V$, and the ratio of C to V reflects the relative proportions in which labor power is used in conjunction with the means of production.

It should be noted that when we compare C to V we are comparing the *value* of the labor power to the *value* of the means of production. Marx also called this ratio the "value composition" of capital, which is perhaps clearer. We are *not* comparing the number of workers to the physical quantities of means of production. This latter ratio is what Marx calls the "technical composition of capital" and is similar to the capital-labor ratio in neoclassical economics. Marx decides to use the phrase "organic composition" instead of "value composition" because the latter is inherent in the basic physical and technical character of capital. The organic composition "grows out of," that is, is organically inherent in, the technical composition of capital.

Finally, as we would expect, the organic composition of capital will vary from industry to industry, depending on the technical features of production. One would surmise, therefore, that the production of automobiles would have a higher organic composition of capital than the production of custom-made furniture.

12.1B(2) The rate of exploitation. The rate of exploitation is the ratio of surplus value to variable capital, or S/V. It shows the amount of value created by labor during surplus labor time relative to the amount of value created during necessary labor time. In fact, the latter begets the former.

If, for example, the amount of socially necessary labor time required to produce a day's means of subsistence is 4 hours, and if the workday is 8 hours, the rate of exploitation is 100%. The ratio only signifies the relative exploitation of labor. If the ratio of S to V is 6 to 6, the rate of exploitation is still 100% but workers are now required to labor an extra 6 hours instead of 4.

According to Marx, the rate of exploitation will tend to equalize among industries, unlike the organic composition of capital. There are two reasons for this. First, the workday tends to be the same for all workers. Suppose this is 8 hours. Second, wages tend to be uniform for a homogeneous work force in freely competitive markets.

If this is the case, then each worker is capable of purchasing an identical share of the total means of subsistence. Suppose this share represents 4 hours of labor. The rate of exploitation, in this case 4/4, or 100%, will be the same in all industries since the total workday, and the division of that workday, is also the same.

12.1B(3) The value rate of profit. The capitalist advances capital valued at $C + V$. The capitalist receives, after production has taken place, a sum of value equal to $C + V + S$. The value rate of profit is simply the capitalist's "reward" S, expressed as a percentage of $C + V$, the capital invested. Letting π stand for the value rate of profit, we have

$$(2) \qquad \pi = \frac{S}{C + V}$$

Dividing each of the three elements on the right-hand side of this equation by V, we obtain

$$(3) \qquad \pi = \frac{S/V}{C/V + 1}$$

Since S/V is the rate of exploitation and C/V is the organic composition of capital,

$$(4) \qquad \text{Value rate of profit} = \frac{\text{rate of exploitation}}{\text{organic composition} + 1}$$

12.2 The transformation problem

12.2A The transformation problem stated

The value rates of profit in any two or more industries are the same only if (a) the rate of exploitation is the same and (b) the organic composition of capital is the same. This can be confirmed by examining equation (4) above.

Now, it would be reasonable to expect condition (a) to hold true, as we have already seen in the previous section. However, condition (b) could not be expected to hold true in all industries. The technical conditions of production in various industries differ significantly, as do the relative proportions of labor and means of production necessary. Thus, the organic compositions of capital also vary.

Because of the variability of organic compositions of capital, the value rates of profit among industries would also vary. Some capitalists will be generating a higher-than-average rate of surplus value; some will be generating a lower-than-average rate of surplus value; others will be generating the average rate of surplus value.

Suppose, now, that all commodities sell at prices that are in direct proportion to values. We call these prices *direct prices*.[1] Thus, if the value of a ton of iron is 100 hours and a ton of steel is 200 hours, the money price of iron will be half that of steel. Suppose that the monetary system consists only of gold coins, each $1 coin representing 1 hour of labor. Iron would sell at $100 per ton; steel would sell at $200 per ton.

The money rate of profit, as opposed to the value rate of profit, is simply the difference between M' and M. It represents the *money* value of the surplus value sold, as a percentage of the *money* value of the capital advanced $(C + V)$. We henceforth denote the money rate of profit as r. If all prices are proportional to values, then it stands to reason that the value rate of profit (a percentage) will be equal to the money rate of profit (also a percentage).

We may conclude, therefore, that if all commodities sell at direct prices (prices always proportional to values) then $r = \pi$ *within* each firm. However, since the organic composition of capital varies, r and π will vary *among* firms and industries.

We already know from our analysis of prices of production in the previous chapters that this is an unsatisfactory conclusion, since money rates of profit will tend to equalize among industries because of business competition. They cannot remain unequal. The only way money rates of profit can equalize is if prices deviate from direct prices. We must find a set of prices—prices of production—that will redistribute the surplus value produced in a way which equalizes r in all industries. The problem, in a formal mathematical sense, is identical to the problem we solved in the Sraffa model. It is the "transformation problem."

In summary, values determine *direct prices*; direct prices get transformed into *prices of production*; and *market prices* will fluctuate around these prices of production. The transformation problem is therefore not a problem of transforming values into prices. Instead, it is a problem of transforming direct prices into prices of production.

Finally, the transformation problem is not a problem with the labor theory of value. It is instead a problem which the market mechanism actually solves in reality. Marx fully recognized that prices are in actuality related to values in a very complicated way. He knew quite well that neither prices of production, nor market prices, would ever be proportional to labor values. Significant deviations should be expected.

Deviations of market prices from production prices, however, *tend* to be eliminated by the automatic forces of the marketplace. But they may not actually be eliminated; they only *tend* to be. However, if such a tendency does not exist, then the competitive capitalist economy would be unable to reproduce itself from one period to the next.

We know that, in order for a competitive capitalist society to survive at a given level of output, certain key commodities (means of subsistence and means of production) must be continually produced in certain definite proportions. Because there exists no mechanism with which people consciously plan and regulate their productive activities, these critical proportions cannot be expected to be always in existence. Decision making under uncertainty, errors in judgment, and the like will always result in the movement of market prices away from the necessary proportions reflected by prices of production. Thus, the deviation of market prices from production prices creates *disproportionalities* and is characterized by excessive growth in some sectors and excessive declines in others.

However, when disproportionalities arise because of excessive expansion or contraction of certain sectors, competitive market prices will respond. Too rapid expansion will spell unsold goods, increasing inventory costs, lower profits, and, ultimately, lower market prices. Too rapid contraction will cause the opposite to occur, driving prices upward. Other capitalists, responding to these price signals, will rechannel the resources under their command away from the excessively expanding sectors to the excessively contracting sectors until proportionality is once again achieved.

Value, therefore, indirectly regulates prices of production and hence market prices. The forces of supply and demand tend to insure that market prices stabilize around prices of production. If disproportionalities arise, changes in the scale of production will occur and, as a result, market prices will adjust. In this way, Marx claimed that value regulates production.

12.2B The transformation problem solved

Because the organic composition of capital varies from industry to industry, the value rates of profit will also vary. If the prices at which the commodities produced by these industries are strictly proportional to their values, then the money rates of profit will vary in precisely the same way.

Because competition exists among capitalists, one would expect the money rates of profit to tend toward uniformity. It is after all these money rates and not the value rates which directly induce capitalists to direct the flow of capital from low profit industries to high profit industries. Capitalists do not consciously make their decisions on the basis of values; they make their decisions on the basis of dollar prices and money rates of profit.

The only way these money rates of profit can change is if the capitalists change the prices at which their commodities sell. Thus, the equality of money rates is brought about by price changes. Prices cannot remain proportional to labor values.

We view this movement of prices as an iterative process which occurs over time and which begins with direct prices. The process then goes through a series of intermediate stages, and ends with a final equilibrium stage. In this final stage the prices of production yield an equalized money rate of profit. This approach is a continuation of the approach Marx took in his third volume of *Capital*. He only took the process of price adjustment part way, however. The solution below completes Marx's analysis and follows the one provided by Shaikh but is of a general class of solutions which includes those of Bortkiewicz, Seton, and Winternitz.[2]

While this process of successive price transformations takes place, the *value structure* of output stays the same. This is to reflect the notion that a certain mass of value is produced with a certain mix of labor and means of production (also measured in value terms). The prices at which this mass of value circulates throughout the system do not, and cannot, alter the value of this mass.

To see how this process works, suppose we have only two industries. The first industry, which we call Department I, produces means of production. The second industry, Department II, produces the means of subsistence.

In Table 12.1 we summarize all of the necessary data. Department I employs 100 hours' worth of means of production (constant capital) and 100 hours of labor. Of the 100 hours of labor, only 50 hours is paid for (variable capital); the other 50 hours represents surplus value. The total value produced is 200 hours.

In Department II the total value produced is 300 hours, which breaks down into 100 hours C, 100 hours V, and 100 hours S. The total mass of value produced in both sectors is 500 hours. The value rates of profit (π) in Department I and II are 33% and 50%, respectively.

A close examination of the numbers selected for this illustration reveals that this is a simple no-growth economy. To see this, note first of all that the total value of means of production produced in Department I (200) is entirely used up by both sectors (100 in each department). Now, note that the total value of the means of consumption produced in

The Transformation Process: The Iterative Approach

		Value Accounts					Money Price Accounts					
		Value of Means (C)	Value of Labor Power (V)	Surplus Value (S)	Total Value	Value Rate of Profit (π)	Money Price of Means	Money Price of Labor	Total Cost Price (M)	Total Dollar Sales (M')	Total Money Profits ($\Delta$$M$)	Money Rate of Profit (r)%
Comments:												
Exchange occurs at direct prices. $\pi = r$	Dept. I	100	50	50	200	33%	$100	$ 50	$150	$200	$ 50	33.33
	Dept. II	100	100	100	300	50%	$100	$100	$200	$300	$100	50.0
		200							$350	$500	$150	
Initial change is in direct prices in order to equalize r.	Dept. I	100	50	50	200	33%	$100	$ 50	$150	$214.28	$ 64.28	42.86
	Dept. II	100	100	100	300	50%	$100	$100	$200	$285.72	$ 85.72	42.86
$\psi_1 = 1.071$ $\psi_2 = 0.952$									$350	$500.00	$150.00	
Above output price changes alter cost prices in current period.	Dept. I	100	50	50	200	33%	$107.10	$ 47.60	$154.70	$214.28	$ 59.58	38.51
	Dept. II	100	100	100	300	50%	$107.10	$ 95.20	$202.30	$285.72	$ 83.42	41.23
									$357.00	$500.00	$143.00	
Above output prices change to equalize money profit rate r.	Dept. I	100	50	50	200	33%	$107.10	$ 47.60	$154.70	$216.67	$ 61.97	40.06
	Dept. II	100	100	100	300	50%	$107.10	$ 95.20	$202.30	$283.33	$ 81.03	40.06
$\psi_1 = 1.011$ $\psi_2 = 0.992$									$357.00	$500.00	$143.00	
Final solution: any further iterations will have no effect on money prices.	Dept. I	100	50	50	200	33%	$108.56	$ 47.15	$155.71	$217.13	$ 61.42	39.44
	Dept. II	100	100	100	300	50%	$108.56	$ 94.29	$202.85	$282.87	$ 80.02	39.44
$\psi_1 = 1.086$ $\psi_2 = 0.943$									$358.56	$500.00	$141.44	

Department II (300) is also entirely used by both workers and capitalists. The workers in both sectors receive a wage equivalent to 150. The capitalists' income is represented by the total surplus value appropriated in both sectors, or 150. Thus, capitalists as well as workers spend their entire aggregate income (300) on the output of Department II.

Such a situation is a no-growth situation because capitalists use all of their surplus value on consumption. Marx calls this situation "simple reproduction." Expansion and growth depend on the ability and willingness of capitalists to accumulate and reinvest their surplus value, not spend it on consumption. In fact, capitalists are characterized by a lust for accumulation and an inner drive to expand the amount of capital under their control. They would therefore not be expected to consume all of their surplus value. Only workers consume their entire income. This arises because market forces tend to drive wages toward a subsistence level. For purposes of illustration, however, we will maintain the assumption that capitalists consume their entire surplus value and proceed to derive prices from values.

If the monetary system consists of only $1 gold coins, each representing 1 hour of labor, then the direct prices are shown in Table 12.1 immediately to the right of the value accounts. Direct prices, it should be remembered, are those which are strictly proportional to values. Since $1 = 1$ hour, the direct money prices are identical in magnitude to values. The total cost prices (M) in Departments I and II are \$150 and \$200, respectively. The selling prices (M') are \$200 and \$300, respectively. Finally, the money rates of profit (r_1 and r_2) are identical to the value rates of profit, or 33% and 50% respectively.

Because the profit rates differ, new prices must be calculated. The total dollar volume of profits is \$150 in both departments. The total cost price of the means of production and of labor power is \$350. The average, overall rate of profit is therefore 42.86%.

Assuming that both departments tend to gravitate toward this average, then clearly prices must change in order to bring this about. In Department I, the cost price is \$150.00; profit must be 42.86% of that, or \$64.28. The sales price must therefore be \$150.00 plus \$64.28, or \$214.28. This is higher than the previous \$200.00. The same reasoning applied to Department II suggests that its sales price must now be \$285.72. This is lower than the previous \$300.00.

The sum of sales is still \$500. It is just redistributed in order to bring about a uniform money rate of profit. The price of the means of production (the output of Department I) increases by a multiplier of 1.071 while the price of the means of subsistence decreases by a multiplier of 0.952. These "multipliers" reflect the fact that Department I was earning a lower money profit rate and Department II was earning a higher rate. The first department must therefore be compensated with a higher price while the second must be penalized with a lower price.

In the next period, these newly "transformed" prices will be reflected in the costs of production. The higher priced means of production are used in both departments and the lower priced means of subsistence are used by the workers in both departments as well. Thus, means of production which first cost $100.00 now cost $107.10 ($100 × 1.071) in Department I. Means of subsistence which first cost $50.00 now cost $47.60 ($50 × 0.952) in that department.

The total cost price has therefore risen to $154.70 from $150.00. With the selling price still at $214.28, the money rate of profit declines again to 38.51%. The same changes occur in Department II, causing its total cost price to rise to $202.30 and its money rate of profit to fall to 41.23%.

With the money rates of profit unequal once again, further price changes must occur. This time the average money rate of profit is 40.06% ($143 ÷ $357). Assuming price changes occur so as to bring each industry's rate into conformity with this average, then Department I must receive $216.67 instead of $214.28; Department II must receive $283.33 instead of $285.72.

In the next round these new prices of production feed back onto the cost side. The means of production have gone up by a factor (ψ_1) of 1.011 (216.67/214.28) and the means of subsistence have gone down by a factor (ψ_2) of 0.992. This will cause profits to change, which will cause prices to change. The process continues to repeat itself until an equilibrium is reached. This equilibrium is shown at the bottom of Table 12.1.

The rates of profit have been equalized at 39.44% and the two departments can continue to exchange their commodities at the indicated prices without any further adjustments. The prices of the commodities produced in Department I are 1.086 times their original direct prices, and the prices of the commodities produced in Department II are 0.943 times their original direct prices. Note also that the total monetary value of the means of production used in both sectors ($108.56 + $108.56) equals the monetary value produced ($217.13). Similarly, the monetary value of the labor purchased ($47.15 + $94.29) plus the monetary value of the profits ($61.42 + $80.02) adds up to the total monetary value of the means of consumption produced ($282.87).

In summary, the transformation problem is one of determining the final prices of production. The initial starting point is direct prices.

These direct prices are based entirely on labor values. From this point on competition among capitalists will change prices in a series of transformations until an equilibrium is reached. At this equilibrium money profit rates are uniform; value profit rates are not.

12.2C The formal solution

Close examination of the solution to the transformation problem reveals a striking similarity between the Ricardian theory of price formalized by Sraffa and the Marxian theory of price described in the previous section. The nature and significance of the relationship between Marx and Sraffa is hotly contested. But before we can begin to introduce the similarities and differences between these two approaches we must describe the method of solving the Marxian system.

In the example of the previous section, we began with a two-sector model in which the inputs were expressed in terms of value (hours of labor). The value of the inputs consisted of (1) the value of the means of production C and (2) the value of labor V. The result of production is a mass of value W which exceeds the value of the inputs by an amount S. In general terms we may write, for a two-sector model,

(5) $$C_1 + V_1 + S_1 = W_1$$
$$C_2 + V_2 + S_2 = W_2$$

Remembering that the value rate of profit π in each sector is $S/(C + V)$, we can rewrite equations (5) as

(6) $$(C_1 + V_1)(1 + \pi_1) = W_1$$
$$(C_2 + V_2)(1 + \pi_2) = W_2$$

Substituting $S_1/(C_1 + V_1)$ for π_1 and $S_2/(C_2 + V_2)$ for π_2 in equations (6) will give us equations (5). The equations (6) are shown in the top left-hand corner of Table 12.2. The illustration of the previous section is shown immediately to the right.

The next step in our calculations was to derive the direct prices for the inputs and outputs. Direct prices, it should be recalled, are "directly" proportional to the labor values. The degree of proportionality depends on the value of a $1 gold coin. In our example, $1 = 1 hour, so 100 hours of labor has a money price of $100. We let the letter D represent the monetary value of one hour of labor. Thus $D = 1$ in the above example.

In order to calculate the direct price of a certain mass of commodities, we simply multiply D times the labor value of that mass. Thus, if $D = 1$, then the direct price of a commodity with a value of 100 hours is $D \times 100$ hours, or $100. If $D = 2$, then the direct price would be $200.

Table 12.2

The Formal Solution to the Transformation Problem

	Formalized System	Illustration
Values	$(C_1 + V_1)(1 + \pi_1) = W_1$	$(100 + 50)(1.33) = 200$
	$(C_2 + V_2)(1 + \pi_2) = W_2$	$(100 + 100)(1.50) = 300$
Direct prices	$(DC_1 + DV_1)(1 + r_1) = DW_1$ $D = \$1/\text{hr}$	$(\$100 + \$\ 50)(1.33) = \$200$
	$(DC_2 + DV_2)(1 + r_2) = DW_2$	$(\$100 + \$100)(1.50) = \$300$
Prices of production	$(\psi_1 DC_1 + \psi_2 DV_1)(1 + r) = \psi_1 DW_1$	$(\$108.56 + \$47.15)(1.3944) = \$217.13$
	$(\psi_1 DC_2 + \psi_2 DV_2)(1 + r) = \psi_2 DW_2$	$(\$108.56 + \$94.29)(1.3944) = \$282.87$
	$\psi_1 DW_1 + \psi_2 DW_2 = DW_1 + DW_2$	$\$217.13 + \$282.87 = \$500$
	$p_1 = \psi_1 D$	$\psi_1 = 1.086$
	$p_2 = \psi_2 D$	$\psi_2 = 0.943$
		$r = 0.3944$
		$p_1 = 1.086$
		$p_2 = 0.943$

Multiplying each of the values in equations (6) by D gives us the monetary value of each of the commodities measured in direct prices. Thus,

(7)
$$(DC_1 + DV_1)(1 + r_1) = DW_1$$
$$(DC_2 + DV_2)(1 + r_2) = DW_2$$

where r_1 and r_2 represent the unequalized money rates of profit in each sector. Equations (7), together with the illustration of the previous section, are shown in the second row of Table 12.2

Because the organic composition of capital differs in each sector, and because competition will drive profit rates toward uniformity, prices will begin to diverge from direct prices. *This is natural and to be expected in a competitive capitalist economy*. Prices will therefore begin to move away from the levels indicated by equations (7). They will converge toward an equilibrium set of prices in which the money rate of profit is equalized.

Because the aggregate mass of value produced stays the same, the monetary value of that mass will also remain the same, given a constant value for D. As prices converge toward this equilibrium, the surplus *value* actually produced in each sector gets redistributed from higher profit sectors to lower profit sectors. The logic behind this is the same as in the Sraffa model. There we saw that any change in price will effectively alter the distribution of the surplus. The same thing takes place here.

The final equilibrium prices will be some multiple of the original direct price. The size of these multipliers depends on the technical and value (organic) composition of production (C/V) and the rate of exploitation (S/V). Let p_1 stand for the equilibrium price of production of means of production (Department I) and p_2 stand for the equilibrium price of production of means of subsistence (Department II). The price p_1 will be some multiple of the direct price of means of production, and p_2 will be some multiple of the direct price of means of subsistence. The former multiplier we call ψ_1 and the latter multiplier we call ψ_2.

The final set of equations describes the system measured at the correct (i.e., equilibrium) prices of production. Hence,

(8)
$$(\psi_1 DC_1 + \psi_2 DV_1)(1 + r) = \psi_1 DW_1$$
$$(\psi_1 DC_2 + \psi_2 DV_2)(1 + r) = \psi_2 DW_2$$
$$\psi_1 DW_1 + \psi_2 DW_2 = DW_1 + DW_2$$

or, using p_1 and p_2

(9)
$$(p_1C_1 + p_2V_1)(1 + r) = p_1W_1$$
$$(p_1C_2 + p_2V_2)(1 + r) = p_2W_2$$
$$p_1W_1 + p_2W_2 = DW_1 + DW_2$$

The first equation in (9) states that the capital advanced for means of production and labor power ($C_1 + V_1$) measured by prices of production (p_1 and p_2) and multiplied by ($1 + r$) yields the output of means of production W_1 measured by p_1. A similar interpretation applies to the consumption goods sector. The third equation states that the mass of output produced by both sectors must remain the same in dollar terms. This forces p_1 and p_2 to take on values which will simply redistribute the existing mass. Equations (8) are reproduced in the last row of Table 12.2. Using the equations $p_1 = \psi_1 D$ and $p_2 = \psi_2 D$, we can easily transform equations (8) into equation (9). The actual solutions when $D = 1$ are indicated on the lower right.[3]

An overview and comparison

Part VI

Marxian vs. post-Keynesian (neo-Ricardian) price theory: an overview   13

> *The different criticisms are but variations on a single theme—that Sraffian analysis can be identified with Ricardian analysis, and thus that Sraffa can be compatible with Marx only if Marx is reduced to Ricardo. In the attempt to prove this, sometimes Sraffa's contribution to economic theory is itself reduced to the solution of the Ricardian problem of the invariable standard of value.*
>
> Alessandro Roncaglia

> *Insofar as some Marxists have pursued a similar line of argument as to the "reduction" of Marx to Ricardo, they have been making an absolutely crucial point: namely, that by attempting to "reduce" Marx to Ricardo, or to neoclassical economics, the impossibility of this reduction will manifest itself as a series of "contradictions" and "irrationalities" in Marx!*
>
> Anwar Shaikh

13.1 Marxian and neo-Ricardian price theory

There is no doubt that Marx chronologically followed Ricardo. This is perhaps the only point with which all economists agree. The relative merits of Ricardian and Marxian theory and the relationship of the latter to the former have always been hotly contested. In 1896 Böhm-Bowerk declared that "the Marxian system has no abiding future." Marshall dismissed him [Marx] as a "tendentious thinker who had mischievously misunderstood Ricardo."[1] Samuelson in more recent times called Marx a "minor post-Ricardian."[2] But Schumpeter came closest to accurately describing the Ricardo–Marx connection:

> Ricardo is the only economist whom Marx treated as a master.... Marx used the Ricardian apparatus: he adopted Ricardo's conceptual lay-out and his problems presented themselves to him in the forms that Ricardo had given to them. No doubt, he transformed these forms and he arrived

in the end at widely different conclusions. But he always did so by starting from, *and criticising*, Ricardo. *Criticism of Ricardo was his method in his purely theoretical work.*³

It is true that Ricardo tilled the soil in which Marx's theory grew. It was after all Ricardo's labor theory of value which presented itself to Marx. But the development of Marx's own theory of value occurred as a result of criticism of Ricardo, as Schumpeter observes in the quotation above. The formulation of Marx's theory was in the final analysis a rejection of Ricardo's.

Ricardo's theory, however, suffered because he was unable to unravel the paradox of distribution. That is, he couldn't construct an invariable standard of value which would allow one to observe the relationship between profits and wages independently of, and unobstructed by, the price disturbances which result from such changes in distribution. In recent times, this paradox was resolved by Sraffa. Sraffa's important contribution thereby reaffirmed the Ricardian theory of price and value, giving rise to a new wave of "neo-Ricardianism."

Marx's theory, on the other hand, was not completed. Specifically, he never fully resolved the "transformation problem." This cast great doubt on the validity of Marx's value theory and caused many to dismiss it as logically inconsistent. But the solution to this problem, and the completion of his theory, came long after Marx's death. As a result of the satisfactory solution to the transformation problem, a renewed interest in Marxian theory has also recently emerged. It has proven to be logically consistent after all.

Because of these theoretical advances, the controversies about the Ricardo-Marx relationship and the relative merits of each have become of vital concern among nonorthodox economists. The controversies are made very complex, however, because in the process of resolving the Ricardian problem Sraffa also made a contribution to the development of Marxian value theory. What, then, do we make of Sraffa? Is there a bridge between Ricardo and Marx? Three schools of thought now exist:

(a) *Neo-Ricardians*. These people, sometimes referred to as post-Keynesians (or by some the Cambridge School) are mostly interested in Sraffa's implicit critique of neoclassical economics. They regard his contribution as an advance over Marx. Many go very far in claiming the superiority of Sraffa over Marx, even to the point of rejecting Marx's theory of value entirely. Ian Steedman, for example, concludes his own Marx-Sraffa analysis with the observation that "Marx's value reasoning—hardly a peripheral aspect of his work—must therefore be abandoned, in the interest of developing a coherent materialist theory of capitalism."⁴

(b) *Marxist fundamentalists*. This group views Sraffa's work as incompatible with Marx. They say that neo-Ricardianism, epitomized by Sraffa, "reduces" Marx to Ricardo and that Marx's analysis, when carried to its completion, requires no alterations or modifications. Representatives of this school are Shaikh and Roosevelt.[5]

(c) *Eclectics*. This group includes those who see Sraffa and the "neo-Ricardians" as operating on a different level from Marx. The two models are not inconsistent and irreconcilable. They are simply governed by different problematics. Sraffa is more concerned with the formation of prices of production and distribution. Marx is more concerned with uncovering the source of profit and explaining the exploitive operation of a capitalist economy. Examples of eclectic positions are the works of Roncaglia and Eatwell.[6]

Because of the introductory nature of this book, we do not enter very deeply into these extremely esoteric debates. It is hoped that the reader, having followed the analysis thus far, will be suitably equipped to explore this complex literature alone. We wish only to point to the most fundamental similarities and differences between Sraffa and Marx in order to permit a basic understanding of the differences between the three schools described above.

13.2 The similarities between Sraffa and Marx

The similarities between Sraffa's model and that of Marx have been itemized in previous chapters. Both models are descendants of early classical thinking and thereby display certain common attributes.

Both Sraffa and Marx base their analyses on the concept of "prices of production." Such prices are in the same tradition as "natural prices" and are defined independently of any notion about supply and demand. Supply and demand determine only market prices. Production prices, on the other hand, are determined by the social and technical conditions of production. This approach contrasts starkly with the orthodox neoclassical subjective theory of value.

The Sraffa model and the Marxian model are also founded on the concept of economic surplus. The existence of a surplus is a fundamental feature of capitalism. Moreover, both claim that exchange at prices of production redistributes the surplus produced in each sector of the economy in a way which provides all capitalists with a uniform rate of profit on their investment. The equalization of the profit rate is brought about by competition among capitalists.

If exchange takes place at prices of production then (1) the replacement of used up means of production and (2) the payment of wages and profits at the specified rates will also be assured. These are the two basic conditons for smooth, uninterrupted reproduction, a concern common to both models.

Also implicit in both approaches is the view that profit is really income that is unavailable to the working class. Additionally, the general rate of profit is determined solely by the existing social and technical relations which describe the system. The technical relations determine the volume of output possible; the social relations determine the share of that output going to capitalists in the form of profit.

The distribution of surplus to capitalists, which takes place through exchange at prices of production, is governed by how much capital is *owned*. The distribution of income to workers is governed by how much they *work*. At the bottom of both models, therefore, is the viewpoint that the interests of the capitalist class are in conflict with the interests of the working class. Class conflict, not class harmony, is the order of the day.

13.3 The differences between Sraffa and Marx

13.3A Features of Sraffa's model

In Figure 13.1 we observe Sraffa's model. The rectangles marked "basics" and "nonbasics" represent physical quantities of actual commodities. Only those commodities which are directly and indirectly used to produce *all* other commodities are included in the basic category. These are Sraffa's means of production.

In the category "nonbasics" we find three subcategories of commodities: (1) means of production used only for the production of nonbasics (i.e., means that do not directly or indirectly enter the production of all other commodities); (2) subsistence commodities for workers and capitalists; (3) luxury goods for workers and capitalists.

The surplus produced in the various basic sectors of the economy is the source of income for both capitalists and workers. That is, both classes receive an income, the value of which is represented by a specified share of the surplus.

Because we are speaking of heterogeneous commodities, and because reproduction takes place by way of commodity exchange, prices of production must be determined. These prices are represented by the cells of the two rectangles in the center of the diagram. When the physical commodities on the left are multiplied by these prices we obtain the monetary value of the basics and nonbasics. These monetary values

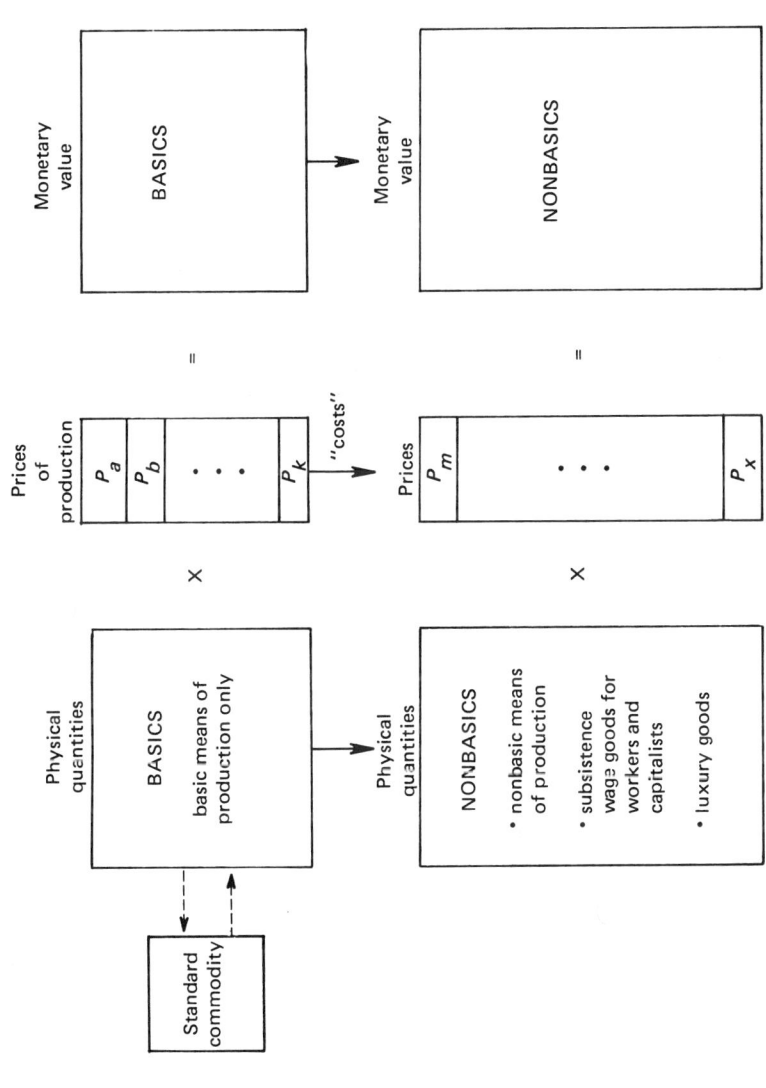

Figure 13.1

Sraffa's Ricardian Model

are represented by the rectangles on the right of Figure 13.1.

Two broad features of this model are noteworthy. First, it is possible to construct a perfectly balanced "standard system" by mathematically transforming the actual *basic* system. One may then use the surplus of this standard basic system as a numeraire. The value of this numeraire, called the *standard commodity*, will be unaffected by alterations in distribution. The standard commodity is shown on the extreme left-hand side of the diagram. By measuring all prices in terms of the standard commodity, we see that the wage–profit relation is linear and free from the price distortions which otherwise result when distribution changes.

Secondly, the Sraffa model shows that prices of production of basic commodities determine the costs of production of nonbasics, and not the other way around. Because each of the basics directly or indirectly enters into the production of all nonbasics, the monetary value of the basics acquired by nonbasic industries represents, strictly speaking, a cost of production. But fur coats are not used to produce steel; so, too, nonbasics are not used to produce basics. Thus, no matter what the price of nonbasics, they cannot affect in any way the costs of producing basics.

The implication of this is that prices p_a to p_k are determined independently of prices p_m to p_x. This reflects the notion that it is the social/technical conditions of production in the basic sector which determine overall profit rates and prices of production.

13.3B Sraffa's wage theory

A great concern among critics of Sraffa's model is that subsistence commodities are included among nonbasics. In this way, it is felt, Sraffa breaks from the spirit of much of classical thinking. Classifying subsistence commodities as nonbasics denies the possibility that changes in the way these goods are produced can influence profits or prices of production. Surely subsistence commodities are basic and indirectly enter the production of everything else. Would not an improvement in the production of such commodities automatically permit higher profits to be earned? And would not the resulting increase in surplus require a change in prices in order to pay the new profit rate?

Many Marxists feel that this treatment of wages obscures a fundamental attribute of the capitalist system. Wage rates, so it is claimed, are really determined by the amount of socially necessary labor time required to produce these subsistence commodities. Sraffa has nothing to say about what determines wages. He leaves it open-ended.

Moreover, if wage rates are determined in the way specified by Marx, then, say the Marxists, profits come from selling the surplus value *produced by labor*. This is what constitutes exploitation in the Marxian system. Profits originate in the exploitation of workers. But exploitation, the ultimate source of capitalist profits, can only be observed when you have a theory of wage determination. Since Sraffa has no theory of wage determination he obscures the exploitive nature of capitalism.

13.3C Sraffa's defense

Defenders of Sraffa claim that the placement of subsistence commodities among nonbasics is purely for ease of exposition. They assert that a Marxian wage theory, based on the notion that labor power is a commodity requiring certain means of subsistence, can be introduced into Sraffa's model without changing the results obtained.[7] Specifically, we can reject Sraffa's approach and reintroduce a "wage dichotomy" in which one portion of the wage is a subsistence wage and another portion is a "social dividend," or a share of the surplus.

Another positive contribution of Sraffa is that he liberated Ricardian wage theory from its Malthusianism. Ricardo accepted Malthus's population law and used it to explain wages. He claimed that whenever wages rose above the subsistence level population growth would increase the supply of labor and drive wages back to subsistence. Sraffa gets away from this naive argument by making wages depend on the outcome of an unspecified social process.

And finally, the defenders point to the fact that Sraffa's model deals with prices and distribution; one should not accuse Sraffa for failing in tasks which he himself did not set out to accomplish.

13.3D Features of Marx's model

In Figure 13.2 we illustrate the Marxian version. In volume 3 of *Capital* Marx makes no distinction between categories of commodities, although elsewhere he distinguishes between means-of-production industries and means-of-consumption industries. Beginning with Bortkiewicz's formulation of the transformation problem in 1907, however, it has become standard to present a three-sector model instead. (see footnote 3 of Chapter 12). Department I continues to represent the sectors which produce the means of production. Department II represents all those sectors which produce the means of subsistence. These are purchased only by workers. Department III represents those industries which produce only luxury commodities. These, in turn, are purchased only by capitalists.

This expanded version can be analyzed in precisely the same way as the two-sector model. We simply need to add a third equation represent-

190　AN OVERVIEW AND COMPARISON

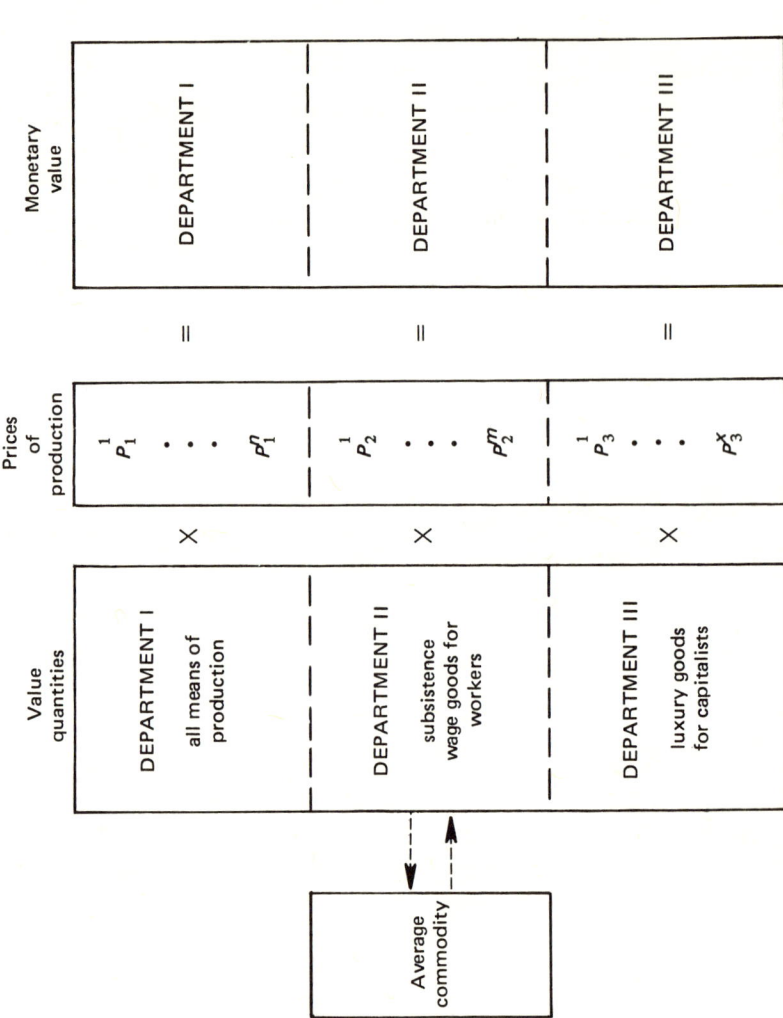

Figure 13.2

The Marxian Model

ing Department III and a third price of production (the price of luxuries). Nothing else changes.

The large rectangle on the left-hand side of Figure 13.2 represents the aggregate mass of values produced in a given period of time. It does not represent physical quantities. Although this total mass of values is partitioned into three sections, all commodities rank equally in terms of price and profit determination. This differs sharply from Sraffa.

In Sraffa's model, only those commodities produced in basic industries enter into the determination of the general rate of profit. In Marx's model, the general rate of profit is an average rate of profit in all industries. This point has come under attack by neo-Ricardians. They ask, How can the conditions of production in the fur coat industry rank equally with the conditions of production in the steel industry in the determination of the overall profit rate and prices?

The middle set of rectangles represents the prices of production for all three sectors. There are n industries in Department I, with equilibrium prices p_1^1 to p_1^n; there are m industries in Department II, with equilibrium prices p_2^1 to p_2^m; and there are x industries in Department III, with equilibrium prices of p_3^1 to p_3^x. Multiplying these prices times the given value gives the monetary value of the output produced.

13.3E Marx's average commodity

Marx attempts to show in volume 3 of *Capital* that the general rate of profit will tend toward the average rate of profit in all industries. The adjustment of prices which occurs to bring this about was demonstrated in the previous chapter.

If we consider a hypothetical commodity whose value composition is equal to the average composition of all industries, then, according to Marx, its price of production should equal its value. Moreover, the surplus value produced in that "average" industry would equal the profit realized. In other words, the average commodity would display a direct proportionality between its value and its price.

If this direct proportionality is to be maintained, then it must be insensitive to changes in the wage–profit relation. In other words, increases (or decreases) in wages must be fully offset by decreases (or increases) in profits. But this can occur only if the composition of the constant and variable capital used to produce the current constant and variable capital is identical. In fact each previous generation of capitals must be identically proportioned. This discussion of an average commodity, insensitive to changes in the distribution between wages and profits, should sound familiar. It is indeed virtually identical to our discussion of the balanced standard commodity in Sraffa's model.

Now, Marx never successfully carried the analysis very far. But it is implicit in his average commodity. That standard commodity possesses all the attributes suggested above. The only difference is that Sraffa's standard commodity, unlike Marx's average commodity, is derived from the *basic sector only*. The average commodity is derived from *all sectors* of the economy.

But just because Marx did not complete the analysis does not imply that an invariable standard cannot be successfully derived in his model. This was done by Medio.[8] He used the Sraffaian method of formally deriving a standard commodity to find a similar commodity—the ω "omega" commodity—which would function the same way in Marx's model.

13.3F Marx's wage theory

Just as Sraffa jettisons Ricardo's Malthusianism from his wage theory, so too does Marx. But Sraffa leaves the determination of wages open-ended whereas Marx replaces it with a theory of his own.

As we already know, Marx's wage theory is based on the idea that labor power is a commodity and is sold on markets like any other commodity. The wage is going to be regulated by the value of this commodity. This value, in turn, will be equal to the amount of socially necessary labor used to produce the means of subsistence.

The actual money wage will not be directly proportional to the labor embodied, however. This occurs because the wage is a money price, and, like all other prices of production, will deviate from labor values. These deviations occur because (1) the composition of capital differs among industries and (2) the money rate of profit must be equalized. This concept was explored in depth in the previous chapter.

Once labor is purchased by the capitalist, however, the latter gets to use that labor for an extended period of time. During this period of time the worker produces surplus value, and it is this surplus value which gives rise to profit, since the surplus value belongs to the capitalist, who is free to realize (if he or she can) the full monetary value of this surplus.

The main conclusion reached by Marx's theory of wages is, therefore, that *profits arise from the employment and subsequent exploitation of living labor*. This conclusion is *not* reached in Sraffa's analysis. In Marx, to raise the rate of profit the capitalist must increase the rate of exploitation. In Sraffa, to raise the rate of profit the capitalist need only "squeeze the share of wages in the net product [surplus]."[9]

This is the most important difference between the neo-Ricardian, or post-Keynesian, branch and the Marxian branch of value and price theory. Are these two views irreconcilable? Is Marx's theory really different from Sraffa's or is any difference pure semantics? Can a simple appeal to the facts resolve the controversy, or are these differences more fundamental? And finally, is it really legitimate to classify post-Keynesian and Marxian theories of value and price into one "school" with diverse branches, or should they be kept separate? We shall let the reader decide on the answers to these questions.

Recommended Readings

The following works are categorized according to the six parts of this book. I have excluded from this compilation the original works of the Physiocrats, Smith, Ricardo, and Marx. A basic knowledge of these classics is essential to understanding the post-Keynesian/Marxian approach, and they need not be listed below.

Many books and articles are relevant to several categories and are therefore listed more than once. Most should be readily accessible in college and university libraries and ought to be well within the capabilities of the reader. This listing should by no means be viewed as a complete and comprehensive one.

There is a core of books which the reader is encouraged to pursue if he or she wishes to get more deeply into the post-Keynesian and Marxian tradition. These are:

Maurice Dobb, *Theories of Value and Distribution Since Adam Smith*, Cambridge University Press, Cambridge, 1973.

Alfred S. Eichner, ed., *A Guide to Post-Keynesian Economics*, M. E. Sharpe, Inc., White Plains, New York, 1978.

————, *Macrodynamics of the American Economy*, M. E. Sharpe, Inc., Armonk, New York, forthcoming.

————, *The Megacorp and Oligopoly: Micro Foundations of Macro Dynamics*, Cambridge University Press, Cambridge, 1976.

Donald J. Harris, *Capital Accumulation and Income Distribution*, Stanford University Press, Stanford, California, 1978.

Martin Hollis and Edward Nell, *Rational Economic Man*, Cambridge University Press, Cambridge, 1975.

E. K. Hunt, *History of Economic Thought*, Wadsworth Publishing Company, Belmont, California, 1979.

E. K. Hunt and Jesse G. Schwartz, eds, *A Critique of Economic Theory*, Penguin Books, Middlesex, England, 1972.

Michal Kalecki, *Selected Essays on the Dynamics of the Capitalist Economy*, Cambridge University Press, Cambridge, 1971.

J. A. Kregel, *Rate of Profit, Distribution and Growth: Two Views*, Aldine-Atherton, Inc., Chicago, 1971.

Ronald Meek, *Studies in the Labour Theory of Value*, 2nd ed., Laurence and Wishart, London, 1973.

I.I. Rubin, *Essays on Marx's Theory of Value*, Black and Red, Detroit, 1972.

Jesse Schwartz, ed., *The Subtle Anatomy of Capitalism,* Goodyear Publishing Company, Santa Monica, California, 1977.

Piero Sraffa, *Production of Commodities by Means of Commodities*, Cambridge University Press, Cambridge, 1960.

Vivian Walsh and Harvey Gram, *Classical and Neoclassical Theories of General Equilibrium*, Oxford University Press, New York, 1980.

Part I: Competing Traditions

Kenneth E. Boulding, *Economics As a Science*, New York, 1970.

Alfred S. Eichner and J. A. Kregel, "An Essay on Post-Keynesian Theory: A New Paradigm in Economics," *Journal of Economic Literature*, vol. 13, December 1975.

Raymond Franklin, "Ideology in Economic Thinking," *American Capitalism: Two Visions*, New York, 1977, Chapter 1.

N. Kaldor, "Alternative Theories of Distribution," *Review of Economic Studies*, vol. 23, no. 2, 1956, pp. 83–100.

Thomas S. Kuhn, *The Structure of Scientific Revolutions*, 2nd ed., Chicago, 1970.

Oscar Lange, "The Scope and Method of Economics," in D. R. Starleaf, ed., *Economics: Readings in Analysis and Policy*, Glenview, Illinois, 1969, pp. 1–6.

R. L. Meek, "Economics and Ideology," *Economics and Ideology and Other Essays*, London, 1967, pp. 196–224.

Edward Nell, "Economics: The Revival of Political Economy," in Robin Blackburn, ed., *Ideology in Social Science*, New York, 1972, pp. 76–95.

Joan Robinson, "Metaphysics, Morals and Science," *Economic Philosophy*, Garden City, New York, 1962, Chapter 1.

Part II: Two Value Traditions

Maurice Dobb, *Studies in the Development of Capitalism,* London, 1946.

Maurice Dobb, Paul Sweezy, et al., *The Transition from Feudalism to Capitalism*, London, 1976.

Maurice Dobb, *Theories of Value and Distribution Since Adam Smith*, Cambridge, 1973.

E. K. Hunt, *Property and Prophets: The Evolution of Economic Institutions and Ideologies*, 2nd ed., New York, 1975.

Ronald Meek, *Studies in the Labour Theory of Value*, 2nd ed., London, 1973.

Isaak I. Rubin, *Essays on Marx's Theory of Value*, Detroit, 1972.

Joseph A. Schumpeter, *History of Economic Analysis*, New York, 1954, Chapters 1–4.

George Stigler, "The Development of Utility Theory, "*Journal of Political Economy*," vol. 63 (August and October, 1950); reprinted in George Stigler, *Essays in the History of Economics*, Chicago, 1975.

George Stigler, "The Ricardian Theory of Value and Distribution," *Journal of Political Economy*, vol. 60 (June 1952); reprinted in George Stigler, *Essays in the History of Economics*, Chicago, 1975.

R. H. Tawney, *Religion and the Rise of Capitalism*, New York, 1963.

Part III: An Organizing Principle: Economic Surplus

William J. Barclay and Mitchell Stengel, "Surplus and Surplus Value," *Review of Radical Political Economics*, vol. 7, Winter 1975, pp. 48-64.

S. J. Chapman, "The Remuneration of Employers," *Economic Journal*, vol. 16, 1906, pp. 523-528.

John Bates Clark, *The Distribution of Wealth*, New York, 1899.

John Eatwell, "Controversies in the Theory of Surplus Value: Old and New," *Science and Society*, vol. 38, no. 3, 1974, pp. 281-287.

Peter M. Lichtenstein, "Social Planning and Social Surplus: An Essay," *Economic Forum*, vol. 10, no. 1, Summer 1979.

Alfred Marshall, *Principles of Economics*, 9th ed., New York, 1961, Book III, Chapter 6, Appendix K.

Karl Marx, *Theories of Surplus Value*, Part II, Moscow, 1968, Chapters 15 and 16.

Ron Stanfield, *The Economic Surplus and Neo-Marxism*, Lexington, Massachusetts, 1973.

Ron Stanfield, "A Revision of the Economic Surplus Concept," *Review of Radical Political Economics*, vol. 6, Fall 1974, pp. 69-74.

George Stigler, "Euler's Theorem and the Marginal Productivity Theory," *Production and Distribution Theories*, New York, 1941, Chapter 12.

Part IV: Post-Keynesian Theories of Value and Price

Raford Boddy and James Crotty, "Class Conflict and Macro-Policy: The Political Business Cycle," *Review of Radical Political Economics*, vol.7 (Spring 1975).

John Eatwell, "Mr. Sraffa's Standard Commodity and the Rate of Exploitation," *Quarterly Journal of Economics*, vol. 89, 1975.

Eugene F. Fama and Arthur B. Laffer, "The Number of Firms and Competition," *American Economic Review*, vol. 62, September 1972, pp. 670-674.

E. K. Hunt, "Religious Parable Versus Economic Logic: An Analysis of the Recent Controversy in Value, Capital and Distribution Theory," *Intermountain Economic Review*, vol. 2 (Fall 1971).

J. A. Kregel, *Rate of Profit, Distribution and Growth: Two Views*, Chicago, 1971.

Paul J. McNulty, "A Note on the History of Perfect Competition," *Journal of Political Economy*, vol. 75, August 1967, pp. 395-399.

Paul J. McNulty, "Economic Theory and the Meaning of Competition," *Quarterly Journal of Economics*, vol. 82, November 1968, pp. 639-656.

Edward Nell, "Property and the Means of Production: A Primer on the Cambridge Controversy," *Review of Radical Political Economics*, vol. 4 (Summer 1972).

Peter Newman, "Production of Commodities by Means of Commodities: A Review," in Jesse Schwartz, ed., *The Subtle Anatomy of Capitalism*, Santa Monica, California, 1977.

Luigi L. Pasinetti, *Lectures on the Theory of Production*, New York, 1977, Chapter 7.

Joan Robinson, "Prelude to a Critique of Economic Theory" in E. K. Hunt and Jesse G. Schwartz, eds., *A Critique of Economic Theory*, Middlesex, England, 1972, pp. 197-204.

Joan Robinson, "What Is Perfect Competition?" *Quarterly Journal of Economics,* November 1937, pp. 104-120; reprinted in William Breit and Harold M. Hochman, eds., *Readings in Microeconomics,* New York, 1968, pp. 229-238.

Joan Robinson and John Eatwell, *An Introduction to Modern Economics,* London, 1973, Chapter 6.

Alessandro Roncaglia, "Sraffa and Price Theory," in Jesse Schwartz, ed., *The Subtle Anatomy of Capitalism,* Santa Monica, California, 1977.

Alessandro Roncaglia, *Sraffa and the Theory of Prices,* New York, 1978.

Frank Roosevelt, "Cambridge Economics as Commodity Fetishism," *Review of Radical Political Economy,* vol. 7 (Winter 1975); also in Jesse Schwartz, ed., *The Subtle Anatomy of Capitalism,* Santa Monica, California, 1977.

Piero Sraffa, "The Laws of Returns Under Competitive Conditions", *Economic Journal,* vol. 36, December 1926, pp. 535-550.

George J. Stigler, "Perfect Competition, Historically Contemplated," *Journal of Political Economy,* vol. 65, no. 1, February 1957, pp. 1-17.

Jeffrey T. Young, *Classical Theories of Value: From Smith to Sraffa,* Boulder, Colorado, 1979.

Part V: Marxian Theories of Value and Price

Lucio Colletti, "Some Comments on Marx's Theory of Value," in Jesse Schwartz, ed., *The Subtle Anatomy of Capitalism,* Santa Monica, California, 1977, pp. 458-473.

Economic Forum: Special Issue on Value Theory, vol. 13, no. 2, Fall 1982.

Diane Elson, ed., *Value: The Representation of Labour in Capitalism,* London, CSE Books, 1979.

Erich Fromm, *The Sane Society,* New York, 1965.

Herb Gintis and Samuel Bowles, "Structure and Practice in the Labor Theory of Value," *Review of Radical Political Economics,* vol. 12, no. 4, Winter 1981, pp. 1-26.

David Golding, "Appearance and Reality in Marx's *Capital,*" *Science and Society,* vol. 31, no. 4, Fall 1967, pp. 428-447.

E. K. Hunt, "Marxian Values, Prices and Profits," *Intermountain Economic Review,* vol. 9, Spring 1978, pp. 1-20.

David Laibman, "Values and Prices of Production: The Political Economy of the Transportation Problem," *Science and Society,* vol. 37, 1973.

Karl Marx, "Alienated Labor, " in *Economic and Philosophic Manuscripts (1844),* reproduced in Lloyd D. Easton and Kurt H. Guddat, eds., *Writings of the Young Marx on Philosophy and Society,* Garden City, New York, 1967, pp. 287-301.

Review of Radical Political Economics: Special Issue on Modern Approaches to the Theory of Value, vol. 14, no. 2, Summer 1982.

Issak I. Rubin *Essays on Marx's Theory of Value,* Detroit, 1972.

Jesse George Schwartz, "There is Nothing Simple About a Commodity," in Jesse Schwartz, ed., *The Subtle Anatomy of Capitalism,* Santa Monica, California, 1977, pp. 474-500.

Anwar Shaikh, "Marx's Theory of Value and the 'Transformation Problem,' " in Jesse Schwartz, ed., *The Subtle Anatomy of Capitalism,* Santa Monica, California, 1977, pp. 106-139.

Piero Sraffa, *Production of Commodities by Means of Commodities*, Cambridge, 1960.

Part VI: An Overview and Comparison

John Eatwell, "Controversies in the Theory of Surplus Value: Old and New," *Science and Society*, vol. 38 (1974).

Alfredo Medio, "Profits and Surplus-Value: Appearance and Reality in Capitalist Production," in E. K. Hunt and Jesse G. Schwartz, eds., *A Critique of Economic Theory*, Middlesex, England, 1972, pp. 312-346.

Luigi L. Pasinetti, *Lectures on the Theory of Production*, New York, 1977.

Alessandro Roncaglia, *Sraffa and the Theory of Prices*, New York, 1978.

Frank Roosevelt, "Cambridge Economics as Commodity Fetishism," *Review of Radical Political Economics*, vol. 7, no. 4, Winter 1975, pp. 1-32.

Ian Steedman, *Marx After Sraffa*, London, 1977.

Notes

Preface

[1] Paul Samuelson, *Economics*, 11th ed., McGraw-Hill, New York, 1980, p. 786.

[2] Alfred Marshall, *Principles of Economics*, 8th ed., Macmillan, London, 1961, p. 140.

[3] Mark Lutz and Kenneth Lux, *The Challenge of Humanistic Economics*, Benjamin/Cummings, Menlo Park, California, 1979.

[4] For an excellent overall introduction to post-Keynesianism see Alfred S. Eichner, ed., *A Guide to Post-Keynesian Economics*, M. E. Sharpe, Inc., White Plains, New York, 1978; see also the new *Journal of Post Keynesian Economics*.

Chapter 1

[1] For a more comprehensive survey of the meaning of the word "ideology" see, for example, John Plamenatz, *Ideology*, New York, 1970.

[2] A good example of such an institution is education. One of its main functions is to perpetuate the ideology of our society. See Samuel Bowles and Herb Gintis, *Schooling in Capitalist America*, Basic Books, New York, 1976.

[3] Joan Robinson, *Economic Philosophy*, Garden City, New York, 1962, p. 3.

[4] Joseph A. Schumpeter, *History of Economic Analysis*, New York, 1954.

[5] Ibid., pp. 41-43.

[6] Says Schumpeter: ". . . the way in which we see things can hardly be distinguished from the way in which we wish to see things." Ibid., p. 42.

[7] The term "paradigm" is borrowed from Thomas S. Kuhn, *The Structure of Scientific Revolutions*, 2nd ed., Chicago, 1970.

[8] Kai Birket-Smith, *Eskimos*, New York, 1971, pp. 62-74.

Chapter 2

[1] Vivian Walsh and Harvey Gram, *Classical and Neoclassical Theories of General Equilibrium*, Oxford University Press, New York, 1980, pp. 404-405.

[2] Ibid., p. 182.

[3] Donald J. Harris, *Capital Accumulation and Income Distribution*, Stanford University Press, Stanford, California, 1978, p. 20.

[4] This model is based on the one developed by Martin Hollis and Edward Nell, *Rational Economic Man*, Cambridge University Press, Cambridge, 1975.

[5] See, for example, Alfred S. Eichner, *The Megacorp and Oligopoly*, Cambridge University Press, Cambridge, 1976; see also Peter Kenyon, "Pricing," in Alfred S. Eichner, ed., *A Guide to Post-Keynesian Economics*, M. E. Sharpe, Inc., White Plains, New York, 1978, pp. 34-45.

[6] N. Kaldor, "Alternative Theories of Distribution," *Review of Economic Studies*, vol. 23, no. 2, 1956, pp. 83-100.

[7] M. Kalecki, *Selected Essays on the Dynamics of the Capitalist Economy*, Cambridge University Press, Cambridge, 1971, p. 13.

Chapter 3

[1] This example is adapted from Maurice Dobb, *Theories of Value and Distribution Since Adam Smith*, Cambridge, 1973, pp. 49-50.

[2] Piero Sraffa, ed., *The Works and Correspondence of David Ricardo*, Cambridge, 1970, vol. 4, p. 375.

³Ibid., vol. 1, p. 11.

⁴Ibid,. p. 12. An example of the commodities referred to here are "rare statues and pictures, scarce books and coins, wines of a peculiar quality . . . ."

⁵Alternatively we may reduce all types of skilled labor to simple unskilled labor.

⁶George Stigler, "Ricardo and the 93 Per Cent Labor Theory of Value," *American Economic Review*, vol. 48, June 1958.

⁷Just before he died, Ricardo wrote: "I have been thinking a good deal on this subject lately but without much improvement—I see the same difficulties as before and am more confirmed than ever that strictly speaking there is not in nature any correct measure of value nor can any ingenuity suggest one, for what constitutes a correct measure for some things is a reason why it cannot be a correct one for others." Sraffa, *The Works and Correspondence of David Ricardo*, vol. 9, p. 397.

⁸See Isaak I. Rubin, *Essays on Marx's Theory of Value*, Detroit, 1972.

Chapter 4

¹John Stuart Mill, *Utilitarianism*, Indianapolis, Indiana, 1957, p. 10.

²Although these books appeared at about the same time, all three authors were unaware of the others' work. Mark Blaug, *Economic Theory in Retrospect*, Homewood, Illinois, 1968, p. 298.

³Maurice Dobb, *Theories of Value and Distribution Since Adam Smith*, Cambridge University Press, Cambridge, 1973, p. 184.

⁴William S. Jevons, *Theory of Political Economy*, London, 1871, p. 142–143.

⁵Blaug, op. cit., pp. 309–310.

⁶Dobb, op. cit., p. 186.

⁷Joseph A. Schumpeter, *History of Economic Analysis*, New York, 1954, pp. 1057–1058.

⁸Ibid., p. 1057.

⁹John O'Neill, ed., *Modes of Individualism and Collectivism*, St. Martin's Press, New York, 1973; Ellen Wood, *Mind and Politics: An Approach to the Meaning of Liberal and Socialist Individualism*, University of California Press, Berkeley, California, 1973.

¹⁰David R. Kamerschen and Lloyd M. Valentine, *Intermediate Microeconomic Theory*, South Western Publishing Co., Cincinnati, Ohio, 1977.

Chapter 5

¹Treatments of these models in greater depth can be found in Alfred S. Eichner, *Macrodynamics of the American Economy*, M. E. Sharpe, Inc., White Plains, New York, chapters 5 and 6, forthcoming and Luigi L. Pasinetti, *Lectures on the Theory of Production*, Columbia University Press, New York, 1977.

²These equations can be solved as follows. Let p_w be the price of wheat in terms of iron and p_i be the price of iron in terms of wheat. Using these variables we transform equations (1) to:
$$2{,}240 p_w + 12 p_i = 3{,}200 p_w$$
$$960 p_w + 8 p_i = 20 p_i$$
Solving for p_i, we readily obtain $p_i = 80 p_w$.

³See, for example, Maurice Dobb, *Studies in the Development of Capitalism*, London, 1946; Rodney Hilton, *The Transition from Feudalism to Capitalism*, London, 1976; and *The Cambridge Economic History of Europe*, Cambridge University Press, various volumes.

⁴In post-Keynesian/Marxian economics the term "fixed capital" refers to produced means of production, such as machines, tools, buildings, etc., whereas "circulating capital" refers to items which have to circulate among producers in order to be useful. Examples of the latter are raw materials, provisions, etc.

⁵Maurice Dobb, *Theories of Value and Distribution Since Adam Smith*, Cambridge University Press, Cambridge, 1973, pp. 59–64.

⁶Karl Marx, *Capital*, vol. 2, New York, 1967, p. 235.

⁷Sweezy notes that "[w]hat is specific to capitalism is thus not the *fact* of exploitation of one part of the population by another, but the *form* which this exploitation assumes . . ." Paul Sweezy, *The Theory of Capitalist Development*, New York, 1970, p. 62.

⁸The term "constant" signifies the fact that the commodities which Marx considers here do not create more value than what these commodities themselves contain. Thus, a machine containing 100 labor hours can contribute no more than 100 hours of value to output over its life. "Variable" capital, however, applies to labor, a resource which can produce more value than what it is "worth" on the market. How much more depends on the length of the workday. Hence, the value which labor produces is variable.

Chapter 6

¹In Part IV we deal with these conditions in greater depth. There it will be seen that the failure of these conditions to hold does not alter the fact that prices are regulated by values. The only change is that prices would no longer be *proportional* to values.

²Paul Baran, "Economic Progress and Economic Surplus," *Science and Society*, vol. 17, Fall 1953, pp. 289-317; see also Baran's *The Political Economy of Growth*, New York, 1957; Paul Baran and Paul Sweezy, *Monopoly Capital: An Essay on the American Social and Economic Order*, New York, 1966.

³The definition of potential surplus provided here follows that of Ron Stanfield, *The Economic Surplus and Neo-Marxism*, Lexington, Massachusetts, 1973. See also Stanfield's "A Revision of the Economic Surplus Concept," *Review of Radical Political Economics*, Vol. 6, Fall 1974, pp. 69-74.

⁴Alfred Marshall, *Principles of Economics*, 9th ed., New York, 1961, p. 124.

Chapter 7

¹A more advanced treatment of production models would require that we divide the post-Keynesian branch into two additional subbranches, the Ricardian branch, which serves as the basis for Sraffaian models, and another branch derived from Quesnay. This latter branch serves as the basis for Leontief-type models.

²Piero Sraffa, *Production of Commodities by Means of Commodities*, Cambridge University Press, Cambridge, 1960.

³To be more consistent with the modern tradition, we abstract in the following pages from the presence of a landowning class. This emphasis is more in line with Marx than with Ricardo, because the latter's primary concern was the antagonism between the capitalists and the landowners. Ricardo felt that landowners would encroach on the capitalists' profits, slowing down the accumulation process. Marx, of course, gave prominence to the capitalist-worker antagonism.

⁴See, for example, Fredy Perlman, "The Reproduction of Daily Life," in Jesse Schwartz, ed., *The Subtle Anatomy of Capitalism*, Santa Monica, California, 1977.

⁵See, for example, Mark Blaug, *Economic Theory in Retrospect*, rev. ed., Richard D. Irwin, Inc., Homewood, Illinois, 1968 and G. J. Stigler, "Perfect Competition, Historically Contemplated," *Journal of Political Economy*, vol. 65, no. 1, February 1957, pp. 1-17.

⁶See Paul J. McNulty, "A Note on the History of Perfect Competition," *Journal of Political Economy*, vol. 75, August 1967, pp. 395-399 and "Economic Theory and the Meaning of Competition," *Quarterly Journal of Economics*, vol. 82, November 1968, pp. 639-656.

⁷Augustin Cournot, *Researches into the Mathematical Principles of the Theory of Wealth*, translated by Nathaniel T. Bacon, Augustus M. Kelly, Publishers, 1960.

⁸The neoclassical assumption that there must exist a large number of firms is challenged by Eugene F. Fama and Arthur B. Laffer, "The Number of Firms and Competition," *American Economic Review*, vol. 62, September 1972.

⁹The introduction to fixed capital would not change the results which we wish to obtain. Since it substantially complicates the analysis, we abstract from fixed capital. The issue of how best to incorporate fixed capital remains, however, a controversial one. See Sraffa, op. cit., Chapter 10.

[10] There are only two independent equations in the above illustration since one equation can always be deduced from the sum of the others. But since we set the price of iron equal to unity, there are only two unknowns, allowing a solution to be easily obtained.

[11] The different treatment of profits is best explained by Adam Smith: "The profits of stock, it may perhaps be thought, are only a different name for the wages of a particular sort of labour, the labour of inspection and direction. They are, however, altogether different, regulated by quite sufficient principles, and bear no proportion to the quantity, the hardships, or the ingenuity of this supposed labour of inspection and direction. They are regulated altogether by the value of the stock employed, and are greater or smaller in proportion to the extent of the stock." Adam Smith, *An Inquiry into the Nature and Causes of the Wealth of Nations*, Edwin Cannan, ed., Modern Library reprint, New York, 1937, p. 48.

[12] The solution is rather difficult to obtain, requiring two theorems from matrix theory (Frobenius and Perron). Moreover, the method of successive approximations was employed. Hence the solutions are approximations and, because of rounding errors, will not be exact. See, for example, F. R. Gantmacker, *Applications of the Theory of Matrices*, New York, 1969, Chapter 3 and Luigi L. Pasinetti, *Lectures on the Theory of Production*, New York, 1977, Mathematical Appendix.

Chapter 8

[1] The implication of treating wages in this way is that it differs significantly from most of the early classical writings. This issue will be introduced in our discussion of Marx's approach. It is also true that it would make more sense to assume that there is a technologically determined subsistence level of wages and that the distribution of the surplus is between the workers, in the form of a wage in excess of subsistence, and the capitalists, in the form of the residual. However, Sraffa's approach is followed here. This approach makes the whole wage variable.

[2] This is not to say, however, that the marketplace and the marginalist principles have nothing to do with the personal distribution of income, as between different kinds of labor.

[3] The relationship between wages and profits and their effects on macroeconomic activity are examined in a series of articles appearing in the *Review of Radical Political Economics*: Raford Boddy and James Crotty, "Class Conflict and Macro-Policy: The Political Business Cycle," vol. 7 (Spring 1975); Howard Sherman, "Class Conflict and Macro-Policy: A Comment," vol. 8 (Summer 1976); Raford Boddy and James Crotty, "Wages, Prices and the Profit Squeeze," vol. 8 (Summer 1976).

[4] According to Adam Smith, for example, "[t]axes upon luxuries have no tendency to raise the price of any other commodities except that of the commodities taxed. Taxes upon necessaries, by raising the wages of labour, necessarily tend to raise the price of all manufactures, and consequently to diminish the extent of their sale and consumption." A. Smith, *An Inquiry into the Nature and Causes of the Wealth of Nations*, ed. R. H. Campbell and A. S. Skinner, London, 1976, p. 873.

[5] Perhaps the most extensive critique of the Cambridge School is M. Blaug, *The Cambridge Revolution: Success or Failure*, London, 1974.

[6] A complete development of this theory of pricing is Alfred S. Eichner, *The Megacorp and Oligopoly*, Cambridge University Press, Cambridge, 1976. See also Peter Kenyon, "Pricing in Post-Keynesian Economics," *Challenge*, vol. 21 (July/August 1978).

[7] See Eichner, op. cit.

Chapter 9

[1] For mathematical proofs of these propositions, see Luigi L. Pasinetti, *Lectures on the Theory of Production*, New York, 1977 and Peter Newman, "Production of Commodities by Means of Commodities: A Review," in Jesse Schwartz, ed., *The Subtle Anatomy of Capitalism*, Santa Monica, California, 1977.

Chapter 10

[1] Piero Sraffa, *Production of Commodities by Means of Commodities*, Cambridge, Cambridge University Press, 1960, pp. 36–37.

[2]This term can be derived by taking the derivative of the labor term, setting it equal to zero, and solving for r. Let v be the value term, so that

$$v = L\left\{1 - \frac{r}{R}\right\}(1 + r)^n$$

$$\frac{dv}{dr} = -\frac{L}{R}(1 + r)^n + nL\left\{1 - \frac{r}{R}\right\}(1 + r)^{n-1} = 0$$

Solving this expression for r, we get

$$-\frac{1}{R}(1 + r) + n\left\{1 - \frac{r}{R}\right\} = 0$$

$$r + nr = nR - 1$$

$$r(n + 1) = nR - 1$$

$$r = R - \frac{1 + R}{n + 1}$$

[3]Consider the following example. Suppose you are to receive three equal payments of $C every year for three years. Your first payment comes at the end of the first year and you keep it in a bank for the remaining two years at r%. At the end of the second year you then have $C + $Cr, or $C(1 + r)$. At the end of the third year the first payment compounds again and you get $C(1 + r)^2$. The second payment of $C is kept for one period, after which time you receive $C(1 + r)$. At the end of the third year you receive the third payment of $C. The total amount received after three years will then be $C(1 + r)^2 + C(1 + r) + C$. Call this sum S_3. Generalizing,

(1) $\quad S_n = C + C(1 + r) + C(1 + r)^2 + \ldots + C(1 + r)^{n-1}$

Multiply both sides of the equation by $(1 + r)$:

(2) $\quad S_n(1 + r) = C(1 + r) + C(1 + r)^2 + C(1 + r)^3 + \ldots + C(1 + r)^n$

Subtract equation (2) from (1);

(3) $\quad S_n - S_n(1 + r) = C - C(1 + r)^n$

or

(4) $\quad S_n[1 - (1 + r)] = C[1 - (1 + r)^n]$

which equals

(5) $\quad S_n(-r) = C[1 - (1 + r)^n]$

and

(6) $\quad S_n = \frac{C[1 - (1 + r)^n]}{-r} = C\left\{\frac{(1 + r)^n - 1}{r}\right\}$

where C is the periodic annuity and S_n the sum of all the annuities after n years.

Chapter 11

[1]Alfred Medio, "Profits and Surplus—Value: Appearance and Reality in Capitalist Production," in E. K. Hunt and Jesse G. Schwartz, eds., *A Critique of Economic Theory*, Penguin Books Ltd., Middlesex, England, 1973, p. 312.

[2]This observation does not imply that Sraffa's model is in any respect inferior to Marx. Neither is it inconsistent with Marx's theory. It just has a different and more narrow focus, as we shall see.

[3]Friedrich Engels, "Speech at Karl Marx's Funeral," in Erich Fromm, *Marx's Concept of Man*, Frederich Ungar Publishing Co., New York, p. 258.

[4]The reader should be aware that Marx's theory of alienation is much more comprehensive than the simplistic explanation given above and that there are other causes and types of alienation

which Marx explains in great depth. This is a very complex matter and it is hoped that the reader will appreciate the need to avoid it at this point. See Karl Marx, "Alienated Labor," in "Economic and Philosophic Manuscripts (1844)," reproduced in Lloyd D. Easton and Kurt H. Guddat, eds., *Writings of the Young Marx on Philosophy and Society*, Doubleday and Company, Garden City, New York, 1967, pp. 287–301; Herbert Marcuse, *One-Dimensional Man*, Beacon Press, New York, 1964; Bertell Ollman, *Alienation, Marx's Conception of Man in Capitalistic Society*, Cambridge University Press, Cambridge, 1971; and Walter A. Weisskopf, *Alienation and Economics*, Dutlon, New York, 1971.

[5]This does not at all suggest that life in feudal societies is pleasant and self-actualizing. Quite the contrary is true. All we wish to do is show how, according to Marx, a certain kind of alienation arises out of the historically unique way in which society is ordered under capitalism.

[6]Marx, op. cit., p. 292.

[7]Karl Marx, *Capital*, vol. 1, Progress Publishers, Moscow, p. 51.

[8]This notion also serves as the basis for Marx's theory of commodity fetishism. See I. I. Rubin, *Essays on Marx's Theory of Value*. Black and Red, Detroit, 1973.

Chapter 12

[1]This term is used by Anwar Shaikh, "Marx's Theory of Value and the 'Transformation Problem,'" in Jesse Schwartz, ed., *The Subtle Anatomy of Capitalism*, Goodyear Publishing Company, Santa Monica, California, 1977. Much of this and the next section is based on this excellent article.

[2]Shaikh, op. cit.; L. V. Bortkiewicz, *Appendix to Karl Marx and the Close of His System by E. von Böhm-Bawerk and Böhm-Bawerk's Criticism of Marx by Rudolf Hilferding*, Paul Sweezy, ed., New York, 1949; F. Seton, "The Transformation Problem," *Review of Economic Studies*, vol. 24, 1956–57, pp. 146–60; J. Winternitz, "Values and Prices: A Solution of the So-Called Transformation Problem," *Economic Journal*, vol. 58, 1948, pp. 276–280.

[3]More standard versions of the Marxian model contain three sectors instead of two. The first, Department I, produces means of production. The second, Department II, produces wage goods for workers. The third, Department III, produces luxury goods for capitalists. All we need to do in order to extend the above model to the more popular case is to add the third departmental equation and a third price of production, the price of luxury goods p_x. The formal model would be as follows:

$$\text{Department I} \quad (\psi_1 DC_1 + \psi_2 DV_1)(1 + r) = \psi_1 DW_1$$
$$\text{Department II} \quad (\psi_1 DC_2 + \psi_2 DV_2)(1 + r) = \psi_2 DW_2$$
$$\text{Department III} \quad (\psi_1 DC_3 + \psi_2 DV_3)(1 + r) = \psi_3 DW_3$$
$$\psi_1 DW_1 + \psi_2 DW_2 + \psi_3 DW_3 = DW_1 + DW_2 + DW_3$$

or, using prices of production,

$$\text{Department I} \quad (p_c C_1 + p_v V_1)(1 + r) = p_c W_1$$
$$\text{Department II} \quad (p_c C_2 + p_v V_2)(1 + r) = p_v W_2$$
$$\text{Department III} \quad (p_c C_3 + p_v V_3)(1 + r) = p_x W_3$$
$$p_c W_1 + p_v W_2 + p_x W_3 = DW_1 + DW_2 + DW_3$$

Chapter 13

[1]Maurice Dobb, *Theories of Value and Distribution Since Adam Smith*, Cambridge University Press, Cambridge, 1973, p. 141.

[2]Paul Samuelson, "Wages and Interest: Marxian Economic Models," *American Economic Review*, vol. 47, no. 6, December 1957, p. 911.

[3]Joseph Schumpeter, *History of Economic Analysis*, Oxford University Press, New York, 1968, p. 290; emphasis added.

[4]Ian Steedman, *Marx After Sraffa*, NLB, London, 1977, p. 207.

[5]Anwar Shaikh, "Marx's Theory of Value and the 'Transformation Problem,'" in Jesse Schwartz, ed., *The Subtle Anatomy of Capitalism*, Goodyear Publishing Company, Santa

Monica, California, 1977; Frank Roosevelt, "Cambridge Economics as Commodity Fetishism," *Review of Radical Political Economics*, vol. 7, no. 4, Winter 1975, pp. 1-32.

[6] Allessandro Roncaglia, *Sraffa and the Theory of Prices*, John Wiley & Sons, New York, 1978; see also his "Sraffa and Price Theory" in Jesse Schwartz, ed., *The Subtle Anatomy of Capitalism*, Goodyear Publishing Company, Santa Monica, California, 1977, pp. 371-380; J. Eatwell, "Controversies in the Theory of Surplus Value: Old and New," *Science and Society*, vol. 38, no. 3, 1974, pp. 280-303, and "Mr. Sraffa's Standard Ccmmodity and the Rate of Exploitation," *Quarterly Journal of Economics*, vol. 89, no. 4, November 1975, pp. 543-55.

[7] See Roncaglia, op. cit., Chapter 5.

[8] Alfredo Medio, "Profits and Surplus-Value: Appearance and Reality in Capitalist Production," in E. K. Hunt and Jesse G. Scwartz, eds., *A Critique of Economic Theory*, Penguin Books, Middlesex, England, 1972, pp. 312-346. For additional parallels between Sraffa and Marx see J. Eatwell, "Mr. Sraffa's Standard Commodity and the Rate of Exploitation," *Quarterly Journal of Economics*, vol. 89, no. 4, November 1975, pp. 543-555 and Luigi L. Pasinetti, *Lectures on the Theory of Production*, Columbia University Press, New York, 1977.

[9] Medio, op. cit., p. 326.

About the Author

Peter M. Lichtenstein is an associate professor of economics at Boise State University in Idaho. He was educated at Union College and the University of Colorado where he received his Ph.D. in 1974. During 1982-83, Professor Lichtenstein was Visiting Fellow at Cornell University in the Program on Participation and Labor-Managed Systems.